Issues in Providing Services to Trauma-Affected Veterans In and Out of Veterans Treatment Courts

Justice-involved veterans face a number of challenges in the criminal-legal system, including receiving the proper care and treatment for trauma experienced during their service to the nation. This book examines novel approaches to care for veterans and identifies some of the barriers they face. One strategy toward ameliorating these challenges was the formation of specialized Veterans Treatment Courts (VTCs) in 2008. Now numbering well over 600 courts nationwide, VTCs streamline the justice process and provide the necessary structure, services, and support to address the underlying issues behind their offending behaviors. The project upon which this volume is based involved in-depth interviews with 145 stakeholders in 20 geographically dispersed and characteristically unique VTCs in the United States. Interviewees included judges, court coordinators, prosecutors, treatment providers, defense counsel, probation officers, and others working as coordinated teams to provide a network of care enabling the justice-involved veterans to address their specific criminogenic needs and to promote behaviors resulting in subsequent desistence from crime. In addition to the voices of those working daily in the specialty court realm, the book also includes chapters on an issue that was broached often during semi-structured interviews: military sexual assault. Survivors of sexual abuse in the military report substantial trauma associated with in-service victimization, and these final chapters shed light on the extent of military sexual assault and its impacts on veterans as they transition to civilian life.

This book will be an invaluable resource for scholars, researchers, and practitioners of law, criminology and criminal justice, public affairs, and psychology. It was originally published as a special issue of *Victims & Offenders.*

Faye S. Taxman is University Professor at the Schar School of Policy and Government and Director of the Center for Advancing Correctional Excellence at George Mason University. Taxman has expertise in corrections, supervision, implementation science and intervention science.

Don Hummer is a faculty member in the School of Public Affairs at Penn State Harrisburg. His research is centered on corrections policy, offender treatment and control, institutional and community violence, and the implications of technological advances for justice system personnel. He is co-editor of four previous volumes.

Issues in Providing Services to Trauma-Affected Veterans In and Out of Veterans Treatment Courts

Edited by
Faye S. Taxman and Don Hummer

Routledge
Taylor & Francis Group
LONDON AND NEW YORK

First published 2025
by Routledge
4 Park Square, Milton Park, Abingdon, Oxon OX14 4RN

and by Routledge
605 Third Avenue, New York, NY 10158

Routledge is an imprint of the Taylor & Francis Group, an informa business

British Library Cataloguing in Publication Data
A catalogue record for this book is available from the British Library

ISBN13: 978-1-032-87687-0 (hbk)
ISBN13: 978-1-032-87688-7 (pbk)
ISBN13: 978-1-003-53393-1 (ebk)

DOI: 10.4324/9781003533931

Typeset in Minion Pro
by Newgen Publishing UK

Publisher's Note
The publisher accepts responsibility for any inconsistencies that may have arisen during the conversion of this book from journal articles to book chapters, namely the inclusion of journal terminology.

Contents

Citation Information

The following chapters in this book were originally published in the *Victims & Offenders*, volume 19 issue 1 (2024), except Chapters 8 and 9, which were published in volume 19, issue 4 (2024). When citing this material, please use the original page numbering for each article, as follows:

Chapter 2

New Research on Veterans Treatment Courts: An Overview of the Community Participatory Research on Veterans in Specialized Programming Project
James M. Byrne, Don Hummer, Kimberly R. Kras, Sabrina S. Rapisarda, and Kelly M. Socia
Victims & Offenders, volume 19 issue 1 (2024), pp. 5–31

Chapter 3

Veterans Treatment Courts: A Nationwide Review of Enacting and Eligibility State Statutes
Sabrina S. Rapisarda, Kimberly R. Kras, Grace LeMoyne, Don Hummer, Kelly Socia, and James M. Byrne
Victims & Offenders, volume 19 issue 1 (2024), pp. 32–58

Chapter 4

No Veteran Left Behind? Perspectives on VTC Eligibility Criteria for Justice-Involved Veterans in Multiple Jurisdictions Across the United States
Don Hummer, James M. Byrne, J., Sabrina S. Rapisarda, Kelly M. Socia and Kimberly R. Kras
Victims & Offenders, volume 19 issue 1 (2024), pp. 59–79

Chapter 5

SNAFU, Situation Normal All Forces United in Veterans Court: From the Perspective of a California Court of Appeal Justice and Mentor
Eileen C. Moore
Victims & Offenders, volume 19 issue 1 (2024), pp. 80–94

Chapter 6

At Risk and Underserved: Veterans Treatment Court Team Member Perspectives on Service Delivery Challenges
Kimberly R. Kras, Sabrina S. Rapisarda, Kelly M. Socia, Don Hummer, and James M. Byrne
Victims & Offenders, volume 19 issue 1 (2024), pp. 95–118

Chapter 7

"God, I Hope It Doesn't Fade Out": Team Member Perspectives on the Future of Veterans Treatment Courts
Kelly M. Socia, Sabrina S. Rapisarda, Kimberly R. Kras, Don Hummer, and James M. Byrne
Victims & Offenders, volume 19 issue 1 (2024), pp. 119–136

Chapter 8

Protecting but Not Protected: Sexual Assault in the Military
Emily K. Meinert and Ericka A. Wentz
Victims & Offenders, volume 19 issue 4 (2024), pp. 671–691

Chapter 9

Military Sexual Assault, Post-Service Employment, and Transition Preparation among U.S. Military Veterans: New Directions for Research
Adam J. Pritchard
Victims & Offenders, volume 19 issue 4 (2024), pp. 692–708

Notes on Contributors

James M. Byrne, School of Criminology and Justice Studies, University of Massachusetts Lowell, Massachusetts, USA.

Don Hummer, School of Public Affairs, Penn State Harrisburg, Middletown, Pennsylvania, USA.

Kimberly R. Kras, School of Public Affairs, San Diego State University, California, USA.

Grace LeMoyne, School of Public Affairs, San Diego State University, California, USA.

Emily K. Meinert, School of Criminology & Criminal Justice, University of Nebraska Omaha, Nebraska, USA.

Eileen C. Moore, Fourth District, California Court of Appeal, Santa Ana, California, USA.

Adam J. Pritchard, D'Aniello Institute for Veterans and Military Families, Syracuse University, Syracuse, New York, USA.

Sabrina S. Rapisarda, School of Criminology and Justice Studies, University of Massachusetts Lowell, Massachusetts, USA.

Kelly M. Socia, School of Criminology and Justice Studies, University of Massachusetts Lowell, Massachusetts, USA.

Faye S. Taxman, Schar School of Policy and Government; Center for Advancing Correctional Excellence, George Mason University, Fairfax, Virginia, USA.

Ericka A. Wentz, Department of Civic Engagement and Public Service, University of West Georgia, Carrollton, Georgia, USA.

Notes on Contributors

Introduction

Faye S. Taxman and Don Hummer

The Challenges of Being a Veteran in the Criminal Legal System

A hidden population of the criminal justice system are veterans; they are currently serving or have served in the military and are now civilians. While there are 16 million veterans in the United States (Census Bureau, 2021), about 5% of the prison population or around 131,500 are veterans with known military background. There are no available estimates of the number of veterans on probation or parole or those that encounter the criminal-legal system but are diverted. In essence, we have an uneven picture of the size of the justice-involved veteran population. The military experience is not accounted for in typical criminal justice processes in terms of risk assessment and/or classification systems, instead the veterans are typically invisible to the system. Existing evidence suggests that veterans have particular risk factors contributing to criminality, suicide, and homelessness that either originated or were exacerbated by their military service (e.g., Edwards et al., 2023: Olenick et al., 2015; Tsai & Rosenheck, 2015). Historically, veterans frequently attempted to deal with lived trauma themselves, believing they could handle it without help. As a result, by the time issues in a veteran's background became manifest as offending behavior, they are older than the typical offender and have complex treatment and/or service needs. Almost no systematic data is collected that pertains to the military status of individuals in the justice system. Veterans Treatment Courts (VTCs) were developed in response to a perceived need to better identify veterans, especially those that need substance use, mental health, housing, and employment services, and to better improve the veteran's quality of life.

The discharge status of individuals who served in the military is a critical factor to consider when discussing service provision for justice-involved veterans. The Veteran's Administration (VA) has recognized that veterans have special needs when reentering civil society. There are two major types of military discharge: those who are honorably discharged (85% of all discharges each year), and those who leave military service with a dishonorable discharge or some other status (other than honorable discharge, or OTH, account for (about 15% of all discharges). The discharge status is an important issue because eligibility for VA benefits is often tied to this status. Those who are honorably discharged are eligible for many of the benefits provided by the VA including case management, housing supports, employment assistance, medical care for physical and behavioral health needs, and other social services. Honorably discharged veterans typically have fewer behavioral health and homelessness issues than those who are dishonorably discharged (Holiday & Pedersen, 2017). Those that are dishonorably discharged often have had problems during their military service in terms of substance use, mental health, post-traumatic stress syndrome, housing instability, and other issues, but they are often denied services due to their discharge status (Veterans Legal Clinic, 2016).

In response to the special needs of veterans who are in the justice system, two special services were established: the VA's Veterans Justice Outreach program (VJOs) and nearly 600 VTCs. The VA designed the VJO program to provide specialized case managers that serve veterans who are justice-involved, in or out of VTCs. The VJO program is set up to be voluntary in that the veteran must desire case management services. The VJO is primarily for those individuals who were honorably discharged.

VTCs are locally administered which means that there is tremendous variation in who is eligible for the VTC in terms of arrest offense, arrest history, and military status. Some of these courts allow those that are dishonorably discharged but because the individual receives minimal benefits from the VA or VJO, the service resource gap must be filled using local community resources that may not be on par with the services and support provided by the VA. The VTC model adopts the ten principles of problem-solving courts with a focus on providing veterans with a supportive environment that honors them and their military service. In essence, VTCs are a vehicle to address the punishment of individuals with a focus on providing services for the individual.

Organization of the Text

Many of the chapters in this text emanated from a nationwide, five-year study of VTCs. The Bureau of Justice Assistance (BJA) was interested in understanding how VTCs serve the needs of justice-involved veterans. They commissioned a study via a transfer of federal funds from BJA to the National Institute on Drug Abuse's Justice Community Opioid Innovation Network (JCOIN). The study was conducted by the JCOIN Coordination and Translation Center (CTC) under the leadership of Drs. Faye S Taxman and James M. Byrne. The VA participated in the study as members of the Advisory Board as well as a representative from All Rise (formerly the National Association of Drug Court Professionals). This study is the largest study of VTCs, conducted to date, with an emphasis on the service delivery features in 20 VTCs and treatment process data in 3 VTCs. It also uncovers some of the strengths of the VTC model as well as identifies hiccups in the implementation process. The role of the VJO is highlighted to illustrate what a collaborative VTC model looks like.

There are six chapters that pertain specifically to the aforementioned research project. The first by Dr. James M. Byrne and his research team, "New Research on Veterans Treatment Courts: An Overview of the Community Participatory Research on Veterans in Specialized Programming Project", provides an overview of this two-phase study. Dr. Byrne addresses the question of "why VTC" to provide context as to what the problem-solving court model offers to the justice system, and to individuals with military service that have been arrested. It is an important piece because it furnishes a justification for the need of the VTC, as well as special emphasis on the needs of veterans.

Sabrina S. Rapisarda is the lead author of the chapter "Veterans Treatment Courts: A Nationwide Review of Enacting and Eligibility State Statutes" and Don Hummer is the lead author for "No Veteran Left Behind? Perspectives on VTC Eligibility Criteria for Justice-Involved Veterans in Multiple Jurisdictions Across the United States". These two chapters provide an in-depth review of the eligibility for participation in VTCs in terms of state-level statutes and eligibility criteria of the courts participating in the VTC study. Eligibility criteria determines who can benefit from the VTC, and as with most criminal justice initiatives, the eligibility criteria identifies whether the program is targeting certain types of individuals. The greater the extent of the eligibility criteria (the number of requirements) in a VTC usually signifies a more constrained participation whereas fewer criteria indicates that the emphasis is on trying to serve a larger number of veterans. One often looks at the eligibility criteria to understand the "rationale" behind a particular program like the VJO.

Judge Eileen C. Moore provides her insight into the value provided by the VTC in the chapter "SNAFU, Situation Normal All Forces United in Veterans Court: From the Perspective of a California Court of Appeal Justice and Mentor". The unique perspective of a judge that champions the VTC and works with other VTCs to assist them in delivering their services is outlined in this chapter. More importantly, Judge Moore helps the reader understand why veterans need a supportive environment, and how the judge, VTC staff, and other VTC participants can offer to the men and women that served in our military and now have legal system issues.

Kimberly R. Kras is the lead author of the chapter "At Risk and Underserved: Veterans Treatment Court Team Member Perspectives on Service Delivery Challenges". In this piece, she details the service delivery interface with the VTCs. This in-depth analysis of the VTCs and their access to—and use of—various service types reveals the complexity of service delivery. The linkage to care notion is one of the tenets of problem-solving courts; in the ideal situation this should be relatively easy but the different funding streams, eligibility criteria for services, geographic location, and services provided complicates access. This chapter underscores some of the systemic barriers that affect which services justice-involved veterans can avail themselves of.

Next, Kelly M. Socia is the lead author of " 'God, I Hope It Doesn't Fade Out': Team Member Perspectives on the Future of Veterans Treatment Courts". This chapter details how the team members of the VTCs view what lies ahead for, and the challenges faced by, these courts. The VTC, like most problem-solving courts, consists of a judge, coordinator, prosecutor, defense attorney, treatment provider(s), probation officer, and other community providers with each having a different role and perspective about the VTC. While most articulate support for the VTC and the need to provide our veterans with the best quality care, the VTC can be very fragile in some communities. The fragility is due to lack of funding, competition with other specialty courts, and unmet needs of the veterans. This chapter ultimately provides a vision for how to improve the VTC concept from the eyes of those that work in the system.

While conducting the interviews with VTC stakeholders in jurisdictions nationwide, one of the themes that emerged repeatedly was the prevalence of justice-involved veterans who had experienced sexual trauma while serving. Military sexual assault (MSA) is underreported for both males and females, much as it is in society generally, however the proportion of justice-involved veterans reporting sexual assault while on active duty is significant. The text concludes with two chapters that shed light on this heretofore understudied problem, and highlight its effects on military personnel both while serving and after separation. The first of these chapters by Emily K. Meinert and Ericka A. Wentz, "Protecting but Not Protected: Sexual Assault in the Military", discusses how elements of military culture have allowed MSA to continue on, with failures of leadership particularly blameworthy. The authors outline several policy recommendations and strategies that military leaders could implement to reduce the number of MSA incidents going forward.

The text concludes with a chapter by Adam J. Pritchard that details the effects of the trauma brought about by MSA for veterans. In "Military Sexual Assault, Post-Service Employment, and Transition Preparation among U.S. Military Veterans: New Directions for Research", the author details how MSA affects the service member after separation in terms of employment and other aspects of transition to civilian life. The piece demonstrates how the trauma of MSA leads to risk behaviors, such as substance misuse, that are also correlates of the criminal behaviors exhibited by many participants in VTCs. Recommendations made by the author are aligned with many of the types of support services offered within VTCs as treatment regimens to assist survivors of MSA as they continue their lives in the civilian world.

This text provides both a glimpse into the inner workings and functioning of the VTC, and how the courts and other entities strive to help veterans dealing with past trauma, such as MSA. VTCs and VJOs can challenge the local criminal justice system to do a better job at helping individuals who need specific behavioral health services but they can also provide opportunities to help the criminal justice system develop better, integrated services for veterans in need.

References

Edwards, E. R., Epshteyn, G., Connelly, B., Redden, C., Moussa, C. E. H., Blonigen, D. M., Stimmel, M., Holliday, R., & Osterberg, T. (2023). Understanding Criminogenic Risk Factors Among United States Military Veterans: An Updated Literature Review. *Criminal Justice Review*. (online first). https://doi.org/10.1177/07340168231160862

Holliday, S. B. & Pedersen, E. R. (2017). The Association between Discharge Status, Mental Health, and Substance Misuse among Young Adult Veterans, *Psychiatry Research*, *256*, 428–434.

Olenick, M., Flowers, M., & Diaz, V. J. (2015). US Veterans and Their Unique Issues: Enhancing Health Care Professional Awareness. *Advances in Medical Education and Practice*, *6*, 635–639.

Tsai, J. & Rosenheck, R. A. (2015). Risk Factors for Homelessness among US Veterans, *Epidemiologic Reviews*, *37*(1), 177–195.

U.S. Census Bureau. (2021). *American Community Survey 1-Year Estimates, Table DP02: Selected Social Characteristics in the United States*. https://data.census.gov/table?tid=ACSDP1Y2021.DP02

Veterans Legal Clinic at the Legal Services Center of Harvard Law School. (2016). *Underserved. How the VA Wrongfully Excludes Veterans with Bad Paper*. www.nvlsp.org/images/uploads/ NVLSP__Swords_to_Plowshares_Underserved.pdf

New Research on Veterans Treatment Courts: An Overview of the Community Participatory Research on Veterans in Specialized Programming Project

James M. Byrne, Don Hummer, Kimberly R. Kras, Sabrina S. Rapisarda, and Kelly M. Socia

ABSTRACT

Justice-involved veterans return to civilian life with a variety of mental and physical health challenges that often go untreated and increase their risk for self-harm and involvement in the criminal-legal system. Veterans Treatment Courts (VTC) were created to respond to the unique problems of justice-involved veterans by attempting to coordinate services and support with the U.S. Department of Veterans Affairs (VA), local treatment providers, and the VTC. Our research has two distinct phases. In Phase 1, we conducted qualitative interviews with VTC team members in twenty (20) VTCs from each USA region; in each VTC, we gained the perspectives of team members – judges, prosecutors, defense attorneys, VJOs, VTC program coordinators, mentors, probation officers, and treatment providers – on the operation of VTCs, with a focus on how to improve service provision for justice-involved veterans. A total of 145 interviews were conducted. We begin by describing the unique problems and treatment needs of justice-involved veterans, and briefly summarize the findings from previous research on the implementation and impact of VTCs. We then present our research study protocol and highlight findings from our phase 1 qualitative interviews with VTC team members. In addition, we describe phase 2 of our project, which will include focus groups with VTC graduates, and quantitative analyses of the service provision networks of three VTCs.

Introduction

Several recent studies have attempted to document the link between veteran status and criminal-legal system involvement (Council on Criminal Justice, 2022; Lucas et al., 2022; Snowden et al., 2017). According to the U.S. Census Bureau (2021), there are currently about 16 million veterans in the United States; and it is estimated that 200,000 service members return from military service to civilian life each year (Orak, 2023; U.S. Government Accountability Office, 2019). A recent review by the Council on Criminal Justice (2022) noted that the majority of active-duty service members successfully transition out of the armed services without engaging in behaviors that invoke criminal-legal system involvement; but that is not the case for *all* returning veterans, due to struggles with "mental health challenges, substance abuse, homelessness, and criminality" which are likely exacerbated by lack of access to services and support due to the discharge status of veterans (e.g., other than honorable and dishonorable discharges).[1] Unfortunately, accurate up-to-date data on the extent of post-service criminal-legal system involvement by veterans are not available for each stage of the criminal justice process(i.e., arrest, prosecution, and conviction) .[2] We do have recent survey data suggesting[3] that about 5% of our Federal and state prison and jail population are veterans (n = 181,500). Although somewhat older, researchers also estimate that "roughly one third of veterans report having been arrested and booked into jail at least once in their lives, compared to fewer than one fifth of non-veterans."[4] However, it is not known whether these arrests occurred before or after an individual enters the military.[5] Accurate estimates of the number of veterans on probation are not available. We highlight this veteran-specific criminal-legal system data gap to underscore a simple point: the case for more government resources targeting the unique problems and needs of veterans – already compelling – would be even stronger if we had the necessary data available to document not only their mental health and physical health challenges post-service, but also to describe the nature and extent of their criminal-legal system involvement (National Institute of Corrections 2022).[6]

Justice-involved veterans are unlike other groups of justice-involved individuals due to their unique military experiences. They encounter the criminal-legal system when they are arrested for engaging in a range of criminal behavior, including driving under the influence, theft, substance use, domestic violence, and assault. While the criminal-legal system responds to individuals who are arrested for these crimes regularly, the traditional court process is ill-equipped to address the unique problems and needs of justice-involved veterans. These individuals often have a litany of concerns: military trauma, including military sexual trauma and post-traumatic stress disorder (PTSD), co-occurring mental health and substance use disorders, and diagnosed psychiatric conditions (Clary et al., 2020; Finlay et al., 2019; Tsai & Seamone, 2019; Tsai et al., 2017), as well as physical health problems, including traumatic brain injuries (Logan et al., 2021). For post-9/11 veterans, these concerns appear to be more prevalent than in earlier cohorts of veterans (Parker et al., 2019). According to a recent review by the Council on Criminal Justice (2022), "veterans, and especially post-9/11 veterans, face unique risk factors for criminal justice involvement, ranging from multiple combat deployments to high PTSD rates and housing insecurity. For the 200,000 people who annually transition out of the military, the exit programs that await them often fail to meet expectations. In addition, increasing numbers of service members are leaving the armed forces with other than honorable discharges, which in almost all cases bar VA benefits" (p. 20). While the court system cannot ignore justice-involved veterans' involvement in criminal activity, the general consensus within the U.S. is that veterans deserve special treatment, given their service.[7]

Why do we need VTCs?

There has been a recent debate over the need for specialty courts (see, e.g., Lucas, 2021; Pratt & Turanovic, 2019, 2021), which has implications for the VTCs examined here. Pratt and Turanovic (2019) describe the justification for specialty courts as follows: "The purported benefits of specialized courts ... hinge on the idea that certain groups of offenders are unique – and therefore different from others – so having their own unique court process will increase the odds that their particular offending tendencies might be curbed" (p. 376). Citing the "generality of deviance" thesis (Hirschi & Gottfredson, 1994; Pratt et al., 2016), they point out that, "offenders do not specialize in any particular form of misbehavior," and they go on to argue that specialty courts are not designed to reduce recidivism; instead, they are, "largely intended to provide administrative benefits in terms of system efficiency and ease of case processing" (Pratt & Turanovic, 2019, p. 376). While they do make a valid point about organizing specialty courts around the latest conviction offense of an individual (e.g., substance use, domestic violence), this point does not – in our view – apply to veterans' courts, which focus on a specific subgroup of individuals rather than specific *offense types*. As we demonstrate in the following review, while justice-involved veterans may indeed be generalists in terms of their criminal behavior, they do have special problems that will require veteran-specific treatment; that alone justifies the creation of this type of specialty court.[8]

The implementation and effectiveness of VTCs: what do we currently know?

It has been fifteen years since the first VTC was established. During this period, the number of VTCs has grown annually, and there are currently over 600 VTCs operating across the country; only Vermont and Connecticut do not have VTCs in place (Rapisarda et al., 2024 volume). These programs vary in size, scope, target population, VTC team composition, VA and non-VA service provision networks, and intervention models. The above-mentioned variations make a simple description of a "typical" VTC program virtually impossible. However, these differences in VTC program models provide a unique opportunity for evaluators to compare the effectiveness of different VTC models, based on a full range of in-program and post-program outcomes related to service provision and improvement in designated need areas (i.e., mental health, physical health, housing stability, family, relationships/disruption, substance use, and recidivism). In 2022, the National Institute of Justice (NIJ) provided a total of $6 million in funding for a large multi-site evaluation of VTCs, which is currently underway; the results of this multi-site evaluation will be released in FY2027.[9] Given the proposed reduction in federal funding support for VTCs included in the Office of Justice Programs FY 24 Budget request, there is certainly a need for rigorous evaluation research to determine whether government support for the VTC imitative should continue. In that 2024 budget proposal, funding for VTCs was reduced from $35 million to $25 million, with at least some of this funding targeted to diversion/deflection programs.[10] It seems that at the national level, support for the continued development and expansion of VTCs is waning. Perhaps this will change if the results of the multi-site evaluation are positive; but realistically, this study is years from completion. In the interim, it makes sense to briefly summarize the current body of VTC evaluation research because this is the research that Congress will be able to review when these funding priorities are established over the next several years.

Despite the growth of VTCs nationwide in recent years, the evaluation research supporting the continued development of VTCs is remarkably limited. Our research team has conducted a systematic review of all published evaluations on VTCs since their inception.[11] Table 1 highlights the results of our review. We have identified fifteen separate research studies that examined VTC processes and outcomes, including four (level 2) quasi-

Table 1. An overview of veterans treatment court program evaluation research.

Author(s) (Year)	Program Under Review (State)	Research Design & Sample Size	Quality Ranking: Low (1) – High (5)	Key Findings
Derrick et al. (2018)	The San Diego Veterans Treatment Review Calendar (SDVTRC) Pilot Program	Longitudinal study (pre-post design) – participants measured at baseline, 6 months and 12 months. 82 Veterans accepted into the program: 49 participants with a program outcome at the close of the study time period.	Level 2 quasi-experimental design: Pre-post comparisons of changes in substance use, and several psychological well-being measures; no comparison group	With 49 participants having an outcome (i.e., graduated from the program, voluntarily terminated, or were involuntarily terminated), the successful completion rate was 71%. Overall, participants reported a decline in drug use ($p < .01$); depressed mood ($p < .001$); total trauma and stress and all three subscales ($p < .001$); total anger and aggression ($p < .001$); physical aggression toward objects ($p < .05$); and physical aggression toward self ($p = .052$). There was no statistically significant reduction in physical aggression toward others. There were no differences in treatment outcomes based on factors of military service, underscoring the importance of considering an individual's service history when developing their treatment plan, in lieu of a one size fits all approach for participants. The court has effectively achieved a 0% criminal recidivism rate among its participants.
Hartley and Baldwin (2019)	Large urban VTC program	144 VTC program participants who entered the VTC between 2010 and 2014 and remained in program for at least 6 months were compared to a group of veteran nonparticipants ($n = 157$) who were accepted into the VTC but opted out. Graduates: 128 Terminations: 16 General treatment group: 144 Comparison group: 157 Sample size for recidivism analyses varied significantly by year: Year 1: 126 grads, 14 terminations, 109 comparisons Year 2: 70 grads, 14 terminations, 44 comparisons Year 3: 30 graduates, 11 terminations, 12 comparisons	Level 2, quasi-experimental design: Comparison group identified but matching techniques were not employed; participants who dropped out of the VTC in first 6 months were excluded from the analyses; comparisons included for completers and terminations and the comparison group without controlling for known differences between groups. Significant missing data problem makes comparisons potentially misleading. Note: 9.4% of treatment group were designated high risk, compared to 17.1% of control group; no controls for risk level	No overall differences in recidivism: At 1-year post-program re-arrest, no difference between treatment and control groups (14% vs 16%) At 2-years post-program, the difference is 20.2% program participants vs. 34.1% comparison group. At 3-years post-program, the difference is 31.7% program participants vs. 50.0% for comparison group. However, Positive findings reported when terminations excluded from the analyses at 1-year post-program: 8.7% VTC program completers vs. 16.6% comparison group (see p. 64). Note: Researchers stated that matching "could not be employed due to the limited sample sizes of the groups" (see p. 71)

(*Continued*)

Table 1. (Continued).

Author(s) (Year)	Program Under Review (State)	Research Design & Sample Size	Quality Ranking: Low (1) – High (5)	Key Findings
Knudson and Wingenfeld (2016)	1 large urban, Midwestern VTC	Mixed-methods research design (assessments at baseline, 6 months and 12 months, in person interviews); 86 veterans	Level 2 quasi-experimental design: Includes pre-post psychological well-being and treatment recovery measures; no separate non-VTC comparison group	PTSD symptoms decreased significantly during treatment (F = 36.93, $p < .001$). Results revealed significant improvements over the course of treatment in recovery orientation (F = 12.25, $p < .001$), sleep (F = 7.94, $p < 001$), family relations (F = 5.60, $p < .004$), substance abuse (F = 21.36, $p < .001$), depression (F = 28.29, $p < .001$), emotional wellbeing (F = 17.59, $p < 001$), self-harm (F = 3.26, $p < .041$), and overall energy (F = 5.11, $p < .007$). The mental health outcome in terms of functioning (F = 25.34, $p < .001$), social connectedness (F = 14.74, $p < .001$), and social functioning (F = 14.65, $p < .009$), and emotional limitations (F = 14.65, $p < .001$) measures also evidenced significant improvement over time. The BASIS relationship factor (F = 7.33, $p = .001$) and the general health factor (F = 3.99, $p = .02$) each showed significance, as well Of the 86 participants, 9 were rearrested during their time in the program while 7 veterans were rearrested after 6 months, and 4 after 12 months, two were arrested at both 6 and 12 months
Slattery et al. (2013)	Colorado Springs VTC (Colorado)	Longitudinal evaluation: 200-item in person interviews at baseline, 6 months, and 12 months; 83 veteran participants	Level 2 quasi-experimental design: Pre-post comparisons of intermediate outcomes, including psychological well-being, employment, housing, sand substance use	Although VTC participation did not significantly improve unstable housing or unemployment, mental health did improve. Improvements in PTSD, depression, self-harm, emotional lability, substance use, and social reintegration were significant from baseline to 6-month interview and sustained from 6- to 12-month interview

(Continued)

Table 1. (Continued).

Author(s) (Year)	Program Under Review (State)	Research Design & Sample Size	Quality Ranking: Low (1) – High (5)	Key Findings
Tsai et al. (2017)	VJO program participants were extracted from the VA's Homeless Operations Management and Evaluation System (HOMES)	Secondary data analysis of 22,708 veterans (*N* = 8,083 VTC participants, 680 participants in other treatment courts and 13,945 participants in neither VTCs nor treatment courts)	Level 2 quasi-experimental design	VTC participants had better independent housing outcomes, and they had better employment outcomes, than non-tx court participants. However, VTC and other tx court participants were also more likely to have jail sanctions and new incarcerations compared with non-TC participants. VTC participants were more likely than other VJO participants to have served in Iraq or Afghanistan, but there were no sociodemographic disparities in access to VTCs.
Baldwin and Hartley (2022)	8 VTC programs operating in 3 Southern USA states (Florida, North Carolina, Texas)	Mixed-method research design	Level 1 non-experimental design: No comparison groups	Graduation rates: 75% or higher for 6 of 8 VTCs Self-report arrest data only included for a subset of interview participants: 10% self-reported re-arrest (see summary, p. 28)
Blonigen et al. (2017)	VJP (veterans justice outreach program) Specialists nationwide	Qualitative, in-depth interviews; 41 Veterans Justice Outreach Specialists, 13 Health Care for Reentry Veteran Specialists, and nine "hybrid" Specialists who served justice- involved veterans through both VJPs	Level 1 non-experimental design: Qualitative study	Of the 6 RNR-based risk factors (1-substance abuse, 2/3-lack of + school or work involvement, 4-family/marital dysfunction, 5-lack of prosocial activities/interests, 6-antisocial tendencies), VJP specialists reported having services and resources 100% of the time to address risk factors 1–3, 94% of the time for risk factor 4, 86% of the time to address risk factor 5, and only 57% of the time for risk factor 6. VJPs discussed services and resources along 3 cross-cutting themes: (1) peer-based services, (2) motivational interviewing/ cognitive behavioral techniques (brief/ informal), &; (3) cognitive behavioral interventions (structured groups)

(*Continued*)

Table 1. (Continued).

Author(s) (Year)	Program Under Review (State)	Research Design & Sample Size	Quality Ranking: Low (1) – High (5)	Key Findings
Erickson (2016)	3 VTC programs operating in 3 U.S. cities/counties (Broward County FL, Colorado Springs CO, Anchorage AL)	Case study including interview data, agency records, and evaluation stories; participants included: (1) the VTC coordinators in the Colorado Springs VTC and the Anchorage, Alaska VTC; and (2) the VTC judge of the Broward County VTC	Level 1 non-experimental design: Single-site case study; no comparison group	Broward County: Of the 264 active cases, 197 veterans were receiving services, seven were awaiting services, and 43 were in of need assistance (as of May 2015). Recidivism rate was less than 3%, according to the judge. Colorado Springs: Of approximately 289 cases, 159 veterans have graduated from the program and 35 veterans were either removed or opted out. The recidivism and/or re-arrest rate of the VTC is not tracked but was anecdotally reported as having a "very low" recidivism rate. Anchorage: 74 of 133 eligible veterans opted in; and, out of those, 38 graduated (51% graduation rate). 17 of the 38 graduates of this VTC (45%) reoffended within 3 years. The Anchorage VTC began collecting data with regard to recidivism in 2013 and since then not one veteran involved who has completed the VTC program has recommitted.
Himes (2019)	2 VTCs (Jefferson and Hardin Counties, Kentucky)	Secondary data analysis (exploratory descriptive study) of a mixed methods process evaluation project; 58 participants – 22 from Hardin County and 36 from Jefferson County	Level 1: Small-sample non-experimental design; no comparison group	46.6% (27/58) completed the program, 36.2% of participants recidivated. Gender ($\chi 2 = 3.639$, $p = .056$), sanctions ($t = 2.42$, $p = .019$), drug screens ($t = 2.702$, $p = .011$), and treatment sessions ($t = 55.54$, $p = .015$) each have a significant association with program completion, and both age ($\chi 2 = 7.817$, $p = .005$) and housing status ($\chi 2 = 5.974$, $p = .015$) have a significant association with recidivism. With reduced recidivism as one of the program's primary goals, 77.7% ($n = 21$) of those who completed the program did not recidivate.

(*Continued*)

Table 1. (Continued).

Author(s) (Year)	Program Under Review (State)	Research Design & Sample Size	Quality Ranking: Low (1) – High (5)	Key Findings
Holbrook and Anderson (2011)	14 VTCs	Cross sectional survey (participants were invited to submit any internal reports, operating procedures, or other information they believed would be helpful) between 2009 and 2010; participants were also asked to participate in follow-up interviews	Level 1: Non-experimental design; survey data collected from 11 VTCs	Responding courts (11/14 VTCs) reported a total of 59 graduates, eight voluntary withdrawals from the program, and 21 early terminations. Of the 59 reported graduates among all responding courts, only one had reoffended following graduation, a recidivism rate under 2%.
Johnson et al. (2016)	Each of the existing US veterans' courts over a period of 4–5 months by the VJO National Program Office	Cross sectional phone survey consisting of 107 questions on court structural classification, admission eligibility criteria, admissions/terminations/completions from the program, court sanctions and rewards, mentor component, and barriers to treatment; 302 VTCs	Level 1 non-experimental design	The following were associated with *higher rates of termination* from the VC program: (a) programs that offered phase progression based on measurable goals, (b) programs that permitted post-plea veteran defendants, (c) programs that accept veterans from outside jurisdictions, (d) programs that conduct frequent drug and alcohol testing, (e) programs for which sanctions are more severe for failing immediate goals (e.g., sobriety) versus long-term ones (e.g., training), and (f) programs that are classified as veterans' courts as opposed to mental health or drug courts The following were associated with *lower rates of termination* from the VC program: (a) programs that allow reserve/national guard veterans, (b) programs in which later phases permit less stringent testing, (c) programs utilizing behavioral contracts, (d) programs utilizing brief incarcerations, and (e) programs that work in close partnership with a VA Health Care Network

(Continued)

Table 1. (Continued).

Author(s) (Year)	Program Under Review (State)	Research Design & Sample Size	Quality Ranking: Low (1) – High (5)	Key Findings
Russel (2009/2015)	Buffalo NY VTC	Case study	Level 1 non-experimental design	As of 2011, there have been 71 graduates of the Veterans Treatment Court in Buffalo and, of those, we have had a zero percent recidivism rate Graduates of Buffalo's Veterans Treatment Court have experienced drastic, positive life changes (i.e., sober and actively addressing any mental-health needs). All of them are either employed or pursuing further education. Many have been able to mend strained relationships with family and friends, and those who were homeless have all been able to attain stable housing.
Shannon et al. (2017)	2 VTC programs (Jefferson and Hardin Counties, Louisiana)	Mixed-methods research design: Qualitative process evaluation and quantitative performance data on veteran participants ($n = 19$) served during the first year; 25 participants (21 VTC stakeholders, 4 veteran participants)	Level 1 non-experimental design	Qualitative data from both stakeholders and veteran participants suggest that offering rehabilitation via various program components, services/referrals, and accountability are critical to the success of the VTC. Data also provides valuable lessons learned for VTC implementation including communication, collaboration, information/protocols, and resources. Performance data shows that a variety of services are utilized and that frequent judicial interaction, drug testing, and sanctions are major fixtures within the court
Smith (2012)	1 VTC program (Anchorage, Alaska)	Analysis of data records on Veterans Court cases from July 1994 through December 2010; 147 veterans	Level 1 non-experimental design	Of the 147 individuals, 133 were eligible for the veterans court program, 74 opted in, and 38 graduated; 17 of the 38 graduates of Veterans Court (45%) reoffended within three years

(Continued)

Table 1. (Continued).

Author(s) (Year)	Program Under Review (State)	Research Design & Sample Size	Quality Ranking: Low (1) – High (5)	Key Findings
Tsai et al. (2018)	Veterans Affairs (VA) Veterans Justice Outreach program across 115 VA sites nationwide who entered a VTC from 2011 to 2015	Secondary data analysis of National VJO program data extracted from the VA's Homeless Operations Management and Evaluation System (HOMES); 7931 veterans	Level 1 non-experimental design	From program admission to exit, 10% more participants were in their own housing, 12% more were receiving VA benefits, but only 1% more were employed Controlling for background, characteristics, a history of incarceration predicted poor criminal justice, housing, and employment outcomes. Participants with property offenses or probation/parole violations and those with substance use disorders were more likely to experience a new incarceration. Participants with more mental health problems were more likely to be receiving VA benefits and less likely to be employed at program exit Although 20% of VTC participants received jail sanctions during the program, only 14% experienced a new incarceration during an average of nearly 1 year in the program

experiments with significant research design flaws, and eleven (level 1) studies that provide data on VTC operations and preliminary effects, which include secondary analyses of VA data related to veterans in VTCs, case studies, telephone surveys of VTC team members, interviews with staff and VTC program participants, and other studies with no control groups. Only one of the four level 2 quasi-experiments included a comparison group; in this study, significant differences in the risk levels of VTC and comparison groups were identified as a likely threat to the validity of the study (Hartley & Baldwin, 2019). The authors offer the following self-assessment, which applies to all evaluations of programs when participation is voluntary[12]: "Our finding that participation in the VTC was related to reduced recidivism could be confounded by unobserved differences between those who chose to participate and those who did not" (Hartley & Baldwin, 2019, p. 70). Unfortunately, none of the evaluations on VTCs conducted to date employ a rigorous research design, which leads us to conclude that at present and using Campbell Collaborative standard review criteria, the impact of the VTC court model on recidivism is currently classified as unknown.[13]

The studies highlighted in Table 1 provide a preliminary snapshot of program implementation challenges, while also presenting some interesting data on service provision outcomes. For example, several studies provided data on program completion rates. In a recent multi-site process evaluation of eight VTCs, Baldwin and Hartley (2022) highlighted the diversity of VTC models currently operating in these jurisdictions in terms of target population, selection criteria, referral pipeline, program conditions and supervision requirements, availability of treatment and rehabilitative support, and the level of service coordination with the Veterans Health Administration. There was significant variation in the graduation rates of the programs they reviewed, with successful completion rates ranging from 44% to 84.6% (Baldwin & Hartley, 2022).[14] Variations in graduation rates across VTC sites was also identified by Erickson (2016), while Johnson et al. (2016) identified factors related to both higher and lower VTC program termination rates (see our summary of these factors in Table 1).

We were particularly interested in the attempts by researchers in several jurisdictions to measure the impact of VTC services on various behavioral, mental health, and physical health outcomes. Derrick et al. (2018) identified improvements in several need areas, based on pre-post comparisons of a cohort of 49 VTC participants who completed the program. According to the research team, graduates of the program reported a decline in drug use, depressed mood, trauma, and aggression toward physical objects or self-aggression. Similarly, Knudson and Wingenfeld (2016) reported pre-post improvements in various psychological well-being and treatment recovery measures for 86 veterans who completed a VTC program, while Slattery et al. (2013) reported that 83 VTC program participants showed improvements (also via pretest posttest comparisons) in PTSD symptoms, depression, self-harm, substance use, and social integration. These preliminary research studies suggest that VTCs in these jurisdictions appear to be working as designed, but more rigorous research is necessary before these findings can be presented as "evidence" that VTC programs have their desired effects in terms of service provision.

It is obvious that there is much that we simply do not know about how VTCs are being implemented and operated across the country, but the studies highlighted in Table 1 still provide useful preliminary information on a handful of the 600 plus VTCs. Unfortunately, only a small number of low-quality impact evaluations of VTCs have been conducted to date, so we currently know more about implementation challenges than program effectiveness.[15]

Our research study: an overview

The purpose of our research study is two-fold: first, we are interested in understanding the perspectives of VTC team members on how their VTCs operate, and to document their recommendations on how to improve services and support for justice-involved veterans; second, we hope to provide our assessment of VTC service provision based on our examination of the service provision networks in three different VTC models. Throughout this project, our research has been guided by the advice and suggestions of our advisory board, which includes representatives from the VA's Veterans Justice Program, judiciaries, veterans advocacy groups, probation, and academia.[16]

Phase 1 interviews with VTC team members

Our research aims to document and understand the nature of VTCs' inner workings and collaboration with various entities such as community service providers and the VA.[17] We take a qualitative approach to uncovering these processes and relationships and focus on in-depth interviews with 145 VTC team members from 20 unique courts across the U.S. Key VTC team members include court staff, judges, attorneys, probation officers, community treatment providers, and Veterans Justice Outreach (VJO) coordinators.[18]

Table 2 provides a brief overview of our interview sample. The study sample is comprised of 34 attorneys (prosecutors, public defenders, and private defense attorneys), 15 judges, 16 community corrections officers, 17 community mental health or substance

Table 2. Sample characteristics across 20 sites.

Variable	n (%) or mean (sd)
Gender (*n* = 97)	
Female	58 (60%)
Male	38 (40%)
Race/Ethnicity (*n* = 97)	
White	67 (70%)
Black or African American	17 (18%)
Hispanic or LatinX	5 (5%)
Multi-Racial	6 (6%)
Asian	1 (1%)
Age in Years (*n* = 93)	49.8 (12.6)
Highest Educational Attainment (*n* = 119)	
*JD, EdD, MD, PsyD, and/or PhD**	54 (45%)
Master's degree	40 (34%)
Bachelor's or associate degree	22 (18%)
No higher degree	3 (3%)
Prior Military Experience (*n* = 103)	
Yes	36 (35%)
No	67 (65%)

Due to the semi-structured nature of the interviews, personal characteristics for each variable were not collected from every participant. *The vast majority of participants reporting having received a doctorate acquired a JD (*n* = 47), while 2 earned a PhD, 2 acquired an MD, 1 both a PhD and JD, 1 a PsyD, and 1 an EdD.

use treatment providers, 21 VJOs, 6 VA personnel (e.g., Veterans Benefits Administration representatives, VA peer support specialists, and veteran employment counselors), 18 court coordinators/managers, 6 social service providers, 9 mentor coordinators, and 3 "other" individuals, including a paralegal, a law enforcement officer, and a court clerk. Interviewees were majority women (60%), white (70%), and had an average age of 49.8 years. Additionally, 80% had advanced degrees and 35% were veterans with prior military experience.[19]

Phase 1 site selection

Twenty (20) VTCs were selected for this study using a purposive sampling approach. Our goal was to engage with VTCs across the U.S. that represented a range of characteristics including VTC size (i.e., the number of veterans served in each court), geographic location, and availability of court information. The research team developed an initial list of 54 possible court jurisdictions that served municipalities, counties, or regions, and then settled on 30 sites for initial recruitment. Researchers conducted outreach to court coordinators or VJOs to present the research study and provide additional information to court staff. In some cases, members of the research team met with court team members via Zoom to discuss the details of the research study, answer questions, and outline a process for obtaining any court approvals. Ultimately, 20 sites agreed to participate in the current study.[20]

We do not identify these specific courts or provide identifiable data on the team members we interviewed to maintain privacy and confidentiality of participants. However, we have collected data on key court and respondent characteristics that are worth considering at the outset of our review. Table 3 provides an overview of the key characteristics of our 20 VTC sites. The VTCs in our study vary in several key program characteristics, including program size, geographic region, and whether they operate in urban, suburban, or rural settings.[21] While the majority of the VTCs we studied were post-adjudicatory programs ($n = 11$), several had the capacity to provide both pre-adjudicatory and post-adjudicatory options for justice-involved veterans ($n = 8$), while one program was solely pre-adjudicatory. In terms of program models, there was variation in:

(1) The use of program phases (e.g., 2 programs had no unique phases, while 6 required veterans to complete five phases).
(2) Length of the program (e.g., 11 were 18 months or longer, 5 were 12-17 months, and the remainder had no set duration).
(3) Phase progression and program completion requirements (e.g., the amount of time a veteran is required to be abstinent from drugs and alcohol varied across sites, as did community service requirements, and payment of fees).
(4) The extent to which the VTC court integrated military symbols and protocols into hearings (e.g., some jurisdictions placed an emphasis on military protocols, such as referring to participants by their rank and branch of service[22]; others did not).

One characteristic of the VTCs in Phase 1 that is important to consider is the typical offense types that brought the veteran into the criminal-legal system: DUIs, domestic violence, drug possession, and theft. Many of the veterans referred to these programs did not have extensive

Table 3. Characteristics of veterans treatment courts in our multi-jurisdictional review.

Site #	Region[a]	Program Type & Length[b]	Estimated Average # Veteran Participants[c]	Military Discharge Exclusions[d]	Crime Exclusions[e]	Nexus Requirement[f]	Pre- or Post- Adjudicatory[g]	Typical Offenses[h]
1	West	12 months	33–49	No exclusions	None	None	Both	DUI, Domestic Violence, Assault, Drug Possession
2	Midwest	4 phase, 24 months	30	No exclusions	Current offense is a violent offense; convicted of a crime of violence within the past 10 years excluding incarceration	No	Post	Drug Possession, Misdemeanor Domestic Violence
3	South	5 phase, ≥ 12 months –3 years	40–45	No exclusions	Violent crimes (depends upon the severity); sexual crimes	Yes	Both	DUI, Domestic Violence, Other violent crimes accepted including gun crimes
4	South	5 phases, 18–24-month program	12	No exclusions	Violent & sex offenses	No	Both: most post-adjudicatory	Drug Possession, Domestic Violence
5	Midwest	5 phase, ≥ 18 months	17	Excludes dishonorable discharges	sex offenses are not allowed nor are prior registered sex offenders	No	Post; beginning a pre-disposition component	DUI, Domestic Violence, Drug Possession
6	South	4 phases, minimum of 18 months +6 months of aftercare	30–35	Must have "Honorable Discharge or general discharge."	A current charge or previous conviction for a violent crime (other than aggravated assault) or sexual assault; a prior conviction for delivery of a controlled substance	Yes	Both	DUI, Domestic Violence, Drug Possession
7	Midwest	3 phase, 18–24 months	40–50	Must have "an honorable, less than honorable or general discharge from the service"	Must "have a nonviolent misdemeanor and/or felony (up to level 2) offense"	No	Post	DUI, Domestic Violence, Alcohol-fueled crimes such as theft

(Continued)

Table 3. (Continued).

Site #	Region[a]	Program Type & Length[b]	Estimated Average # Veteran Participants[c]	Military Discharge Exclusions[d]	Crime Exclusions[e]	Nexus Requirement[f]	Pre- or Post- Adjudicatory[g]	Typical Offenses[h]
8	East	12 months +12 months aftercare	30	Dishonorable discharges	Sex offenses; violent crimes (homicide)	No	(Pre-sentence, plea into the court); sentenced upon completion of the program – dismissal or reduction of their charges upon successful completion (enter 2 pleas on the record; if they do not complete the program, they get the sentence)	Bulk of participants have some type of theft charges: retail theft, theft by deception, unlawful taking, generalized theft crimes. DUI
9	Southwest	6 months	131	No Exclusions	Violent crime; or multiple prior convictions	Yes	Pre; mostly misdemeanor offenses	All misdemeanor offenses considered. Typical offenses include: DUIs, domestic violence, harassment, shoplifting, theft, drug paraphernalia, prostitution
10	Midwest	5 phase, 14 months	52	Exclude individuals discharged while in Entry Level Status (boot camp)	Sex offenses (1st or 4th degree)	No	Post	DUI, Domestic Violence, Trespassing, Disorderly Conduct
11	West	5 phases, 18-month program	49	Discharge must be honorable, yet some courts make exceptions; must be eligible for VA benefits	Sex offenses; homicide	Yes	Post	Driving under the influence (DUI), and domestic violence are two main categories, but hate crimes, threats, assault cases and drug offenses are also accepted
12	South	6–18 months	35	Discharge must be honorable and must be eligible for VA benefits	Sex offenses, first degree felonies, crimes against children	Yes	Both	Majority of cases are DUIs, but some DV, drug, and theft cases as well; lower-level felony cases that are nonviolent

(Continued)

Table 3. (Continued).

Site #	Region[a]	Program Type & Length[b]	Estimated Average # Veteran Participants[c]	Military Discharge Exclusions[d]	Crime Exclusions[e]	Nexus Requirement[f]	Pre- or Post- Adjudicatory[g]	Typical Offenses[h]
13	West	4 phases, 18–24-month program	20	No exclusions	Violent Only sex offense convictions that require an evaluation and/or registration	Yes	Post	Drug offenses, burglary, shoplifting, domestic violence, trespassing and DUIs
14	East	4 phases, 12 months	80	Discharge must be honorable and must be eligible for the VA benefits	No specific crimes, however most violent crimes likely to be excluded on a case-by-case basis	Yes	Both (mostly pre)	Majority of cases are DUIs and Domestic Violence; or a combination of DUI and DV. District court only includes misdemeanors, unless there is a felony case taken as an exception (DV with a prior DV)
15	South	12–18 months	4	No exclusions	Violent crimes and sex offenses	No	Both (mostly pre because most offenses are misdemeanors)	Shoplifting, drug, and property offenses
16	West	3 phases, 18–24 months	35	Discharge must be honorable, yet some courts make exceptions; must be eligible for VA benefits	Sex offenses; homicide	Yes	Both	DUIs, Domestic Violence, non-DV assault and battery, and drug possession, and a small number of drug sales
17	West	18–24 months	40	Discharge must be honorable, yet some courts make exceptions; must be eligible for VA benefits	No specific crimes, however most violent crimes likely to be excluded on a case-by-case basis	No	Both	Majority of cases are DUIs or drop-down versions of DUIs like reckless driving; and domestic violence case and substance use offenses
18	West	9–18 months	40–45	No exclusions	Sex offenses; homicide	Yes, but not always enforced	Both	Substance use, DUIs, and a range of serious crimes

(Continued)

Table 3. (Continued).

Site #	Region[a]	Program Type & Length[b]	Estimated Average # Veteran Participants[c]	Military Discharge Exclusions[d]	Crime Exclusions[e]	Nexus Requirement[f]	Pre- or Post- Adjudicatory[g]	Typical Offenses[h]
19	Midwest	5 phases, 18 months	15	No exclusions	Violent & sex offenses	No	Both	DUIs, assault, and drug possession, and some distribution cases
20	East	5 phases; 18 months	20–25	No exclusions	Sex offense arson	No	Post	Substance use, DUIs, and drop-downs to negligent operation of MV

[a]We identify the Region of the VTC based on the US Census regions. https://www2.census.gov/geo/pdfs/maps-data/maps/reference/us_regdiv.pdf.

[b]Data on VTC program phases and length reflect the program in place at the time of our interview at each site.

[c]Participant numbers often changed drastically within individual VTCs during the COVID-19 pandemic and were slow to recover at the time interviews took place (January – August 2022). These program size estimates provided by VTC team members were not official program data, but they do represent the approximate size of each VTC at the time of our interview. We have contacted each site to get a current estimate (as of August 2023) of VTC program size. These data will be examined in an upcoming report.

[d]There are several types of possible discharge. According to a recent report by the Council on Criminal Justice (2022): "[t]he military discharges enlisted personnel with one of five designations: honorable, general, other than honorable, bad conduct, and dishonorable. Bad conduct and dishonorable discharges are punitive in nature and are assigned through a military court martial, where service members retain legal representation. With other than honorable discharges, however, commanders make the designation outside of a legal process to regulate misconduct that has not led to a military-court conviction" (pp. 9–10).

[e]For a variety of reasons, VTC programs that indicate that they exclude individuals charged with violent offenses typically include veterans charged with domestic violence when the charges are misdemeanors.

[f]Nexus Requirement involves a connection between the criminal offense and the mental health condition resulting from military service.

[g]Pre-adjudicatory includes pre-sentence/post-plea decisions where the individual has pleaded guilty but not received a sentence, as well as pre-plea diversion options. Post-adjudicatory refers to cases where the individual has been sentenced and assigned to the VTC as part of the sentence. These data reflect the program operating at the time of our interview; it is possible that some sites have expanded their VTC program model since the time of our interview.

[h]Typical offense profiles for each site are based on interviews with team members at each site; they represent the interview subjects' perceptions of the offense mix, but they are not based on official data from each site. However, several sites do include these data in their annual reports. We plan to compare these data to interviewee estimates in a future report.

criminal histories, which certainly raises questions when selection criteria target high risk individuals. The question becomes: at risk for what? For crime commission? Or for behavioral health problems? In this regard, it is interesting to consider OJP's target population for VTCs, which is described in their FY2024 Budget Justification for VTCs (2023):

> Veteran's treatment courts are focused on their scope and target audience. They serve veterans who have criminal justice involvement who have been assessed as being **high risk** to commit crimes with high levels of behavioral health needs. This means that no more than about 10– 15 percent of the overall number of persons with criminal justice involvement could be served by this court-based intervention. (p. 268)

We suspect that OJP may be conflating high risk (for recidivism) with high need (for services and support), given the estimate of the likely size of the high-risk population provided.[23] The designation of the high-risk category for the types of risk assessment instruments used in probation departments typically draws a cutoff point to include around 10–15%, of the overall population, as noted by OJP. If decisions on funding levels for VTCs are targeting only the subgroup of veterans who are high-risk for recidivism, this will result in a significant proportion of justice-involved veterans who will not be included in VTCs that rely solely (or mainly) on this funding source, because many justice-involved veterans are low risk for recidivism, but high risk for a variety of negative behavioral health outcomes (in other words, low-risk but high-need).

Our review of VTCs also revealed that program acceptance and admission vary by a veteran's discharge status. In half the programs we studied, only veterans who were eligible for VA services were accepted into the program; in the remaining programs, VA eligibility for services was not required. Similarly, half of the VTC sites required a nexus between the veteran's service-related mental health concerns and diagnoses and the current criminal behavior that has brought them into the criminal-legal system.

Phase 1 data collection procedure

After agreeing to participate in the research as a court, we recruited individual members of each VTC team to engage in an in-depth virtual interview. The court coordinator or manager provided a list of contact e-mails for individuals in key roles within the VTC. Not all courts had all roles as part of their organizational structure or had those positions filled. We directly emailed individuals to recruit them for participation in the interview, describing the interview process and providing a consent form for review. Participants who agreed to participate in an interview were then scheduled to meet on Zoom with one or two members of the research team.

Virtual in-depth interviews were conducted using Zoom web-conferencing software due to restricted travel during the COVID-19 pandemic. We believe the virtual platform increased our access (both time and place) to interviewing team members, but it is possible that the nature and course of interviews differed from what might have taken place if the interviews had been conducted in person (Oliffe et al., 2021). We constructed three semi-structured interview guides specific to various roles in the court.[24] All three interview guides asked participants about their role in the court, aspects of the court process, the makeup of the court clientele, perspectives on the strengths and weaknesses present in their particular court's service provision network, and the future of VTCs in general. The first interview guide was for team members who are engaged in elements of direct service (e.g., mentors, VA, or community-based treatment providers) or coordinating direct services and court engagement (e.g., court coordinators, probation officers, mentor coordinators) with the veteran client. The second interview guide was formulated for VJOs and contained questions specific to the VA's relationship with VTCs, and the process and function of brokering services for clients. The third interview guide focused on team members who perform legal functions including the judge, prosecutor, and defense counsel. This interview guide contained broader questions about relationships with other court team members and legal specifics about the VTC.

Interviews were scheduled for one hour but lasted between 45 and 90 minutes. All participants were provided the approved research ethics documents in advance of the meeting and consented to the interview prior to beginning recording. All but one participant agreed to be audio-recorded. In this case, detailed interview notes were taken by one member of the research team. We relied on Zoom's audio recording function to capture the audio, and these files were uploaded to a transcription service for verbatim transcribing. We did not rely on Zoom's auto-transcribe feature due to accuracy and data management concerns. Once audio recordings were transcribed verbatim, we deidentified participant names and other potentially identifying information (including names of other people in the court, aspects of the court itself, location specifics, or references to specific organizations) to protect participant and court privacy and confidentiality. Instead, we report our findings using a unique identification number and generic role/title. We met weekly as a research team to tackle logistical concerns related to collecting data from many sites, as well as debrief about emergent issues and topics from the interviews.

Phase 1 analytic strategy

All interview transcripts were imported into the qualitative software program, NVivo, for coding and analysis. We adopted a thematic analysis approach to coding the data, which included deductive procedures followed by inductive coding through an iterative process (Braun & Clarke, 2006). Thematic analysis is a qualitative strategy for coding and analyzing qualitative data that uses deductive and inductive approaches and is theoretically flexible, meaning researchers can engage in analysis steps that are tightly tied to specific theoretical propositions or enter the analysis phase *a priori* (Braun & Clarke, 2006). This allowed us to enter the analysis phase, which began after we collected interviews from the first two sites, with a robust list of possible codes and domains built on our post-interview debriefing sessions, the questions from the interview guide, and the prior research on VTC service provision. We complemented this deductive coding strategy with an inductive approach whereby new or unexpected actions, relationships, and processes were coded. Two members of the research team conducted the initial coding process, collaborating on where new codes were needed, as well as to confirm interrater agreement.

We produced analytic memos reflecting the larger themes emerging from this round of coding, which were collectively reviewed by the entire research team to produce the final iteration of the findings. This consensus approach to distilling our findings allowed for sufficient probing of the data and development of new conceptual framing about service delivery. We also engaged in a version of member checking by presenting our findings to the larger study's Advisory Board' who provided rich and detailed feedback on the veracity of our conclusions (Kornbluh, 2015).

Initial findings from phase 1's interviews

We will be presenting the results of the Phase 1 interviews in a series of research articles highlighting the unique perspectives of VTC team members. The four articles included in this issue present the results of our Phase 1 research in four areas: (1) the influence of enacting and enabling state statutes on the design and operation of VTCs (Rapisarda et al., 2024); (2) team member perceptions of eligibility criteria and target population (Hummer et al., 2024); (3) team member perceptions of service delivery and coordination with the VA (Kras et al., 2024); and (4) team member perceptions on the future of VTCs (Socia et al., 2024).

A summary of the key findings and take-aways from these four reviews is provided below:

(1) **A Nationwide Review of Enacting and Eligibility State Statutes**: Our nationwide statutory review revealed interstate variation in enacting and eligibility statutes that can be viewed as one factor impacting veteran eligibility and participation in VTCs. However, we found that most state statutes do *not* provide explicit language restricting the eligibility of veterans to only those who are VA eligible for services. Instead, we found that restricting prospective participant access into VTCs by VA service eligibility status is primarily shaped not by state legislation, but rather by the court and its team members, funding agency restrictions, and other state and local authorities outside the purview of state legislation.

(2) **Team Member Perceptions of Eligibility Criteria and Target Population**: VTC team members highlighted several issues related to eligibility for participation in VTCs and offered recommendations for improving the identification and decision-making process. Team members did not favor rigid eligibility criteria, and regularly mentioned a desire to be able to serve more justice-involved veterans. In courts without eligibility criteria codified by statute, high on their wish lists for the future would be additional resources and treatment options for veterans who are ineligible for VA benefits, or for services that supplement current VA offerings. In most jurisdictions where we conducted interviews, the VTCs were typically under capacity for participants (in some cases significantly so), with numbers not rebounding post-COVID, and courts were actively trying to bring more eligible veterans into the VTCs, but recruitment was an ongoing challenge.

(3) **Team Member Perceptions of Service Delivery and Coordination with VA**: VTC team members identified several service delivery challenges and offered recommendations for improving service delivery to justice-involved veterans. Across the interviews, team members identified where and why the needs of veterans were not being met, both before and after VTC court participation. Team members pointed out that a veteran's discharge status directly affected veteran's access to VA support services.[25] Team members also noted that current eligibility requirements for participation in VTCs may exclude a sizable subgroup of veterans that need the most help and support. In terms of service availability, team members noted the lack of residential mental health services available in their jurisdictions, and particularly from VAs, resulted in long waiting lists and an extended time to treatment for justice-involved veterans. They recommended developing veterans-only transitional

and long-term housing options. Similar strategies employing veterans-only mental health and substance use treatment programs were also recommended. Finally, team members felt that information sharing is a continuing challenge, in large part due to the siloing of client data across two large bureaucracies – the court and the VA – which renders any assessment of VTC program fidelity based only on one of these data sources incomplete.

(4) **Team Member Perceptions on the Future of VTCs**: Team members were hopeful about both the short-term and long-term future of VTCs, expecting them to continue to treat justice involved populations. This optimism, however, was tempered by concerns about the stability of funding sources, availability, and expansion of treatment resources, and the continued buy-in of key personnel and political supporters.

In addition to these articles, we also plan to highlight the unique perspectives of team members based on their roles and responsibilities on the VTC team, in a series of forthcoming articles on the perceptions of VJO specialists, judges, probation officers, mentors, VTC program coordinators, and other team members.

Next steps: phase 2 research

The initial component of Phase 2 of the current project has focused on collecting quantitative data on VTC processes and outcomes in three of the 20 VTCs within which team members were interviewed during Phase 1 of the project. Using a comprehensive model data collection instrument developed by the research team, we have worked with the sites to gather information on veterans' progress through, and completion of, various program phases in their respective programs. Examples of variables requested from these sites include:

- Veteran military discharge status for all referrals
- Referral process and reason for acceptance/rejection
- Race/ethnicity/other demographics of accepted VTC participants
- Instrument used to conduct initial risk and needs assessment
- Specific types of substance use, mental health, and other treatment modalities recommended
- Service provision data in each program phase
- Individual progress and time to completion in each program phase
- Overall improvement noted in designated need areas
- Legal system status
- Incentives for VTC program completion at each VTC

We are conducting a series of focus groups with program graduates in the three courts that are also providing Phase 2 quantitative data. We think it is critical to provide the perspective of justice-involved veterans on the design, implementation, and impact of these programs, and to carefully consider their recommendations for improving service provision, both inside and outside the VTC.

Concluding comments

The overarching goal of this project is to enhance our knowledge and understanding of strategies employed by VJO specialists and VTC staff to provide service to veterans in VTCs. Based on our Phase 1 qualitative research findings, our Phase 2 focus groups with justice-involved veterans, and the results of our quantitative review of service provision in three VTCs, we will be offering actionable recommendations on how to improve service delivery for veterans within VTCs.

We do have a few key take-aways from our initial background research that are worth considering. First, our review demonstrates the need for accurate, up-to-date data on the level of involvement of veterans in our criminal-legal system during their initial transition from the military to civilian life. Specifically, we need to systematically collect data on the post-service arrest, prosecution, conviction, incarceration, and/or community supervision of veterans. Second, we need several rigorous evaluations of the implementation and impact of veterans' treatment programs; we can not simply wait for the results of one multi-site evaluation. Even if the evaluators do successfully conduct a randomized control trial (RCT) at one or more sites, there needs to be a sufficient number of high-quality evaluations available for review. Until this work is done, any discussion of best practices is premature. We currently rely on research from evaluations of drug courts, or from other specialty courts, to develop best practices for veterans treatment courts (Miller et al., 2020); at best, this is a stop-gap strategy. As we highlight in our review of twenty VTCs, there are a variety of VTC models currently operating across the country, but we do not have a single, high-quality evaluation available for review. We have learned – hopefully – from our experience with HOPE-based evaluations that we cannot rely on one boutique evaluation to make critical policy and resource decisions regarding all VTCs; there needs to be much more research conducted and available for review (Pattavina et al., 2023). And third, researchers attempting to evaluate VTCs over the next few years will need to find ways break down the walls between two systems – the court and the VA – that currently tend to silo rather than share critical data on service provision, supervision, and criminal-legal system outcomes. As Tsai et al. (2023) recommend, we need to "Identify mechanisms for sharing of data, information, funding and other resources between federal, state and local criminal justice entities".[26] To be successful, we will need to develop data access and data sharing protocols that address data confidentiality concerns without excluding researchers not working for either system. High-quality, independent, external evaluations of VTCs are needed to assess the effectiveness of VTCs and guide the continued development of this initiative.

Notes

1. https://counciloncj.org/pr-vjc-preliminary-assessment/ See the review by The Council on Criminal Justice (2022). *From Service through reentry: A Preliminary assessment of veterans in the criminal justice system* for an assessment of the negative impact of discharge status on veterans transitioning from military service to civilian life, see Veterans Legal Clinic (2016), and Veterans Legal Clinic (2020).
2. Data are available on cohorts of veterans that allow estimates of lifetime risk of arrests, but these estimates do not distinguish pre-service, in-service, and/or post-service arrests. See Lucas et al. (2022) for an overview of research; and Brooke and Gau (2018) represents one study with estimates, but data are old.
3. By "recent" we mean that the survey data are just a few years old; but accurate data on the current number of veterans in our state prison and jail systems are not available for review. At the Federal

level, the BOP released estimates of the size of BOP's veteran prison population in their most recent update on the implementation of the First Step Act. They note that" At year end 2022, there were 8,627 persons with military service in BOP facilities, accounting for about 5% of the total federal prison population." See Carson (2023).

4. Brooke and Gau (2018) provide these estimates based on 2004 survey data from state correctional facilities. See also Maruschak et al. (2021), who examined the 2016 survey of prison inmates. These estimates are also included in a recent review by Orak (2023): *From Service to Sentencing: Unraveling Risk Factors for Criminal Justice Involvement Among U.S. Veterans.* Council on Criminal Justice. https://counciloncj.org/from-service-to-sentencing-unraveling-risk-factors-for-criminal-justice-involvement-among-u-s-veterans/
5. Orak (2023) summarizes the research suggesting that military service "might attract people with characteristics that make criminal justice involvement more likely in part because service is seen as a pathway out of challenging circumstances."
6. A recent NIC report, *Veteran Intercepts in the criminal justice system* (NIC, 2022) 2022 identified 6 unique justice system intercept points: (1) non-crisis deflection, (2) pre-arrest deflection, (3) initial detention and court hearings, (4) jails/courts, (5) reentry, and (6) community services. While policy options are discussed by the authors of this report for each intercept point, no data are presented on the number of veterans moving through each intercept point. Without this information, federal and state governments cannot make accurate resource allocation decisions.
7. See the Veterans Treatment Court Fact Sheet for background on this initiative: https://obama whitehouse.archives.gov/ondcp/ondcp-fact-sheets/veterans-treatment-courts.
8. This observation on the need for veteran-specific treatment (the responsivity component of the RNR model) is not an original thought on the research team's part; it was offered by the late Alan Lizotte, Professor Emeritus, SUNY Albany, in response to a question the first author raised to him about whether he thought specialty courts were needed for justice-involved veterans. He was a Vietnam veteran with a deep commitment to veterans' issues, and the research team agrees with his assessment. For those unfamiliar with Lizotte's contributions, see the following tribute: https://www.sansonefuneralhome.com/tributes/Alan-Lizotte.
9. NIJ has allocated a total of 6 million for this evaluation effort; an initial award of 4.5 million. For more details click here: https://nij.ojp.gov/funding/awards/15pnij-22-gk-00035-vtcx#supplemental-award-0-0.
10. See U.S. Department of Justice (2023) details on the budget proposal can be found on pages 268–270: https://www.justice.gov/d9/2023-03/ojp_fy_2024_presidents_budget_final_draft_clean_3.17.23.pdf.
11. We will be publishing a separate article detailing the results of our systematic review, but we think it is important to highlight these initial findings here.
12. Failure to account for the potential confounding effect of motivation to change is a limitation dutifully noted by researchers conducting quasi-experimental studies. Of course, noting it as a potential limitation does not solve the problem.
13. Evaluations of criminal justice programs have been reviewed using the Maryland Scientific Methods Scale; see https://whatworksgrowth.org/resources/the-scientific-maryland-scale/For an overview of how evaluation studies in corrections are ranked on a scale of 1–5 based on the quality of the research design, see Aos et al. (2006), available at http://www.wsipp.wa.gov/ReportFile/924/Wsipp_Evidence-Based-Adult-Corrections-Programs-What-Works-and-What-Does-Not_Preliminary-Report.pdf.
14. The authors noted that for a small subsample of 134 participants who completed 12-month follow-up interviews, 10% self-reported being rearrested. However, these self-report data were not officially verified.
15. A recent scoping review of VTCs (McCall et al., 2019) reached similar conclusions about the current state of VTC evaluation research. McCall and colleagues identified 48 written scholarly works on VTCs, but the majority ($n = 37$) were program descriptions, single case studies, or theoretical or policy pieces.
16. Advisory Board members include **Blue-Howells, Jessica** |*Deputy Director, Veterans Justice Programs, U.S. Department of Justice;* **Clark, Sean C.**| *National Director, Veterans Justice*

Programs, U.S. Department of Justice; **Corbett, Ron** |*Retired Commissioner of Probation, Massachusetts, Lecturer in the School of Criminology and Justice Studies, UMass Lowell;* **Moore, Eileen** |*Associate Justice, California Court of Appeal (Fourth District);* **Stewart, Katharine E.** | *National Coordinator, Veterans Justice Programs, U.S. Department of Justice;* **Stimmel, Matthew A.** |*National Training Director, Veterans Justice Programs, U.S. Department of Justice;* **Taxman, Faye*** |*University Professor, Faculty Fellow, Director, Center for Advancing Correctional Excellence!, George Mason University;* **Tirocchi, Scott** |*Director, Justice For Vets, A division of the National Association of Drug Court Professionals (NADCP);* **Tsai, Jack** |*Research Director of the National Center on Homelessness Among Veterans;* **Buchanan, Alec**, *Professor of Psychiatry, Yale School of Medicine.*

17. The current research project was approved by the George Mason University Institutional Review Board.
18. VJO specialists' primary roles entail providing direct outreach, assessment, and case management for veterans throughout the legal system (and not just courts), including in local courts and jails and help them navigate the legal system (U.S. Department of Veterans Affairs, 2021). For example, VJOs serve as a liaison not only between the VA and VTCs, but also between the VA and Crisis Intervention Teams in police departments and probation and parole officers (U.S. Department of Veterans Affairs, 2021).
19. Sociodemographic data were successfully collected during our interviews at 16 of 20 sites. Of the 145 interviews we conducted, these data were complete for 97 respondents (66% of sample).
20. The most common reason courts declined to participate was lack of staff or resources to support engagement with the research project.
21. Our research team has created an up-to-date listing of all current VTCs operating across the United States, which we used to map and examine the distribution of VTCs within states and across regions. Review of this database was instrumental in guiding our initial VTC selection process.
22. In several courts, a variety of military protocols were identified by the VTC team members that we interviewed, including the Pledge of Allegiance, use of military rank, and other military protocols.
23. See Taxman (2017) for a full discussion. The actual cutoff points set for each level of classification are not based on any specific recidivism marker; they vary from system to system and in many jurisdictions, the size of the high -risk category is likely resource-driven, given the closer supervision and lower caseload size linked to high-risk classification. There have been recent efforts to design a veterans-centered risk/needs assessment instrument, but the question remains: should the target population of VTCs include low risk, but high need veterans? See BJA's work in this area: https://bja.ojp.gov/program/veterans-treatment-court-program/resources.
24. Interview guides are available upon request.
25. It is well-documented in the literature that veterans without access to these services are more likely to self-harm and manifest untreated mental health and substance use problems that may result in criminal legal system involvement. For a recent overview, see the 2020 report, Turned Away, available at https://legalservicescenter.org/wp-content/uploads/Turn-Away-Report.pdf.
26. For a detailed collaborative research agenda, see the following summary report by Tsai et al. (2023) developed by the VA National Center on Homelessness among Veterans: https://www.va.gov/HOMELESS/nchav/docs/HVOSC-405_Research_Agenda_for_CJI_among_Veterans_508c.pdf.

Disclosure statement

No potential conflict of interest was reported by the author(s).

ORCID

James M. Byrne http://orcid.org/0000-0001-9216-9871
Don Hummer http://orcid.org/0000-0003-3026-0287

Kimberly R. Kras http://orcid.org/0000-0002-0592-0418
Sabrina S. Rapisarda http://orcid.org/0000-0001-5148-8630
Kelly M. Socia http://orcid.org/0000-0003-0560-3399

References

Aos, S., Miller, M., & Drake, E. (2006). *Evidence-based adult corrections programs: What works and what does not*. Washington State Institute for Public Policy.

Baldwin, J., & Hartley, R. (2022). *Executive summary: National institute of justice's multisite evaluation of veterans' treatment courts*. National Criminal Justice Reference Services.

Blonigen, D., Rodriguez, A., Manfredi, L., Britt, J., Nevedal, A., Finlay, A., Rosenthal, J., Smelson, D., & Timko, C. (2017). The availability and utility of services to address risk factors for recidivism among justice-involved veterans. *Criminal Justice Policy Review*, *28*(8), 790–813. https://doi.org/10.1177/0887403416628601

Braun, V., & Clarke, V. (2006). Using thematic analysis in psychology. *Qualitative Research in Psychology*, *3*(2), 77–101. https://doi.org/10.1191/1478088706qp063oa

Brooke, E. J., & Gau, J. M. (2018). Military service and lifetime arrests: Examining the effects of the total military experience on arrests in a sample of prisoninmates. *Criminal Justice Policy Review*, *29*(1), 24–44. https://doi.org/10.1177/0887403415619007

Carson, A. (2023). *Federal prisoner statistics collected under the first step act,2023*. U.S. Department of Justice, Office of Justice programs, Bureau of Justice Statistics. NCJ 307305. https://bjs.ojp.gov/document/fpscufsa23.pdf

Clary, K. M., Shaffer, P. M., Gaba, A., Pinals, D. A., & Smelson, D. (2020). Comparing the treatment needs of participants with co-occurring mental health and substance use disorders in drug and veterans treatment courts. *Journal of Substance Use*, *25*(3), 277–283. https://doi.org/10.1080/14659891.2019.1683905

Council on Criminal Justice. (2022). *From service to reentry: A preliminary assessment through the system*. Veterans Justice Commission. https://secure.counciloncj.org/np/viewDocument?orgId=counciloncj&id=2c918082829f83c70182b7c346ea0177

Derrick, R., Callahan, L., Vessellinov, R., Krauel, R., Litzenberger, J., & Camp, L. (2018). Serving those who served: Outcomes from the San Diego treatment review calendar (SDVTRC) pilot program. *Psychological Inquiry and the Law*, *11*(2), 171–183. https://doi.org/10.1007/s12207-017-9308-4

Erickson, J. (2016). Veterans' treatment courts: A case study of their efficacy for veterans' needs. *International Journal of Law and Psychiatry*, *49*, 221–225. https://doi.org/10.1016/j.ijlp.2016.10.009

Finlay, A. K., Owens, M. D., Taylor, E., Nash, A., Capdarest-Arest, N., Rosenthal, J. , Blue-Howells, J., Clark, S., & Timko, C. (2019). A scoping review of military veterans involved in the criminal justice system and their health and healthcare. *Health & Justice*, *7*(1), 1–18. https://doi.org/10.1186/s40352-019-0086-9

Hartley, R., & Baldwin, J. (2019). Waging war on recidivism among justice-involved veterans: An impact evaluation of a large urban veterans' treatment court. *Criminal Justice Policy Review*, *30*(1), 52–78. https://doi.org/10.1177/0887403416650490

Himes, M. (2019). Veterans' treatment courts in Kentucky: Examining how personal characteristics and during-program occurrences influence program completion and criminal recidivism, *Theses and Dissertations-Social work 24*. https://uknowledge.uky.edu/csw.etds/24

Hirschi, T., & Gottfredson, M. R. (1994). *The generality of deviance*. Transaction.

Holbrook, J., & Anderson, S. (2011). Veterans' courts: Early outcomes and key indicators for success. *Widener Law School Legal Studies Research Paper No. 11-25*. https://ssrn.com/abstract=1912655

Hummer, D., Byrne, J., Rapisarda, S. S., Socia, K., & Kras, K. K. (2024). No veteran left behind? perspectives on VTC eligibility criteria for justice-involved veterans in multiple jurisdictions across the United States. *Victims & Offenders*, *1*(1). https://doi.org/10.1080/15564886.2023.2288963

Johnson, R. S., Stolar, A. G., McGuire, J. F., Clark, S., Coonan, L. A., Hausknecht, P., & Graham, D. P. (2016). US veterans' court programs: An inventory and analysis of national survey data. *Community Mental Health Journal*, *52*(2), 180–186. https://doi.org/10.1007/s10597-015-9972-3

Johnson, S., Stolar, A., Wu, E., Coonan, L., & Graham, D. (2016). An analysis of successful outcomes and associated contributing factors in veterans court. *Bulletin of the Menninger Clinic, 79*(2), 166–173. https://doi.org/10.1521/bumc.2015.79.2.166

Knudson, K., & Wingenfeld, S. (2016). A specialized treatment court for veterans with trauma exposure: Implications for the field. *Community Mental Health, 52*(2), 127–135. https://doi.org/10.1007/s10597-015-9845-9

Kornbluh, M. (2015). Combatting challenges to establishing trustworthiness in qualitative research. *Qualitative Research in Psychology, 12*(4), 397–414. https://doi.org/10.1080/14780887.2015.1021941

Kras, K. K., Rapisarda, S. S., Hummer, D., Socia, K., Byrne, J., & Taxman, F. (2024). At risk and underserved: Veterans treatment court team member perspectives on service delivery challenges. *Victims & Offenders, 1*(1). https://doi.org/10.1080/15564886.2023.2275195

Logan, M. W., McNeeley, S., & Morgan, M. A. (2021). The effects of traumatic brain injury and post-traumatic stress disorder on prison adjustment and recidivism among military veterans: Evidence from Minnesota. *Psychiatric Quarterly, 92*(3), 1147–1158. https://doi.org/10.1007/s11126-021-09883-1

Lucas, P. A. (2021). A criminological fly in the ointment? a reply to Pratt and Turanovic's misinterpretation of problem-solving court ideology toward participant generality of deviance. *Victims & Offenders, 16*(5), 631–642. https://doi.org/10.1080/15564886.2020.1850583

Lucas, K., Marcum, C., Lucas, P., & Blalock, J. (2022). Military veteran involvement with the criminal justice system: A systematic review. *Aggression and Violent Behavior, 66*, 1–8. https://doi.org/10.1016/j.avb.2022.101721

Maruschak, L. M., Bronson, J., & Alper, M. A. (2021). *Survey of prison inmates, 2016: Veterans in prison*. https://bjs.ojp.gov/

McCall, J., Rodriguez, K., Barnish-Lange, D., & Gordon, A. (2019). A qualitative examination of the experiences of veterans' treatment court graduates in Allegheny County, Pennsylvania. *International Journal of Offender Therapy and Comparative Criminology, 63*(3), 339–356. https://doi.org/10.1177/0306624X18801462

Miller, M. K., Block, L. M., & DeVault, A. (2020). Problem-solving courts in the United States and around the world: History, evaluation, and recommendations. In M. K. Miller & B. H. Bornstein (Eds.), *Advances in psychology and law* (Vol. 5). Springer. https://doi.org/10.1007/978-3-030-54678-6_9

National Institute of Corrections Justice-Involved Veterans Network. (2022). Veteran Intercepts in the criminal justice system: Minimizing Collateral Consequences for veterans in the criminal justice system with deflection, diversion, and intervention. National Institute of Corrections, U. S. Department of Justice, edited by D. Ledbetter, NIC, November 2022 (Project number 22C6002).

Oliffe, J. L., Kelly, M. T., Gonzalez Montaner, G., & Yu Ko, W. F. (2021). Zoom interviews: Benefits and concessions. *International Journal of Qualitative Methods, 20*, 160940692110535. https://doi.org/10.1177/16094069211053522

Orak, U. (2023). *From service to sentencing: Unraveling risk factors for criminal justice involvement among U.S. veterans*. Council on Criminal Justice. https://counciloncj.org/from-service-to-sentencing-unraveling-risk-factors-for-criminal-justice-involvement-among-u-s-veterans/

Parker, K., Igielnik, R., Barroso, A., & Cilluffo, A. (2019). *The American veteran experience and the post-9/11 generation*. Pew Research Center. https://www.pewresearch.org/socialtrends/2019/09/10/the-american-veteran-experience-and the-post-9-11-generation/

Pattavina, A., Long, J., Petrich, D., Byrne, J., Cullen, F., & Taxman, F. (Early view, 2023). Revisiting the effectiveness of HOPE/Swift-certain-fair supervision programs: A meta-analytic review. *Criminology & Public Policy*. https://doi.org/10.1111/1745-9133.12635

Pratt, T. C., Barnes, J. C., Cullen, F. T., & Turanovic, J. J. (2016). 'I suck at everything': Crime, arrest, and the generality of failure. *Deviant Behavior, 37*(8), 837–851. https://doi.org/10.1080/01639625.2016.1147809

Pratt, T. C., & Turanovic, J. J. (2019). A criminological fly in the ointment: Specialty courts and the generality of deviance. *Victims & Offenders, 14*(3), 375–386. https://doi.org/10.1080/15564886.2019.1595247

Pratt, T. C., & Turanovic, J. J. (2021). They're called "specialty courts" for a reason: A criminologically-informed and evidence-based reply to Lucas (2020). *Victims & Offenders*, *16*(5), 643–651. https://doi.org/10.1080/15564886.2021.1902444

Rapisarda, S. S., Kras, K. R., LeMoyne, G., Hummer, D., Socia, K., & Byrne, J. (2024). Veterans' treatment courts: A nationwide review of U.S. enacting and eligibility state statutes. *Victims & Offenders*, *1*(1). https://doi.org/10.1080/15564886.2023.2263451

Russel, R. (2009/2015). Veterans' treatment courts. *Touro Law Review*, *31*(3), 385–402.

Shannon, L., Birdwhistell, S., Hulbig, S., Jones, A., Newell, J., & Payne, C. (2017). Examining implementation and preliminary performance indicators of veterans treatment courts: The Kentucky experience. *Evaluation and Program Planning*, *63*, 54–66. https://doi.org/10.1016/j.evalprogplan.2017.03.003

Slattery, M., Duggar, M., Lamb, T., & Williams, L. (2013). Catch, treat, and release: Veteran treatment courts address the challenges of returning home. *Substance Use and Misuse*, *48*(10), 922–932. https://doi.org/10.3109/10826084.2013.797468

Smith, J. W. (2012). The Anchorage, Alaska veterans court and recidivism: July 6, 2004–December 31, 2010. *Alaska Law Review*, *29*(1), 93–111.

Snowden, D., Oh, S., Salas-Wright, C., Vaughn, M., & King, E. (2017). Military service and crime: New evidence. *Social Psychiatry and Psychiatric Epidemiology (2017)*, *52*(5), 605–615. https://doi.org/10.1007/s00127-017-1342-8

Socia, K., Rapisarda, S. S., Kras, K. K., Hummer, D., & Byrne, J. (2024). "God, I hope it doesn't fade out": Team member perspectives on the future of VTCs. *Victims & Offenders*, *1*(1). https://doi.org/10.1080/15564886.2023.2276321

Taxman, F. (2017). *Handbook on risk and needs assessment: Theory and practice*. Routledge Press.

Tsai, J., Clark, S., Blue-Howells, J., & Hooshyar, D. (2023). *A research agenda for criminal justice involvement among veterans, VA national center on homelessness among veterans*. https://www.va.gov/HOMELESS/nchav/docs/HVOSC-405_Research_Agenda_for_CJI_among_Veterans_508c.pdf

Tsai, J., Finlay, A., Flatley, B., Kasprow, W. J., & Clark, S. (2018). A national study of veterans treatment court participants: Who benefits and who recidivates. *Administration and Policy in Mental Health and Mental Health Services Research*, *45*(2), 236–244. https://doi.org/10.1007/s10488-017-0816-z

Tsai, J., Flatley, B., Kasprow, W. J., Clark, S., & Finlay, A. (2017). Diversion of veterans with criminal justice involvement to treatment courts: Participant characteristics and outcomes. *Psychiatric Services*, *68*(4), 375–383. https://doi.org/10.1176/appi.ps.201600233

Tsai, J., & Seamone, E. R. (Eds.). (2019). *Intersections between mental health and law among veterans*. Springer.

U.S. Census Bureau. (2021). *American community survey 1-year estimates, Table DP02: Selected social characteristics in the United States*. https://data.census.gov/table?tid=ACSDP1Y2021.DP02

U.S. Department of Justice. (2023). *FY2024 performance budget*. Office of Justice Programs. https://www.justice.gov/d9/2023-03/ojp_fy_2024_presidents_budget_final_dra

U.S. Department of Veterans Affairs. (2021). *Fact sheet: Veterans treatment courts and other veteran-focused courts served by VA veterans justice outreach specialists*. https://www.va.gov/HOMELESS/docs/VJO/Veterans-Treatment-Court-Inventory-Update-Fact-Sheet-Jan-2021.pdf

U.S. Government Accountability Office. (2019). *Transitioning servicemembers: Information on military employment assistance centers*. https://www.gao.gov/products/gao-19-438r

Veterans Legal Clinic. (2016). *Underserved: How the VA wrongfully excludes veterans with bad paper*. Legal Services Center, Harvard Law School. https://legalservicescenter.org/wp-content/uploads/Turn-Away-Report.pdf

Veterans Legal Clinic. (2020). *Turned away: How VA unlawfully denies health care to veterans with bad paper discharges*. Veterans Legal Clinic at the Legal Services Center of Harvard Law School, veterans Legal Services, and Wilmer, on behalf of OUTVETS.

Veterans Treatment Courts: A Nationwide Review of Enacting and Eligibility State Statutes

Sabrina S. Rapisarda, Kimberly R. Kras, Grace LeMoyne, Don Hummer, Kelly Socia, and James M. Byrne

ABSTRACT

Veterans Treatment Court (VTC) is the fastest growing type of treatment court in the United States with over 600 VTCs in operation today. Despite this recent proliferation, minimal scholarship has been conducted investigating how the state-level statutory landscape influences VTCs. The current study begins to address this gap by comprehensively reviewing and analyzing state legislation that governs the enactment, operation, and eligibility requirements of VTCs nationwide. Our initial search reveals that 70% of states currently operating VTCs are statutorily authorized at the state-level, of which nearly two-thirds also enumerates operational and eligibility criteria, such as military status and branch, mental health diagnosis, the "nexus," criminal history, military discharge status, offense severity and type, and more. Our analysis indicates considerable variation and nuance across states but coalesced into several unifying themes. The results provide insights on one of the many important powers involved in shaping the operational and eligibility elements of VTCs – state legislatures – and can serve as a catalyst for future research on the myriad factors involved in determining how we conceptualize VTCs are and who is included in them.

Veterans Treatment Courts (VTCs) operate under a collaborative, or often referred to as, therapeutic court model offering specialized court programming to individuals who are involved with the criminal-legal system and are current or former members of the military. VTCs have proliferated in the past decade, with over 600 currently operating in the United States (U.S. Department of Veterans Affairs, 2021). The VTC court model adopts similar principles as drug court and mental health court models, where participants focus on the underlying cause of their criminal behavior, typically through an intensive, phased program that involves treatment, case management, mentoring, and a collaborative courtroom workgroup (see Russell, 2009). This collaborative team is comprised of attorneys and the judge, and has expanded to members from varying disciplines, including Veterans Justice Outreach (VJO) Program specialists from the U.S. Department of Veterans Affairs (VA), clinical staff (from the VA and community), probation officers, court managers and coordinators, and more. According to policy makers and practitioners, VTCs offer a treatment-focused alternative to more traditional forms of punishment (e.g., incarceration) that acknowledges the sacrifice of military service, the propensity for trauma-inducing experiences as a result, and the unique contexts of having military experience that provide a community of support (Hawkins, 2010; Jones, 2013).

There are a variety of federal, state, and local governmental bodies and individuals, as well as funding sources, that can be identified as key drivers or influences on how VTCs are designed and operated across the country (see Figure 1). The U.S. Congress has signaled its support by passing legislation and authorizing federal funding to support the creation, and now the enhancement, of VTCs nationally. The Veterans Court Coordination Treatment Act of 2019 provides some oversight for the current and not yet established VTCs nationwide, alongside a steady stream of federal monies disseminated from the Department of Justice via the Veterans Treatment Court Grant Program (Veterans Court Coordination Treatment Act of 2019, 2019). This federal legislation aims to unify program approaches and establish policy language for states enacting or operating VTCs. The Bureau of Justice Assistance oversees the selection of sites to be federally funded, basing its decisions on the model of VTC being proposed including the individuals to-be-served (i.e., the target population) and key VTC program components (National Association of Drug Court Professionals, 2018). The VA, through the VJO Program and in collaboration with the court, coordinates services for veterans accepted into VTCs, assuming these veterans are eligible for VA services.[1] Yet another federal agency, the Department of Defense, establishes policies and practices regarding the discharge status of veterans that also impact the population of veterans who enter VTCs (Veterans Legal Clinic at the Legal Services Center of Harvard Law School, 2020).

At the state level, legislatures and judiciaries can both contribute to and shape how VTCs are established and who is eligible. Legislation has been passed in many states that are now operating VTCs to authorize and stipulate court operations and eligibility to institute a "checks and balances" of power, especially in reference to judges and how they oversee their courts (Shah, 2014). Another important state-level factor influencing VTC eligibility is

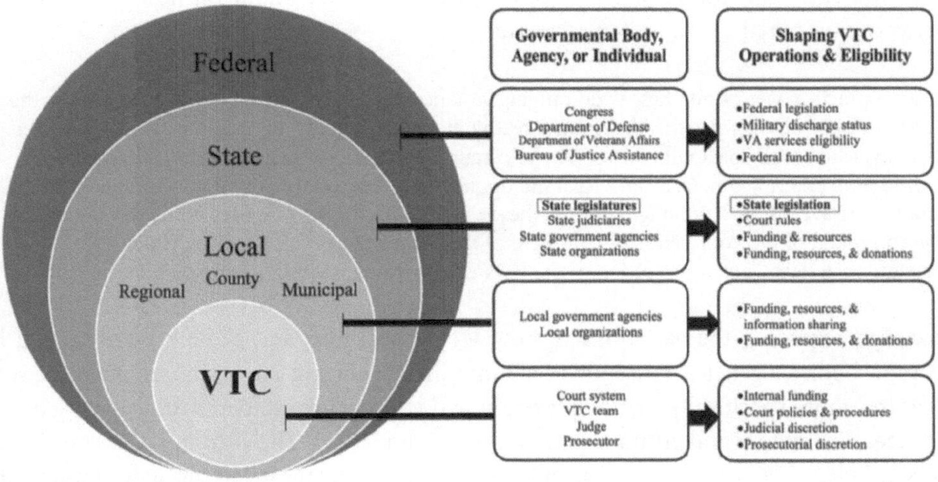

Figure 1. "The powers at play": Shaping VTC operations and eligibility.

funding. In addition to internal funding within the judicial system itself, VTCs can operate with funds that are external to the court, such as state government funding, in addition to other sources like grants and donations, which can either restrict or expand the target population of legal system-involved veterans and service members (Baldwin, 2016). For example, if VTCs are mandated to accept VA-eligible veterans only via legislation or state court rules, then the court need not depend on any external sources of funding (Baldwin, 2016); however, such decisions may be at the expense of serving a wider range of veterans and service members.

At the local level, where VTCs are most immediately situated, there are a variety of individual actors and organizational bodies that can also influence VTC operation and eligibility (Easterly, 2017). As stated above, various funding sources may influence eligibility, which can also originate from local organizations or government agencies. Within the court itself, judges are in some cases granted sole discretion to determine the essential components of VTCs such as the appropriate target population, as opposed to other courts whereby VTC teams collaboratively make decisions about the operational components of the court. In other jurisdictions, it is the prosecutor who is given the authority to determine the target population (Holbrook & Anderson, 2011). To greater or lesser degrees, these influences play important roles in shaping operational and eligibility components within and across VTCs.

While there is general agreement among legislators, funding agencies, and key court team members that VTCs offer positive impact on the lives of legal system-involved veterans, it is less clear precisely how these governmental bodies and agencies, in addition to key court actors, coalesce to shape the operations and eligibility of VTCs. Within this broader question of "*who* influences the operation and eligibility of VTCs, and *how*" lies an important knowledge gap: Namely, a more comprehensive understanding of the underlying legislation that enacts VTCs within states and determines eligibility into those VTCs (Arno, 2015). There is concern that the lack of uniformity in statute and the policies and procedures of VTCs may be producing inequities in the system, where those admitted by the courts become a "privileged class of criminal defendants" (Jones, 2013, p. 307). A lack of standardization may be conducive to an environment that is ripe with unfairness, inequity, and an increased likelihood of bias. Pomerance (2019) sheds light on how this court-to-court variation may be a cause for concern:

> From a practical viewpoint, these wide-ranging variances lead to problematic confusion among the general public about what the "Veterans Treatment Court" label truly means, as justice-involved veterans who are eligible to use the services of certain Veterans Treatment Courts are unequivocally barred from entering others. From a legal standpoint, these elemental distinctions from one court to another are even more troubling. Through these classification-based variances, states risk breaching the command of the Fourteenth Amendment of the United States Constitution, which orders that no state shall deny "equal protection of the laws" to any person within its jurisdiction. (p. 429)

Knowledge regarding the variations in how VTC operations and eligibility are shaped by important bodies, agencies, and individuals, and in the current study, the influence of state legislatures more specifically, can help explain and address impediments to providing access to services for military and criminal populations (Arno, 2015). The current study contributes to this broader endeavor by systematically reviewing and synthesizing the state statutes that govern the enactment, operation, and formulation of eligibility of VTCs across the U.S.

Literature review

Veterans Treatment Courts (VTCs) offer an alternative to traditional processes for individuals who are in contact with the criminal-legal system and hold active-duty or veteran status. These courts are situated in a collaborative or treatment court model, which relies on therapeutic jurisprudence frameworks to focus the role of court intervention on providing treatment for an underlying area of need that is related to the cause of criminal behavior (Rowen, 2020; Winick, 2002). Therapeutic jurisprudence also asserts greater judicial discretion in motivating individuals to succeed where, "judges seek to actively and holistically resolve both the judicial case and the problem that produced it" (Winick, 2002, p. 1061). Under this framework, the law and courts can offer a therapeutic impact through humane and psychologically driven approaches to legal matters.

For over three decades, the drug court model has served as the foundation for the creation and expansion of other treatment court programs, including VTCs, which are ultimately designed to serve specific target populations that have underlying substance use disorders (SUD) contributing to their involvement in the criminal-legal system (DeVall et al., 2022). Among the legal system-involved veteran population, their needs may either predate or stem from their time in the military. Post-traumatic stress disorder (PTSD), traumatic brain injuries (TBI), SUD, military sexual trauma (MST), and other mental and physical health concerns are well-documented in this population (Finlay et al., 2019; Tsai et al., 2018; Wilson, 2018).

VTCs model their "best practices" after drug court best practices established by the National Association of Drug Court Professionals (National Association of Drug Court Professionals [NADP], 2018). Some of these practices include a non-adversarial approach, integration of treatment services, abstinence, early identification, and coordination among court actors and service providers (NACDP, 2018). VTCs also frequently incorporate a mentoring component within their programming, typically on a voluntary basis and managed and carried out by veterans themselves (Douds & Hummer, 2019). VTCs also highlight service provision collaboration with the VA (Clark et al., 2010). Huskey (2017) suggests that VTCs are not just following "in the footsteps of those specialized courts; they are the next step in rehabilitative justice" (p. 179). That is, they have the potential to reform, or currently are reforming, the way courts think about those entering the legal system and the underlying causes of the crimes committed.

While there are limited evaluations on VTC effectiveness and efficacy in extant scholarship (Baldwin & Brooke, 2019; Baldwin & Hartley, 2022; Erickson, 2016; Lux, 2022; McCall et al., 2018), there is a growing body of literature citing VTCs' impacts on the populations they serve and documenting process evaluation metrics (e.g., Shannon et al., 2017). While these studies reveal promising and positive effects of VTCs, in order to move forward with rigorous evaluations that expand the evidence base on VTC operations and eligibility, the various bodies, agencies, and individuals that shape important features of these courts must first be reviewed. Little has been documented in the literature to date on specifically how VTCs are legislated at the state level and how this legislation may be influencing the operation of VTCs, namely the eligibility criteria required for admittance. Below, we highlight some of the definitional and eligibility-related issues that have emerged from the literature to help frame our statutory review.

VTC definitional inconsistencies

Despite that many VTCs claim to operate under "best practices," there is wide variation in how they operate and who they accept (Baldwin et al., 2018; Finlay et al., 2019). Even with federal legislation backing the establishment and funding of VTCs nationwide, considerable differences in operational and eligibility components of VTCs persist. Federal statute does not provide a definition for VTCs or outline their core components. Further, much of the extant literature surrounding VTCs arrives at the same conclusion: there is a lack of consistency in established knowledge or codification of the definition of a VTC and its core criteria for operation and admission (Timko et al., 2016), even with guidance from the Ten Key Components of Drug Courts (NADCP, 2018). It is possible that these operational and eligibility inconsistencies stem from the absence of clear definitions at the federal level.

Existing research provides a backdrop for understanding the current landscape of VTCs. Timko et al. (2016) conducted a longitudinal review of VTC characteristics and criteria for acceptance and participation. Their review of VA data spanning three years, collected through the VJO Program, revealed growing consistency in characteristics and criteria across programs, including primary jurisdiction at the county level, an average of 22–24 participants, and 18–19 months in programming for felony convictions. The results indicated that many courts expressed an "openness to veterans of different backgrounds and status," which included individuals with "other than honorable" (OTH) discharge statuses or prior criminal records (Timko et al., 2016, p. 1). Timko et al. (2016) address the importance of eligibility for allocating resources, ensuring rigorous evaluation of programs, and developing systematic tools for acceptance based on empirical evidence; however, this research fails to mention the limitations that precede acceptance and participation processes, which may be linked to VTC enacting and eligibility legislation. Although Timko et al.'s (2016) study was essential for expanding our understanding and knowledge of VTC characteristics, the data were limited to reports from court personnel, primarily VJO staff.

Attention has also been paid to the front end of the system – or where and how veterans are identified for VTCs. Baldwin et al. (2018) and Baldwin and Hartley (2022) documented the identification and referral processes of eight VTCs in the U.S., finding that an array of practices reflecting much variation in eligibility criteria exists. While their evaluation of these processes is the most comprehensive to date, variation in eligibility criteria came from court-based reviews and the originating statutes were not addressed. In particular, the study focused on identifying and verifying military status, but it did not define the types of military status that are eligible for these courts. Definitional and operational issues may be contributing factors to the lack of documented literature on how or why a potential participant might be excluded from the court.

The only existing study, to our knowledge, that reviewed existing and pending VTC legislation was conducted by Clark et al. (2010) more than a decade ago. Their study revealed considerable variation across statutes, aside from the inclusion criteria that the individual must have a mental health or substance abuse concern. They noted that numerous operational and eligibility elements were "not specified," including, for example, whether the VTC is considered a pre- or post-dispositional program. The lack of specification regarding VTC program components draws attention to the definitional concerns that are related to the vague conceptualization of a VTC (Baldwin & Brooke, 2019). More specifically, their study raises the question as to whether VTCs are true diversionary programs or alternative treatment courts (Arno, 2015). Since Clark et al.'s review in 2010, little has been documented in the literature regarding the legal governance of these specialty courts.

VTC eligibility (and exclusion) inconsistencies

While elements of VTCs' operations may overlap from court-to-court and the emphasis on treatment may be consistent across VTCs, there are important substantive differences in who is eligible and accepted into the court versus who is denied and therefore excluded (Pomerance, 2019). These differences are largely due to a variety of influences, including the existence and interaction of legislation, court rules, and/or the VTC team (Timko et al., 2016). For example, some VTCs may be legislatively constrained in terms of who they can and cannot admit into their courts based on the offense type and severity (Clark et al., 2010; Erickson, 2016). In other cases, veterans and service members may decline admission to VTCs because an operational criterion of the court is that a guilty plea must be entered *prior* to participation (Erickson, 2016).

The summary provided by Timko et al. (2016) not only captures just how varied VTC eligibility criteria can be across courts, but also helps explain why they vary, due in part to the dynamics of and interactions between court rulings and state statutes. Among the core requirements for admission into VTCs documented in studies is the presence of a diagnosed mental health disorder or SUD. This is a common criterion for therapeutic courts, as the model implies, and is the first among the core principles of evidence-based drug court practices (NADCP, 2018). A diagnosis is central and makes inherent in statute and policy the necessary reliance on clinical assessments to classify these individuals.

Another eligibility component referred to in the VTC literature is the "nexus." The nexus most commonly refers to the court's requirement that an explicit connection must be made between the criminal charge and an underlying mental health concern that stems from the defendant's time in the military. In a review of U.S. statutes that include a mitigating factor provision for veteran status and a mental health disorder, Sivanich (2021) found that 50% of states had some statutory language offering punishment alternatives for this population. In Baldwin and Hartley's (2022) evaluation of eight VTCs, five required a nexus to exist for individuals to be eligible for acceptance into the VTC. The nexus is also sometimes linked with criteria restricting admission to only those veterans who have experienced combat (Arno, 2015; Clark et al., 2010; Pomerance, 2019). The rationale reflects both the likelihood of finding a nexus, as well as the moral and legal obligation to offer specialized services to combat veterans (Arno, 2015). However, properly classifying and assessing the nexus, as well as establishing this causal link, has drawn criticism among practitioners and legal scholars (Jones, 2013; Pomerance, 2019).

An eligibility criterion that is intimately linked to this notion of a nexus is the offense type. In many VTCs profiled in the legal literature, violent offenses are excluded from the privilege of treatment court programs and diversionary court processes (Arno, 2015; Hawkins, 2010). Highlighting a similar trend, in an empirical study carried out by Douds and colleagues of 17 Pennsylvania-based VTCs, they found that while every court in this sample reported admission of veterans charged with nonviolent charges, violent crimes were acceptable on a far less consistent basis (Douds et al., 2017). Only a quarter of these VTCs reported definitively allowing for aggravated assault charges, whereas the remaining courts reported making these determinations on a case-by-case basis. Weapons and sexual assault charges were accepted by no VTCs in this sample (Douds et al., 2017). Contrarily, in a review of 461 VTCs across the country, Flatley and colleagues found that the majority of the courts (almost two-thirds) considers a participant with a violent offense charge, while 18% considers domestic violence charges while still excluding other violent offenses (Flatley et al., 2017).[2] One motivation behind this reasoning is that in some courts, domestic violence is not categorized as a "violent offense" and therefore is admissible for those VTCs (Arno, 2015; Pomerance, 2019). While legal scholars question the disparity here, there is some evidence to suggest that this decision is influenced both by perceptions about domestic violence cases compared to other violent offenses, and by local court discretion. For instance, a 2021 survey study by Luna and Redlich found that VTC actors (i.e., judges, coordinators, VJOs) were more likely to accept domestic violence cases than involuntary manslaughter into the court program, suggesting that perceptions of what constitutes "violence" and varying interpretations of statutory requirements may influence local level eligibility determinations (Luna & Redlich, 2021).

Current study

Overall, there is limited research chronicling the evidence-base for the array of VTC eligibility criteria that have already been documented in prior studies. To date, research enumerating the types of veterans that can be treated safely and effectively or the use of evidence-based assessment instruments and systematic procedures has not been the driving force behind establishing and determining eligibility criteria within VTCs at the legislative level and beyond (Timko et al., 2016). Documenting the variation in eligibility criteria across VTCs and linking them closely to evidence-based assessments and justice frameworks may be a step in the right direction for advancing an effective VTC model. Arno (2015) contends that in order to maximize the potential benefits of VTCs, there must be coordination at the state level and a focus on standardizing the VTC model.

The current study fills an important gap in the literature by providing a comprehensive state statutory review of legislation that enacts VTCs and outlines those statutes' operational and eligibility criteria. We review statutory code and records to develop a unique database and analysis of VTC operational and eligibility criteria. It is beyond the scope of this study to review the additional eligibility and operational criteria that exist at state court or local levels; however, where possible, we provide this contextual information to direct readers to additional information and resources.

Methods

This study involves a nationwide statutory review of legislation that enacts the establishment, and/or enumerates the operational and eligibility criteria, of VTCs. To begin, two research team members carried out web-based searches to identify and obtain existing VTC enacting and eligibility statutes across the United States. We gleaned government websites from each U.S. state, in addition to carrying out more general Internet searches of common legal resources like FindLaw, Justia, and Casetext. To ensure that legislation was most current, we conducted individual searches for each state, rather than extracting from websites with statutory compilations (e.g., Government Publishing Office, n.d.).

Currently, 48 of the 50 U.S. states operate VTCs. In the two states researchers could not identify legislation pertaining to veterans' court services or evidence of the operation of VTCs statewide, Connecticut and Vermont, researchers contacted pertinent court stakeholders for corroboration that no VTCs are presently in operation.[3] Of the 48 states with VTCs currently in operation, we identified 34 with statutory backing (see Table 1). In the remaining 14 states, the VTCs are not statutorily endorsed at the state level, but rather are established by the courts and operate under state court rules and local policies and procedures.

To be considered a state with VTC enacting legislation within this study, the statutory language must include explicit language that refers to (1) the establishment, creation, or operation of a veterans or military-specific court or program, including diversion, supervised treatment/probation, or both ($n = 30$), or contain language that allows for (2) the establishment of problem solving, specialty, or treatment courts more broadly, allowing for the creation of veterans courts ($n = 4$) amongst others (e.g., mental health, co-occurring,

Table 1. VTC enacting, operational, & eligibility statutes by state ($N = 34$).

State (N = 34)	Enacting Legislation (n = 38)	Operational & Eligibility Legislation (n = 26)
Arizona	22–601	–
Arkansas	16-10-139	16-101-103
California	**(1)** 1170.9; **(2)** 1001.80	"
Colorado	13-5-144	**(1)** 16-7-207.5; **(2)** 18-1.3-202.5
Florida	**(1)** 394.47891; **(2)** 948.08	"
Georgia	15-1-17	"
Hawaii*	**(1)** SB314; **(2)** 706–605.1	"
Illinois	730–167/5 & 15	730–167/20
Indiana	33-23-16-10	**(1)** 33-23-16-12; **(2)** 33-23-16-13
Kansas	Unnamed	–
Louisiana	13–5366	"
Maine	4-8B-433	–
Maryland	16–207	–
Massachusetts	Acts (2014) 62–33	**(1)** 276A–10; **(2)** 276A–11
Michigan	236 of 1961-12-600.1201	236-1961-12-6.1203
Minnesota	609.1056-1-6	"
Mississippi	9-25-1	"
Missouri	478.008	"
Nevada	176A.280	176A.290
New Hampshire	490-I:1	–
New Jersey	2C:43–24	2C:43–26
New York	Senate Bill S1957A	–
North Carolina	7A–791	–
Oregon	137.680	–
Pennsylvania	42 § 916	–
Rhode Island	8-8-1.1	–
South Carolina	14-29-30	–
Texas	124.002	"
Utah	78A-5-303	"
Virginia	18.2–254.2	–
Washington	2.30.010 (3)	2.3.030 (2–3)
West Virginia	**(1)** 62-16-2; **(2)** 62-16-4	62-16-5" (62-16-4)^
Wisconsin	165.95	"
Wyoming	7-13-1606	7-13-1607
State Total	**34**	**22**

" indicates that the state's enabling and eligibility statutes are one in the same.
– indicates that the state has no existing statute that speaks to VTC eligibility.
*Sunset law that was repealed on June 30, 2022.
^ One of West Virginia's enacting statutes (62-16-4) contains eligibility criteria within, in addition to an entirely separate statute (62-16-5), which speaks solely to VTC eligibility criteria.

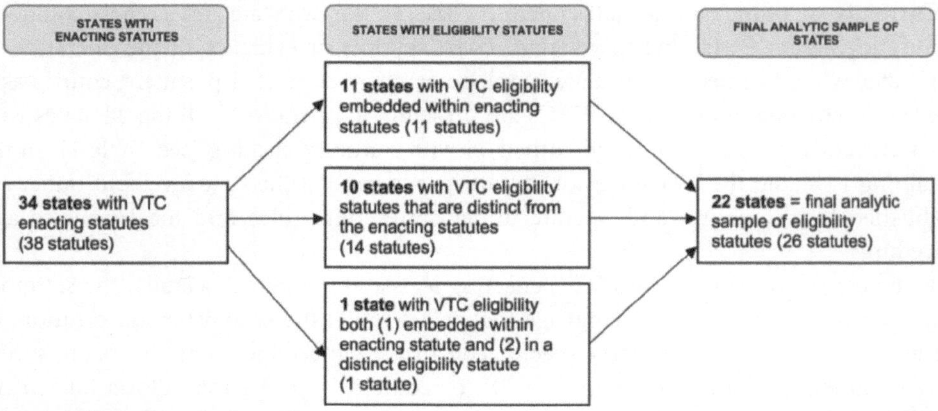

Figure 2. Final analytic sample: Identifying states with VTC statutes that outline operational and eligibility criteria (n=22).

drug, driving while intoxicated (DWI), etc.). We identified 38 statutes across the 34 states with VTC enacting statutes and created a database containing all relevant sections of the statutory language for subsequent analysis.

We reviewed each enacting statute among the 34 states to determine if they contained language pertinent to VTC operations and eligibility (shown in Table 1). We identified these criteria related to VTC admission embedded within the enacting statutes of 12 states. We also identified 11 states with eligibility statutes that were distinct from the previously identified enacting statutes, of which there were 14 statutes total.[4] In West Virginia, elements of eligibility were embedded in both the enacting statute as well as an entirely distinct statute. We noted that 12 of the 34 states with VTC enacting statutes are void of any eligibility criteria. In other words, in these 12 states, the statutory purview extends only to the establishment of the court but does not speak to the operational or eligibility elements of VTCs. Once we identified the distinct eligibility statutes, we stored the full content of all relevant sections of the statutes for subsequent analysis. In the present study, 22 states and their 26 corresponding VTC eligibility statutes were included in our final analytic sample (see Figure 2) for which the findings are presented below.

Analysis

We used an inductive approach to develop codes that identify and track operational and eligibility criteria emerging across states. Following the first read through, we formulated a list of eligibility codes. Using the list as a guide, we iteratively reviewed the statutes to ensure that all codes were applied where necessary. The research team engaged in numerous debriefing sessions after each iteration of coding to ensure the criteria were categorized consistently and in ways that are true to the legislation's meaning (Morse, 2015). To further organize and track the application of codes, we created a second database, where we further distilled categories by presence (1) or exclusion (0), or absence (unassigned) of an eligibility code. This database provided a numerical tabulation to cross-check the qualitative analysis and ensure statutes were included and categories reflected in all instances.

Terminology

As part of the coding and analysis, we rely on prior scholarship and existing statutory language to define and operationalize the terms and concepts present in the statutes, which are further examined as operational and eligibility criteria.

Enacting statutes refer to legislation executed in a state that specifically authorizes the creation and operation of VTCs.

Eligibility statutes refer to the elements within enacting and/or eligibility legislation that provide for the various criteria used to determine who can be admitted to VTCs.

Veterans treatment court refers to specialty or collaborative courts – or dockets, tracks, or divisions within courts – with treatment programming that specifically services either veterans or military servicemembers who are legal system involved, in lieu of alternative carceral outcomes. Despite having substantively similar core elements, the labels of veterans courts range, including "veterans treatment courts," "veterans diversionary courts," "military service members courts," "veterans dockets," "veterans track," and more.

Veteran status refers to the term "Veteran" being present within the statute while describing the treatment/target population of the court. Examples include, "'*Veteran*' [emphasis added] means a person who has served in the military" (Florida Statute § 394.47891) or, "A preadmission screening and evaluation assessment shall include all of the following: (1) A determination of the *individual's veteran status* [emphasis added]. A review of the DD Form 214 'certificate of release or discharge from active duty' satisfies the requirement of this subdivision" (Michigan Compiled Laws 236-1961-12 § 600.1203).

Military status refers to "military service members" being present within the statute while describing the treatment population. One state indicated the following: "A superior or circuit court may establish a veterans track within an existing drug court or mental health court, through which the court monitors veterans and *active duty members of the military* [emphasis added] with mental illnesses, substance abuse issues, or both … " (New Hampshire Revised Statute § 490-I:1).

Armed Forces refers to the United States Air Force, Army, Coast Guard, Marine Corps, Navy, and Space Force.

National Guard refers to state-based military personnel that become part of the reserve components of the United States Army and the United States Air Force when activated for federal missions. Members of the Guard can serve dual missions, state and federal, and can be called into full-time service to support Army combat missions (U.S. Department of Veterans Affairs, 2015).

The Reserve refers to military personnel of the United States Air Force, Army, Coast Guard, Marine Corps, Navy, or Space Force that do not have a state mission and cannot be called to respond to state-based emergencies like floods and hurricanes. Akin members of the Guard, the Reserves can be called on full-time into combat situations (U.S. Department of Veterans Affairs, 2015).

Pretrial diversion concerns the decision of a prosecutor or other authorized party of the court to refer a defendant to a diversion program in lieu of prosecution (usually occurring in the pre-charge disposition stage of the criminal legal system) on the condition that the case shall not be charged at all *or* if charged, that the criminal charges against the defendant shall be either dismissed after a specified period of time, so long as the defendant successfully completes the program.

Post-plea probation indicates that participants are actively enrolled in veterans' treatment programming and are supervised in the community following a plea (i.e., post-adjudication) and usually in lieu of imprisonment. In some cases where court participants are being supervised in the community, a sentence is imposed following a guilty plea to later be dismissed upon successful completion of the VTC (i.e., deferred sentence). Although diverted from incarceration, some court participants on probation who successfully complete the program may be ineligible for expungement of their record.

Mental health diagnosis is conceptualized as encompassing any clinically diagnosed mental health condition or diagnosis directly affecting one's mental state and mental health, including (but not limited to) post-traumatic stress disorder, SUDs (e.g., opioid use disorder, alcohol use disorder), military sexual trauma, and traumatic brain injury.

Nexus refers to determining whether an explicit connection can be made between the criminal charge and underlying mental health concerns that are either a direct consequence of, or stemming from, the defendant's time in the military.

Findings

Our analysis of the statutory language across the states with VTCs in operation revealed considerable variation and nuance but coalesced into several unifying themes. The funnel displayed in Figure 3 illustrates that approximately 71% (34/48) of states with VTCs are statutorily enacted, while the remaining 29% (14/48) operate entirely outside of state statutory purview. Less than half (22/48) of the states with VTCs outline operational and eligibility criteria in statute.

Of the 34 states with VTC enacting statutes, almost two-thirds (65%, $n = 22/34$) also have operational and eligibility criteria outlined, while the remaining 12 states' legislation surrounding VTCs is limited to enactment only (i.e., these states do not outline these criteria in statute). Among the states with any mention of VTC operational elements or eligibility in statute ($n = 22$), half ($n = 11$) include eligibility criteria within existing VTC enacting statutes, 10 states have eligibility criteria that are housed in distinct eligibility statutes, and one state – West Virginia – has eligibility both embedded in its enacting statute and contained within a separate eligibility statute (see Figure 4).

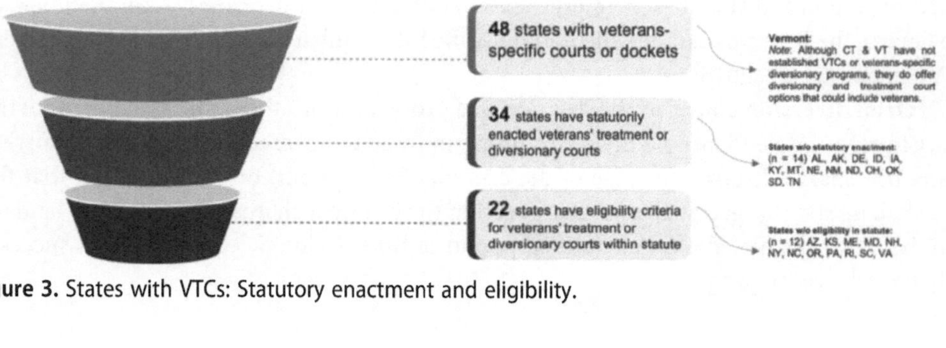

Figure 3. States with VTCs: Statutory enactment and eligibility.

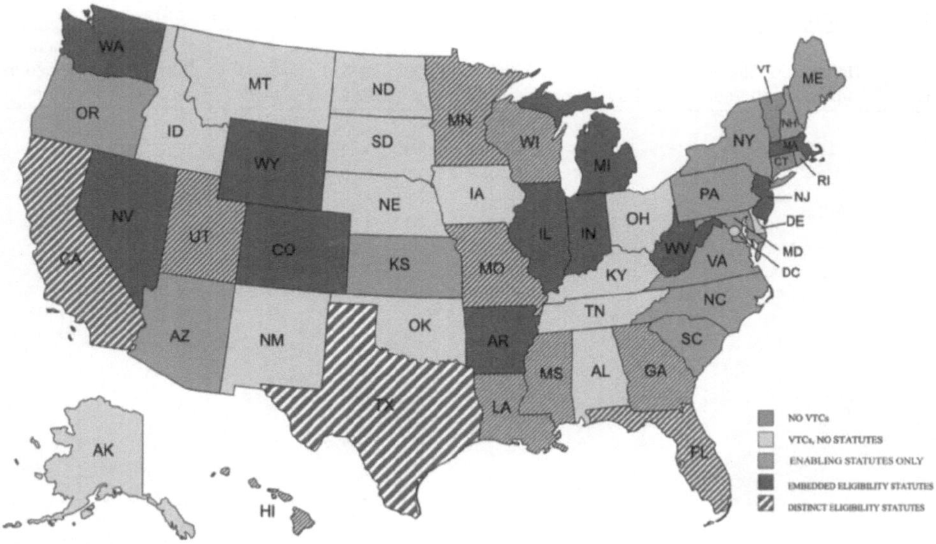

Figure 4. Mapping the VTC legal landscape across the United States.

Key operational & eligibility criteria

Although only 22 states possess VTC eligibility requirements within statute, there are seven states from the group with enacting statutes only (AZ, KS, ME, NH, PA, RI, VA) where the statutory language only briefly speaks to a few surface-level operational and eligibility criteria, such as veteran or active duty status.[5] To include these cases in our review of any operational or eligibility criteria, albeit surface-level only, the sample size of Table 2 was expanded to the original sample size of enacting statutes ($N = 34$). Table 2 displays three surface-level operational and eligibility criteria to begin our analysis: (1) whether the establishment of eligibility criteria and court provisions are explicitly deferred to, or shared with, the courts, (2) whether veterans, active service members, or both are eligible for entry into VTCs, and (3) the specific military branches that are eligible for VTC admission by state. Of the states ($n = 12$) with enacting statutes only, five states (AZ, KZ, ME, PA, VA) made explicit mention of deferment of operational and eligibility standards to the court, while four states (AZ, ME, NH, RI) also referred to the veteran/military status of prospective court participants within their enacting statutes.[6]

Deferred or shared eligibility authority

Of the 34 states with enacting statutes, 15 states explicitly defer or share eligibility-creating authority to/with the courts, of which 10 share authority with the legislative body. For example, despite that Colorado has operational and eligibility criteria outlined in statute, in Colorado Revised Statute § 13-5-144, it is stated that, "In establishing any such program [for the treatment of veterans and military service members], the chief judge, in collaboration with the probation department, the district attorney, and the state public defender, shall establish program guidelines and eligibility criteria." Similarly, Georgia's statute provides eligibility and exclusion criteria related to the types of pleas and offenses accepted into the court, but also denotes the following:

Table 2. Authority of eligibility criteria formulation & military status by state ($N = 34$).

State	Defers to or Shares Eligibility with Court	"Veteran" in Statute	"Active Duty" in Statute	U.S. Armed Forces	National Guard	The Reserve	Branch Unspecified in Statute
AZ	**x**	–	–	–	–	–	x
AR	–	x	x	x	x	–	–
CA	–	x	x	–	–	–	x
CO	x	x	x	x	–	–	–
FL	–	x	x	x	x	–	–
GA	x	x	–	x	x	–	–
HI	–	x	–	x	x	–	–
IL	x	x	x	x	x	x	–
IN	x	x	–	–	–	–	x
KS	**x**	–	–	–	–	–	–
LA	–	x	x	x	x	–	–
ME	**x**	x	x	x	–	–	–
MD	–	–	–	–	–	–	–
MA	–	x	x	x	–	–	–
MI	–	x	–	–	–	–	x
MN	–	x	x	–	–	–	x
MS	–	x	–	x	–	–	–
MO	x	x	x	x	x	x	–
NV	–	x	x	x	x	x	–
NH	–	x	x	–	–	–	x
NJ	–	x	x	–	–	–	x
NY	–	–	–	–	–	–	–
NC	–	–	–	–	–	–	–
OR	–	–	–	–	–	–	–
PA	**x**	–	–	–	–	–	x
RI	–	x	x	x	x	x	–
SC	–	–	–	–	–	–	–
TX	–	x	x	x	x	x	–
UT	x	–	–	–	–	–	x
VA	**x**	–	–	–	–	–	x
WA	x	–	–	–	–	–	x
WV	x	x	x	x	x	x	–
WI	x	–	–	–	–	–	x
WY	x	–	–	–	–	–	x
Total	15	21	16	15	11	6	13

This table includes an "x" only if an eligibility criterion or exclusionary criterion is explicitly stated in statute as applying to prospective participants of VTCs. In other words, the absence of an x does not automatically imply that those criteria aren't applicable to those states, but rather, that they aren't explicitly stated in statute. These criteria may still apply to VTCs but are not written in state legislation. – Indicates that an eligibility or exclusionary criterion is not explicitly enumerated in statute. Bolded x's indicate that eligibility criteria formulation is deferred solely to the courts. Therefore, eligibility criteria are not outlined in state statute.

> Each veterans court division shall establish a planning group to develop a written work plan. The planning group shall include judges, prosecuting attorneys, sheriffs or their designees, public defenders, community supervision officers, and persons having expertise in services available to veterans. The work plan shall include eligibility criteria for the veterans court division. (Georgia Code § 15-1-17b)

Within a handful of enacting statutes (AZ, KS, ME, PA, VA), the establishment of eligibility criteria is deferred entirely to the courts. For example, in Arizona, regardless of the specialty court, eligibility criteria are dictated by the superior court judge (and not based in state legislation): "The presiding judge of the superior court shall establish the eligibility criteria for referral to the homeless court, veterans court, or mental health court" (Arizona Revised Statute § 22-601).

Veteran & military status

Twenty-one states with enacting statutes, eligibility statutes, or both explicitly indicate the populations – veterans and/or active-duty military members – that their VTCs serve. The majority of states with VTC eligibility outlined in statute extend VTC services to both veterans and current members of the military ($n = 16$), while five states appear to restrict services to individuals of veterans-status only. In a handful of cases (e.g., WI, WV) where enacting statutes have broader reach (i.e., statutes that enact problem-solving courts, which can include drug courts, mental health courts, veterans courts and more), the statutory language includes more generic populations like "court participants" or "defendants" as opposed to referring explicitly to "veterans" or "service members."

Military branch

Of states that denoted "veteran" or "active members of the military" within statute ($n = 21$), most ($n = 15$) specify at least one particular branch of military service that is eligible for admission (i.e., Armed Forces, National Guard). Six states specify veteran and or service member status without elaborating further on the types of military service required for admission (CA, IN, MI, MN, NH, NJ), allowing for increased flexibility in the interpretation of military service type. Of the 34 states with VTC enacting and/or eligibility statutes, 13 states do not make any mention of veteran or military status. However, seven of these 13 states (AZ, PA, UT, VA, WA, WI, WY) do not specify this status because they do *not* have eligibility criteria written into statute. Rather, the VTCs within these states are limited statutorily to VTC enactment. Unsurprisingly, the branch most widely and explicitly specified in statute as being eligible for VTC admission is the U.S. Armed Forces ($n = 15$). Following closely behind is the National Guard ($n = 11$), and the least explicitly denoted branch is the Reserves ($n = 5$). Only one-third of VTCs that specify service in the Armed Forces ($n = 15$) as eligible for admission into VTCs also specify accepting members of the National Guard ($n = 5$). It is important to note that the lack of any specification of military branch, or only specifying one branch and not the others, does not necessarily insinuate exclusion from the court, but rather, may be an indication of more leeway and flexibility in interpreting the code.

An in-depth examination of VTC operational & eligibility criteria

Our analysis of the final analytic sample of states ($n = 22$) reveals a variety of domains reflecting both the common and rarer operational and eligibility/exclusion criteria used by VTCs nationwide. These domains include: (1) program type, (2) mental health diagnosis and the nexus, (3) agreement to participate, (4) amenability to treatment, (4) criminal history, (5) military discharge status, and (6) offense severity and type. Throughout our presentation of the findings, we provide example statutory language to illustrate the convergence and divergence of criteria across VTCs and uncover some of the nuances appearing within and across these statutes. We also display the findings across three tables: Table 3 includes adjudication-specific information and basic criteria about court participant characteristics, Table 4 homes in on the types of mental health conditions and related issues initially noted in Table 3 (e.g., PTSD), and Table 5 consists of criteria focused on criminal history, discharge status, and offense severity and type.[7]

Table 3. Key VTC operational & eligibility criteria by states with statutorily outlined eligibility criteria ($N = 22$).

State	Pre-Trial Diversion	Post-Plea Probation	Mental Health Diagnosis^	Nexus	Agree to Participate	Does NOT Demonstrate Amenability to Tx
AR	–	–	x	–	x	–
CA	x	x	x	x	x	–
CO	–	x	x	x	–	–
FL	–	x	x	x	–	–
GA	x	x	–	–	–	–
HI	–	x	x	x	–	–
IL	–	–	–	–	x	x
IN	x	x	x	–	–	–
LA	–	x	–	–	x	–
MA	x	x	x	–	–	–
MI	–	–	x	–	x	–
MN	x	x	x	x	–	–
MS	–	–	x	–	x	x
MO	–	–	x	–	–	–
NV	–	–	x	x	–	–
NJ	x	–	x	x	–	x*
TX	x	x	x	x	x	–
UT	x	x	–	–	–	–
WA	–	–	–	–	–	–
WV	x	x	–	x	–	–
WI	x	x	x	–	–	–
WY	–	x	–	–	x	–
Total	10	14	15	9	8	3

This table includes an "x" only if an eligibility criterion or exclusionary criterion is explicitly stated in statute as applying to prospective participants of VTCs. In other words, the absence of an x does not automatically imply that those criteria aren't applicable to those states, but rather, that they aren't explicitly stated in statute. These criteria may still apply to VTCs but are not written in state legislation. – Indicates that an eligibility or exclusionary criterion is not explicitly enumerated in statute. ^ Includes substance use disorders, traumatic brain injuries, post-traumatic stress disorder, military sexual trauma, and other diagnoses. *In NJ, the prosecutor considers whether the servicemember/veteran IS amenable to change/ treatment, unlike IL and MS whereby an exclusion criterion is a *lack of* perceived amenability to change.

Table 4. VTC eligible mental health-related conditions & considerations by state ($n = 15$).

State	Mental Health "Disorder, Problem or Condition"	Substance Use Disorder	Post-Traumatic Stress Disorder	Traumatic Brain Injury	Military Sexual Trauma	Co-occurring substance use and mental health disorders
AR	x	x	–	–	–	–
CA	x	x	x	x	x	–
CO	x	–	–	–	–	–
FL	x	x	–	x	x	–
HI	x*	–	–	–	–	–
IN	x	–	–	–	–	–
MA	x	–	–	–	–	–
MI	x	x	–	–	–	–
MN	x	x	x	x	x	–
MS	x	x	x	x	x	x
MO	x	x	–	–	–	–
NV	x	x	x	x	x	–
NJ	x	–	–	–	–	–
TX	x	–	x	x	x	–
WI	x	x	–	–	–	–
Total	15	9	5	6	6	1

This table includes an "x" only if an eligibility criterion or exclusionary criterion is explicitly stated in statute as applying to prospective participants of VTCs. In other words, the absence of an x does not automatically imply that those criteria aren't applicable to those states, but rather, that they aren't explicitly stated in statute. These criteria may still apply to VTCs but are not written in state legislation. – Indicates that an eligibility or exclusionary criterion is not explicitly enumerated in statute. *Requires that the mental health condition must be combat-related.

Table 5. Key VTC eligibility & exclusion criteria by states with statutorily outlined eligibility criteria (N = 22).

State	Excludes Having a Criminal History	Excludes Dishonorable Discharge	Felonies Eligible	Misdemeanors Eligible	Violent Offenses Eligible	Non-Violent Offenses Eligible	Excludes Prior Felonies
AR	–	–	–	–	–	–	–
CA	–	–	–	–	–	–	–
CO	–	–	–	–	–	–	–
FL	–	x[g]	x	x	–	–	–
GA	–	–	–	–	–	x[o]	–
HI	x[a]	x[h]	–	x	–	x[p]	x[p]
IL	x	–	x	x	–	x[q]	x
IN	–	–	x	x	–	–	–
LA	x[b]	–	x[k]	x	x[k]	x[k]	x[k]
MA	–	–	–	–	–	–	–
MI	–	x[i]	–	–	x[n]	x[r]	–
MN	–	–	x[l]	x	x	x[l]	–
MS	x[c]	x	x	–	–	x[s]	x[s]
MO	–	–	–	–	–	–	–
NV	–	x	x[m]	x	–	–	–
NJ	x[d]	–	–	–	–	x[r]	x
TX	–	–	x	x	–	–	–
UT	–	–	–	–	–	–	–
WA	x[e]	–	–	–	–	x[r,t]	x[t]
WV	x[f]	x[j]	–	–	–	x[r,u]	x[r]
WI	–	–	–	–	–	x[r]	–
WY	–	–	–	–	–	–	–
Total	7	6	8	8	2	11	7

This table includes an "x" only if an eligibility criterion or exclusionary criterion is explicitly stated in statute as applying to prospective participants of VTCs. In other words, the absence of an x does not automatically imply that those criteria aren't applicable to those states, but rather, that they aren't explicitly stated in statute. These criteria may still apply to VTCs but are not written in state legislation. – Indicates that an eligibility or exclusionary criterion is not explicitly enumerated in statute.

a. HI: kidnapping, 1st degree robbery, sex trafficking; In terms of CH, veterans in HI become ineligible for VTC admittance if they have been convicted of a crime involving serious bodily injury or substantial bodily injury within the past 5 years.

b. LA excludes potential VTC candidates for prior felonies only in cases of homicide and sexual offenses, or cases in which DWI resulted in the death of a person. Veterans charged with DV-related crimes are considered; however, they are required to enroll in a domestic abuse intervention program and surrender their rights to possess a firearm while under supervision.

c. Previous convictions for the following non-exhaustive list of violent felonies in MS are statutorily excluded from admission into VTCs: murder, rape, sexual battery, statutory rape of a child under the age of sixteen, armed robbery, arson, aggravated kidnapping, aggravated assault, stalking, or any offense involving the discharge of a firearm or where serious bodily injury or death resulted to any person.

d. In NJ, the following previous convictions excludes prospective participants from admission: murder, aggravated manslaughter, manslaughter, vehicular homicide, aggravated assault, disarming a law enforcement officer, kidnapping, aggravated sexual assault, sexual assault, robbery, carjacking, aggravated arson, burglary, extortion, strict liability or drug-induced deaths, terrorism, producing or possessing chemical weapons or biological agents, and racketeering.

e. In WA, statute prohibits admission into VTCs for both prior convictions and current charges of the following nature: serious violent offenses; sex offenses; alleging intentional discharge, threat to discharge, or attempt to discharge a firearm; vehicular homicide; or alleging substantial bodily harm or great bodily harm or death of another person.

f. Most violent crimes (of felony status) exclude military personnel (with active or veteran status) from entering VTCs in West Virginia, including sexual offenses; murder of a child by a parent, guardian, etc.; child abuse resulting in injury, use of forced labor, use of persons in debt bondage, malicious or unlawful assault or assault of a child near a school; abduction of a person, kidnapping or concealing a child, felony domestic violence, OR have been previously convicted in WV, another state or federal court of any of the aforementioned crimes, or DWI of alcohol, controlled substances or drugs (exceptions apply).

g. In FL statute, the chief judge and state attorney of the judicial circuit that creates and administers a veterans treatment court program have the exclusive authority to determine whether veterans who have been dishonorably discharged may participate in the veterans treatment court program within the circuit.

h. In HI, the statute defines that a veteran, "is a person who has been discharged honorably," thus, although the statute does not explicitly exclude a type of discharge.

i. MI statute requires that discharge status is disclosed to be considered in determining court admittance; however, a type of discharge is not specified for inclusion or exclusion.

j. While WV excludes dishonorably discharged veterans, it does include those who were discharged as OTH.

Program type: pretrial diversion and post-plea probation

According to statute, participants may gain access to veterans court programming via different pathways, the two most common being pretrial diversion or post-plea probation. The most common path of entrée into VTCs is following a guilty plea ($n = 14/22$). Five states in our analytic sample operate VTCs with post-plea options only (CO, FL, HI, LA, WY). Ten states statutorily enact participants to receive pretrial diversion services (pre-plea), which typically includes sentence deferment so long as participants are enrolled in treatment and successfully complete the program (see Table 3). In seven states with VTC eligibility statutes, it is unclear by viewing only statute whether the courts accept participants on a pre or post plea basis, or both.

Nine states statutorily allow for both pre-trial diversion and probation. A few states offer both pretrial and probation options to veterans in two distinct courts, including California, Florida, and Minnesota, each enacted by separate statutory codes. For example, in California, depending on the criminal charge and criminal history, veterans and military service members may have the option to enter a military diversion court pre-plea

k. LA excludes potential VTC candidates for prior felonies only in cases of homicide and sexual offenses, or cases in which DWI resulted in the death of a person. Veterans charged with DV-related crimes are considered; however, they are required to enroll in a domestic abuse intervention program and surrender their rights to possess a firearm while under supervision.

l. In MN, the types of felony crimes accepted into the court include: (1) Felony DWI, financial exploitation of a vulnerable adult, 2nd degree assault, 1st degree burglary (occupied dwelling), residential burglary, simple robbery, nonresidential burglary, theft crimes (at any amount), check forgery, 4th degree assault, fleeing a peace officer.

m. In NV, most felony charges exclude veterans from entering VTCs including sexual offenses and class A felonies: aiding an act of terrorism, murder (first degree, second degree), kidnapping (first degree), child abuse/neglect, child pornography, and more.

n. Despite explicit language excluding violent individuals from the VTC (" . . . An individual is not eligible for admission into a veterans treatment court if he or she is a violent offender."), statute allows for individuals who have committed intimate partner violence (i.e., "Assault on spouse, former spouse, individual with child in common, dating relationship, or household resident . . . ") to be admissible into VTC programming. See Section 4a of chapter IX of the code of criminal procedure, 1927 PA 175, MCL 769.4a.

o. In statute, GA excludes most veterans from entry into the veterans court division for having committed the following violent crimes: murder, armed robbery, rape, aggravated sodomy, aggravated sexual battery, aggravated child molestation, or child molestation. One exception to this ineligibility criterion is the case of a separate court supervised reentry program designed that more closely monitors veterans returning to the community after having served a term of incarceration.

p. HI: kidnapping, 1st degree robbery, sex trafficking; In terms of CH, veterans in HI become ineligible for VTC admittance if they have been convicted of a crime involving serious bodily injury or substantial bodily injury within the past 5 years.

q. IL excludes otherwise eligible veterans if the defendants were charged with at least one of the following crimes: first degree murder, second degree murder, predatory criminal sexual assault of a child, aggravated criminal sexual assault, criminal sexual assault, armed robbery, aggravated arson, arson, aggravated kidnapping and kidnapping, aggravated battery resulting in great bodily harm or permanent disability, aggravated domestic battery resulting in great bodily harm or permanent disability, aggravated criminal sexual abuse by a person in a position of trust or authority over a child, stalking, aggravated stalking, home invasion, aggravated vehicular hijacking, or any offense involving the discharge of a firearm. Additionally, the statute prohibits veterans who have been charged with aggravated driving under the influence that resulted in the death of another person.

r. In these states, statute doesn't explicitly state the inclusion of certain nonviolent crimes into VTCs; however violent crimes (often felonies) are explicitly excluded from eligibility into the VTCs.

s. Previous convictions for the following non-exhaustive list of violent felonies in MS are statutorily excluded from admission into VTCs: murder, rape, sexual battery, statutory rape of a child under the age of sixteen, armed robbery, arson, aggravated kidnapping, aggravated assault, stalking, or any offense involving the discharge of a firearm or where serious bodily injury or death resulted to any person. Thus, MS VTCs do not accept crimes of violence.

t. In WA, statute prohibits admission into VTCs for both prior convictions and current charges of the following nature: serious violent offenses; sex offenses; alleging intentional discharge, threat to discharge, or attempt to discharge a firearm; vehicular homicide; or alleging substantial bodily harm or great bodily harm or death of another person.

u. Most violent crimes (of felony status) exclude military personnel (with active or veteran status) from entering VTCs in WV, including sexual offenses; murder of a child by a parent, guardian, etc.; child abuse resulting in injury, use of forced labor, use of persons in debt bondage, malicious or unlawful assault or assault of a child near a school; abduction of a person, kidnapping or concealing a child, felony domestic violence, OR have been previously convicted in WV, another state or federal court of any of the aforementioned crimes, or DWI of alcohol, controlled substances or drugs (exceptions apply).

(California Penal Code §1001.80), or veterans treatment court post-plea (California Penal Code § 1170.9). Minnesota has similar statutory guidance:

> *Optional veterans treatment court program; procedures for eligible defendants.*
>
> A county or judicial district may supervise probation under this section through a veterans treatment court .... (Minnesota Statutes 609.1056 § 5)
>
> *Creation of county and city diversion programs; authorization.*
>
> Any county or city may establish and operate a veterans pretrial diversion program for defendants eligible under subdivision 1 without penalty under section 477A.0175. "Pretrial diversion" means the decision of a prosecutor to refer a defendant to a diversion program on the condition that the criminal charges against the defendant shall be dismissed after a specified period of time or the case shall not be charged, if the defendant successfully completes the program of treatment .... (Minnesota Statutes 609.1056 § 6)

Most states that offer pre-plea and post-plea options include multiple paths or tracks within the same court that originate from one statutory code for which veterans or service members can participate in VTC programming, exemplified by the following code:

> (3) In any criminal case in which a defendant is a veteran and the defendant meets the eligibility criteria for the veterans court division, the court may refer the case to the veterans court division: *A. Prior to the entry of the sentence, if the prosecuting attorney consents; B. As part of a sentence in a case; or C. Upon consideration of a petition to revoke probation* [emphasis added]. (Georgia Code § 15-1-17b)

Texas also operates multiple tracks for veterans and servicemembers enacted by one statute and held within the same VTC program:

> A defendant is eligible to participate in a veterans treatment court program established under this chapter only if [...] *the court in which the criminal case is pending or in which the defendant was convicted or placed on deferred adjudication community supervision* [emphasis added] .... (Texas Government Code § 124.0020)

Mental health diagnosis & the nexus

The modal eligibility criterion of the analytic sample is establishing the presence one or more mental health condition(s) (68%, $n = 15/22$). Nine of these statutes allude to the necessity of a nexus between military experience and the criminal charge, often linked to or driven by existing mental disorders. The degree of specificity surrounding the existence or type of mental health condition that must be present for VTC eligibility varies widely across states. In some states (CA, FL, HI, MN, MS, NV, TX), in addition to using encompassing language like "mental illness," their statutory language also explicitly specifies a list of mental health diagnoses (see Table 4 for more detail) that satisfy this eligibility criterion and often make mention of a nexus. Example language includes:

> ...to which [the court] may assign a defendant [...] if the defendant is a veteran or member of the military and: *Is diagnosed [...] as suffering from: (1) Mental illness, alcohol or other substance use disorder, posttraumatic stress disorder or a traumatic brain injury* [emphasis added], any of which appear to be related to military service [...] (2) *Military sexual trauma* [emphasis added] ... (Nevada Revised Statute § 176A.280).

Conversely, the statutory language for the mental health eligibility criterion in a few states (AR, CO, MA) lack the degree of specificity manifested in other states, also insinuating the potential for a wider range of acceptable conditions for VTC entrée. For example, in Colorado, a participant may qualify for VTC program admission, "if the defendant [...] *is suffering from a diagnosable mental health condition* [emphasis added] that is related to the veteran's military service ..." (Colorado Revised Statute § 18-1.3-202.5). Massachusetts's statute is similarly vague and does not require a nexus determination: "...has demonstrated *symptomatology suggestive of a mental illness* [emphasis added] ... " (Massachusetts General Law Part IV, Title II, Chapter 276A § 10–11).

Seven of the 22 states with VTC eligibility criteria do not explicitly specify that prospective participants require a mental health diagnosis for entry. However, the absence of specification does not by default imply that mental health issues need not be present. Six out of 7 of the states without the existence of an explicit mental health eligibility criterion in statute also defer eligibility determinations, in full or in part, to the court (GA, IL, UT, WA, WV, WY). Therefore, the lack of specification in statute could very well be created by the court and present in state and local court rules.

Amenability to treatment

Although infrequently outlined across eligibility statutes, a minority of states include language surrounding the idea of amenability or willingness to treatment and change by participants. Two statutes (IL, MS) briefly outline this criterion as an exclusion criterion, wherein the collaborative court may exclude prospective participants if, "The defendant *does not* [emphasis added] demonstrate a willingness to participate in a treatment program" (730 Illinois Compiled Statutes 167/20; Mississippi Code § 9-25-1). Whereas, in New Jersey's statute, "amenability [...] to participation in the services of the program" is to be considered by the collaborative court in conjunction with other eligibility criteria while making VTC admission determinations (New Jersey Revised Statute § 2C:43–26).

There is considerable variation and nuance in the statutory code surrounding who determines amenability to treatment and change, even of the small number of states (IL, MI, NJ) that make explicit mention of it in their code. Illinois and Mississippi rely on "the court" to make the determination of amenability to treatment/change while also simultaneously considering other legal and extralegal factors (e.g., military discharge status, offense type, etc.), stating that "A defendant may be admitted into a veterans and servicemembers court program only upon the consent of the defendant and *with the approval of the court* [emphasis added] ... " (730 Illinois Compiled Statutes 167/20) and "*The court having jurisdiction over a person for a matter before the court shall have the final determination* [emphasis added] about whether the person may participate in the Veterans Treatment Court program" (Mississippi Code § 9-25-1). In Illinois, while the court is deemed responsible for making admission decisions, if the defendant is charged with a Class 2 (or greater) felony, then, "...the defendant may be admitted into a veterans and servicemembers court program only *upon the agreement of the prosecutor* ... " (730 Illinois Compiled Statutes 167/20).

As is demonstrated by Illinois's statute (above), the "collaborative process" that VTCs are built on appears to have limits (i.e., Class 2 felonies and above). Based on statute and overlooking the collaborative decision-making process entirely, VTCs in New Jersey are required to operate and determine amenability in addition to other important eligibility considerations under prosecutorial discretion:

> *. . .the prosecutor shall have the sole discretion to determine if an eligible service member qualifies for and is admitted to the Veterans Diversion Program* [emphasis added] pursuant to P.L.2017, c.42 (C.2C:43–23 et al.) after consideration of [. . .] the amenability of the servicemember to participation in the services of the program [. . .](New Jersey Revised Statute § 2C:43–26).

Criminal history

A third of the sample ($n = 7/22$) excludes prospective participants with a criminal history from participation in VTCs. Nearly all statutes that exclude participants based on criminal history include a certain profile of felony offenses, most often including serious violent offenses (e.g., homicide, sexual offenses, assaults that result in serious bodily harm, armed robbery, intentional discharging of a weapon) (see footnotes in Table 5 for more detail). The statutes of a few states (i.e., HI, IL) factor in the length of time since the participant's last conviction (if any). For example, participants in Illinois VTCs may be eligible for participation if the crime they were charged with is nonviolent and their most recent prior conviction occurred 5+ years ago:

> A defendant *shall be excluded* from Veterans and Servicemembers Court program if any of one of the following applies: *(1) The crime is a crime of violence [. . .] (3) The defendant has been convicted of a crime of violence within the past 5 years* [emphasis added] excluding incarceration time, parole, and periods of mandatory supervised release. (730 Illinois Compiled Statutes 167/20)

Military discharge status

Only six states' statutes mention military discharge status of any kind as a consideration for VTC admission, of which three explicitly exclude those who have been dishonorably discharged from the military.[8] Of the remaining three, two states' statutes (FL, MI) defer to the court's discretion in determining eligibility based on discharge status, while the remaining state statute (HI) definitionally includes only veterans who have been discharged honorably, which implies – albeit not explicitly stated as an exclusion criterion – that any discharge status besides honorable is excluded. Overall, only one-fourth, or 27.3%, of states ($n = 6/22$) with eligibility outlined in statute are statutorily bound to considering military discharge status at all when determining VTC eligibility. This implies that courts, and not solely the legislative bodies, play a large role (i.e., court discretion) in determining eligibility of prospective participants based on military discharge status.

Offense severity & type

Of the states with operational or eligibility requirements outlined in statute, it is more common for these statutes to *not* specify the severity of eligible offenses – misdemeanor versus felonies. In almost every statute that explicitly noted the severity of the offense committed, it also allows for admission of both misdemeanor and felony offenses ($n = 7$), although researchers observed notable restriction on the types of felonies allowed into the courts (see Table 5) (often excluding sexually violent crimes, homicide, child abuse, DWIs resulting in death, and more).[9] In states that indicate specific crime types ($n = 11/22$) – broadly categorized in Table 5 as violent and nonviolent – it is most common for nonviolent crimes to be eligible for VTC admission, whereas the inverse is much less common ($n = 2/22$). It is common practice for statutes to list offenses that are *ineligible* for entrée into VTCs, rather than indicating the types of offenses that are admissible, especially among felony offense types. Eleven out of 22 states (50%) statutorily specify that *violence* is a key contingency for court exclusion. The most common offenses, most of which are felonies and have a component of violence, statutorily excluded from VTCs include: homicide, aggravated assault, armed robbery, sex crimes and stalking, child abuse and neglect, and DWIs that result in severe bodily harm or death (see footnotes in Table 5 for more detail).

Discussion

This is the first study, to our knowledge, that reviews and descriptively analyzes existing VTC enacting, operational and eligibility statutes across the United States. Understanding the legal landscape of legislation surrounding VTCs brings us closer to developing equitable and evidence-based standards for inclusion in this type of treatment court. Our review of statutes across the country identified the prevailing eligibility criteria for entry into these courts, yet also revealed the substantive gaps in consistency and uniformity that would be necessary for an evidence-based intervention.

First, we found that approximately 70% of states where VTCs are currently in operation are statutorily enacted at the state level, yet less than half have any eligibility criteria for VTC admission outlined in statute. A major implication of this finding is the paramount role of the court in determining eligibility for participant admission into VTC programming. More than half the states with operating VTCs rely entirely on the court for eligibility authority (i.e., no statutory oversight is currently in place), and even the states with eligibility statutes stipulated are still relying in part on the court's discretion. This highlights the importance placed on judicial and prosecutorial discretion in VTC operations. While some scholars have identified judicial discretion as a central tenet of this court model (Hawkins, 2010; Russell, 2009), other scholars suggest that it not only creates a tension between courts' discretion and legislatures' attempt at homogenizing VTC standards and procedures (Edwards et al., 2019; Pomerance, 2018), but it also enables a situation ripe for disparate use of eligibility criteria and due process, as well as unequal treatment claims (Jones, 2013; Pomerance, 2019; Rowen, 2020). Essentially, the absence of statutory uniformity and clarity may mean that a "privileged class" of defendants are created within the court system (Jones, 2013) and within the VTC itself (Pomerance, 2019). As a result of these disparities, some scholars suggest the risk for violating the 14th amendment increases, where some veterans get access to treatment and others do not (Pomerance, 2019).

Considering the variation in statutorily based operational and eligibility criteria across states with legislation in place demonstrates the importance of two overarching themes: (1) the types of criteria most commonly appearing across state statutes often reflects those program components deemed as most pivotal to the VTC model and (2) how eligibility criteria might exclude certain types of veterans. In reference to the former, legislating the presence of a mental health diagnosis for admittance situates VTCs firmly within the treatment court model and therapeutic jurisprudence framework (Winick, 2002). This key eligibility criterion ensures that service member and veteran populations who have made contact with the criminal-legal system are provided with access to a continuum of alcohol use, substance use, and other related treatment services (NADCP, 2018).

Designating the crime profiles also presents a boundary of offense types and histories that the court feels capable of serving or for which the individual is deemed deserving of the court's benefit. However, the dynamic between prospective court participants' needs and the crimes they have committed may in certain circumstances be conflicting, causing a misalignment of treatment and legal goals. Our findings reveal that these circumstances vary widely by state, such that state legislation stipulates an often lengthy, albeit variable, list of criminal offense types (most commonly of a violent nature) that exclude veterans from VTCs. Extant literature also notes a junction of state legislation and prosecutorial discretion, specifically by district attorneys where they played a crucial role in determining eligible offenses, even in cases where legislation and state/local court rules already exclude certain offenses (Holbrook & Anderson, 2011). Restrictions on certain offense types outlined in statute may be misaligned with the therapeutic model of the court. In other words, the type and severity of offenses committed by prospective VTC participants may exclude them from program admission, despite the clinical and social needs they pose following assessment (Baldwin etal., 2016). Further yet, we found that the "nexus" is statutorily required among nearly two-thirds of states with a mental health condition listed as an eligibility criterion for consideration for VTC admission. The requirement of a "nexus" between criminal behavior and a mental health condition linked to military service, and in some cases a specific link to combat experiences, implies that a member or members of the VTC staff are responsible for making these arguably subjective determinations, which could result in disparate determinations and inequity.

To the contrary, scholars have also documented the importance of operational and eligibility diversification across VTCs outside of legislative and executive forces, as it allows for VTC teams the discretion to define eligibility based on the individualized treatment needs of court participants, and considering the variety of pertinent extralegal factors to those specific courts, including the availability of resources to respond to court participants' psychosocial needs (Douds & Ahlin, 2019; Pomerance, 2018). In other words, restricting eligibility to certain veterans and service members may be a consequence of factors beyond the individual, such as resource restrictions (e.g., see Byrne, 2020). These distinctions may be especially important if courts, for example, cannot provide the range of local services necessary to serve certain subpopulations of legal system-involved veterans (e.g., veterans and service members who are ineligible for VA services).

Reviewing state statutes also reveals what eligibility criteria are *not* established or enumerated in legislation. For example, very few state statutes refer to inclusion/exclusion based on military discharge status (and relatedly VA service eligibility) or risk/need profiles. First, our findings show that three states expressly deny entry into the VTC if someone has been dishonorably discharged from the military. Discharge status emerges as an especially important consideration because it is directly related to a veteran's eligibility for VA services and therefore also related to VTC admission (Baldwin etal., 2016). In some locales, VTCs will identify and admit only those veterans who are able to receive VA services, in part to help with gaps that exist in community-based services. Future research should consider the ways in which discharge status affects the inclusion of veterans in VTCs at the local court level and the provision of treatment and other benefits by the VA.

Second, evidence-based principles of correctional intervention guide agencies to rely on risk and need assessment information to determine if the program is appropriate (Bonta & Andrews, 2007). However, only one state in our review, Oregon, which is limited to state legislation that enacts VTCs, stated that "When appropriate, target medium-risk and high-risk offenders" (Oregon Revised Statute § 137.680). This is not to suggest that such a criterion should exist in legislation, rather it speaks to the unknown variation across

VTCs related to inclusion as it pertains to the evidence-based consideration of risk and need. As federal legislation and funding agencies seek to support the implementation of evidence-based practices, criteria on risk and need and how these risks and needs are met will be important to establish in this body of research.

While our study brings forth a systematic review of the current legislative landscape of VTCs in the United States, it is not without limitations. First, our review being focused solely on state level statutes does not account for the impact of other important influences, such as policy and procedure that exists at state or local levels. This is confirmed by our finding that in at least 15 of the 34 states with VTC enacting statutes, there exists explicit language that either defers to or shares the creation of eligibility authority with the court. Furthermore, this study does not explore the dynamic between what is written in statute and how courts establish and determine eligibility in practice, shedding light on the misalignment that may exist between "law on the books" and "law in action" (Douds & Shultz, 2021). This is an important consideration such that VTC eligibility outlined in statute may look very different from the decision-making surrounding eligibility determinations that is carried out by VTC team members, especially alongside varying court-established policies and procedures. Expanding on the research of Baldwin and Hartley (2022), examining the inner workings of VTCs at the local and/or state level may help illuminate where there is convergence with and divergence from current best practices.

This study provides a comprehensive review of the state legislation shaping the establishment, operation, and eligibility of VTCs nationwide. By viewing what is (and is not) enumerated in statute, we are able to offer keen insights into the priorities of legislatures and the many and varied ways in which VTC operations are imparted by local courts and other influences at all levels of the government (see Figure 1). It is essential then to consider the role of state legislatures, among other important influences, when understanding what the best practices for VTCs are and if, and how, they are adopting and implementing them.

Notes

1. Veterans who are not eligible for VA services may still be eligible for VTC participation depending on other criteria, and their service coordination would be addressed by other court team members.
2. An important distinction within this study is that VTCs reported whether they "considered" violent offenses, which may differ from the courts "accepting" violent offenses on a definitive or case-by-case basis.
3. To ensure that our search was thorough and comprehensive, we contacted Vermont's treatment court programs manager and the Attorney General's Office to verify that Vermont does not currently provide diversionary or treatment court services to veterans that are veteran specific. It was relayed that veterans are serviced within the broader mental health, substance use, and DWI court populations. Researchers followed the same process, connecting with a member of the Connecticut Judiciary who confirmed that despite the myriad court services that veterans can access, the state does not provide veterans diversionary or treatment programs that are exclusive to veterans only.
4. Eleven states have 14 statutes because three states (Colorado, Indiana, & Massachusetts) have two eligibility statutes each that are distinct from the statutes that enact VTCs in their respective states.
5. The research team agreed that these 7 states should not be included in the final analytic sample because they only speak to military status and/or whether eligibility criteria should be shared

with the legislature or deferred to the courts. These eligibility criteria are surface-level and do not highlight the core components (e.g., mental health diagnosis, offense type, etc.), and therefore, the corresponding states were excluded from further analysis.

6. Note that these states did NOT outline any eligibility criteria beyond authority of eligibility creation and military status/branch, hence why they were excluded from the final analytic sample displayed in Tables 3 and 4.
7. More detailed information on eligibility for admittance into VTCs can be found in the notes of Table 5.
8. In West Virginia, despite that dishonorably discharged veterans are statutorily barred from entering VTCs, statute explicitly indicates that other-than-honorable (OTH) cases *are* eligible for court admittance.
9. It is important to note that simply because a statute does NOT explicitly indicate a certain crime severity as eligible for admission, does not automatically indicate exclusion. These criteria are not mutually exclusive.

Disclosure statement

No potential conflict of interest was reported by the author(s).

Funding

This study was funded under the Justice Community Opioid Innovation Network (JCOIN) Coordination and Translation Center (CTC) [U2CDA050097, MPI Taxman/Rudes]. The contents of this publication are solely the responsibility of the authors and do not necessarily represent the official views of the NIH, or the participating sites.

ORCID

Sabrina S. Rapisarda http://orcid.org/0000-0001-5148-8630
Kimberly R. Kras http://orcid.org/0000-0002-0592-0418
Don Hummer http://orcid.org/0000-0003-3026-0287
Kelly Socia http://orcid.org/0000-0003-0560-3399
James M. Byrne http://orcid.org/0000-0001-9216-9871

References

Arno, C. (2015). Proportional response: The need for more—and more standardized—Veterans' courts. *University of Michigan Journal of Law Reform*, *48*, 1039–1072. https://doi.org/10.36646/mjlr.48.4.proportional

Baldwin, J. M. (2016). Investigating the programmatic attack: A national survey of veterans treatment courts. *Journal of Criminal Law & Criminology*, *105*(3), 705–751. https://heinonline.org/HOL/Page?handle=hein.journals/jclc105&div=26&g_sent=1&casa_token=5s1QZNBxRtgAAAAA:8uWl41MmpCKfy2cQxO3oA_Ed9VtuHM34XMyjJ_zxiNmwYT-F_f7BID9cdnCL5l2cn6Aihlea&collection=journals

Baldwin, J. M., & Brooke, E. J. (2019). Pausing in the wake of rapid adoption: A call to critically examine the veterans treatment court concept. *Journal of Offender Rehabilitation*, *58*(1), 1–29. https://doi.org/10.1080/10509674.2018.1549181

Baldwin, J. M., & Hartley, R. D. (2022). *Final report: National Institute of Justice's multisite evaluation of veterans treatment courts, systematic assessment of implementation and intermediate outcomes*. National Institute of Justice.

Baldwin, J. M., Hartley, R. D., & Brooke, E. J. (2018). Identifying those who served: Modeling potential participant identification in veterans treatment courts. *Drug Court Review, 1*, 11–32. https://ntcrc.org/wp-content/uploads/2020/05/Drug-Court-Review-Vol-1.pdf#page=16

Bonta, J., & Andrews, D. A. (2007). Risk-need-responsivity model for offender assessment and rehabilitation. *Rehabilitation, 6*(1), 1–22.

Byrne, F. (2020). *Collaborative justice: Survey and assessment of veterans treatment courts.* Judicial Council of California. https://www.courts.ca.gov/documents/lr-2020-collaborative-courts-survey-and-assessment-of-treatment-courts.pdf

Clark, S., McGuire, J., & Blue-Howells, J. (2010). Development of veterans treatment courts: Local and legislative initiatives. *Drug Court Review, 7*(1), 171–208. https://ntcrc.org/wp-content/uploads/2020/06/DCRVolume7-5_Development_of_Veterans_Treatment_Courts_Local_and_Legislative_Initiatives.pdf

DeVall, K., Lanier, C., & Baker, L. J. (2022). *Painting the current picture: A national report on treatment courts in the United States – Highlights and insights.* National Drug Court Resource Center. https://ndcrc.org/wp-content/uploads/2021/08/2020_NDCRC_TreatmentCourt_Count_Table_v8.pdf

Douds, A. S., & Ahlin, E. M. (2019). *The veterans court movement: Striving to serve those who served.* Routledge. https://doi.org/10.4324/9780429401565

Douds, A. S., Ahlin, E. M., Howard, D., & Stigerwalt, S. (2017). Varieties of veterans' courts: A statewide assessment of veterans' treatment court components. *Criminal Justice Policy Review, 28*(8), 740–769. https://doi.org/10.1177/0887403415620633

Douds, A. S., & Hummer, D. (2019). When a veterans' treatment court fails: Lessons learned from a qualitative evaluation. *Victims & Offenders, 14*(3), 322–343. https://doi.org/10.1080/15564886.2019.1595248

Douds, A. S., & Shultz, H. (2021). Are victims' rights honored in veterans courts? A statewide assessment of law on the books versus law in action. *Victims & Offenders, 16*(6), 912–930. https://doi.org/10.1080/15564886.2021.1912871

Easterly, B. (2017). The ties that bind beyond the battlefield: An examination of the diffusion patterns of veterans treatment courts. *Social Science Quarterly, 98*(5), 1622–1641. https://doi.org/10.1111/ssqu.12375

Edwards, B. C., Hinojosa, R., & Hassan, K. (2019). How to transform the judicial system: Lessons from the institutionalization of veterans' treatment courts. *New York University Journal of Legislation and Public Policy, 21*(4), 841–902.

Erickson, J. W., Jr. (2016). Veterans treatment courts: A case study of their efficacy for veterans' needs. *International Journal of Law and Psychiatry, 49*, 221–225. https://doi.org/10.1016/j.ijlp.2016.10.009

Finlay, A. K., Clark, S., Blue-Howells, J., Claudio, S., Stimmel, M., Tsai, J., Buchanan, A., Rosenthal, J., Harris, A. H. S., & Frayne, S. (2019). Logic model of the department of veterans affairs' role in veterans treatment courts. *Drug Court Review, 2*, 45–62. https://pubmed.ncbi.nlm.nih.gov/32016172/

Finlay, A. K., Owens, M. D., Taylor, E., Nash, A., Capdarest-Arest, N., Rosenthal, J., Blue-Howells, J., Clark, S., & Timko, C. (2019). A scoping review of military veterans involved in the criminal justice system and their health and healthcare. *Health & Justice, 7*(1), 1–18. https://doi.org/10.1186/s40352-019-0086-9

Flatley, B., Clark, S., Rosenthan, J., & Blue-Howells, J. (2017). *Veterans court inventory 2016 update: Characteristics of and VA involvement in veterans treatment courts and other veteran focused court programs from the veterans justice outreach specialist perspective.* U.S. Department of Veterans Affairs, Veterans Health Administration.

Government Publishing Office. (n.d.). *Statute compilations.* GovInfo. https://www.govinfo.gov/app/collection/comps

Hawkins, M. D. (2010). Coming home: Accommodating the special needs of military veterans to the criminal justice system. *Ohio State Journal of Criminal Law, 7*(563), 563–573. https://kb.osu.edu/server/api/core/bitstreams/9ad6745f-d65f-506a-8ce3-e140a588123a/content

Holbrook, J. G., & Anderson, S. (2011). Veterans courts: Early outcomes and key indicators for success. *Widener Law School Legal Studies Research Paper No, 11–25*, 1–41. https://ssrn.com/abstract=1912655

Huskey, K. A. (2017). Justice for veterans: Does theory matter. *Arizona Law Review, 59*(697), 697–736. https://arizonalawreview.org/pdf/59-3/59arizlrev697.pdf

Jones, A. E. (2013). Veterans treatment courts: Do status-based problem-solving courts create an improper privileged class of criminal defendants. *Washington University Journal of Law & Policy, 43*(1), 307–331. https://journals.library.wustl.edu/lawpolicy/article/id/1570/

Luna, S., & Redlich, A. D. (2021). A national survey of veterans treatment court actors. *Criminal Justice Policy Review, 32*(2), 132–161. https://doi.org/10.1177/0887403420911414

Lux, F. R. (2022). *Veterans treatment court discretionary participation: A qualitative measure of a court's efficacy* (Order No. 28966429) [Doctoral dissertation, Saint Leo University]. ProQuest Dissertations and Theses Global.

McCall, J. D., Tsai, J., & Gordon, A. J. (2018). Veterans Treatment Court research: Participant characteristics, outcomes, and gaps in the literature. *Journal of Offender Rehabilitation, 57*(6), 384–401. https://doi.org/10.1080/10509674.2018.1510864

Morse, J. M. (2015). Critical analysis of strategies for determining rigor in qualitative inquiry. *Qualitative Health Research, 25*(9), 1212–1222. https://doi.org/10.1177/1049732315588501

National Association of Drug Court Professionals. (2018). *Adult drug court best practice standards.* https://www.nadcp.org/wp-content/uploads/2018/12/Adult-Drug-Court-Best-Practice-Standards-Volume-I-Text-Revision-December-2018-1.pdf

Pomerance, B. (2018). The best-fitting uniform: Balancing legislative standards and judicial processes in veterans treatment courts. *Wyoming Law Review, 18*(1), 179–236. https://doi.org/10.59643/1942-9916.1391

Pomerance, B. (2019). Rational justice: Equal protection problems amid veterans treatment court eligibility categorizations. *Oregon Law Review, 97*(425), 425–475. https://scholarsbank.uoregon.edu/xmlui/bitstream/handle/1794/24699/Pomerance_OLR97%282%29.pdf?sequence=1&isAllowed=y

Rowen, J. (2020). Worthy of justice: A veterans treatment court in practice. *Law & Policy, 42*(1), 78–100. https://doi.org/10.1111/lapo.12142

Russell, R. T. (2009). Veteran treatment court: A proactive approach. *New England Journal of Crime and Civil Confinement, 35*(357), 357–372. https://heinonline.org/HOL/Page?handle=hein.journals/nejccc35&id=361&div=&collection=journals

Shah, S. (2014). Authorization required: Veterans treatment courts, the need for democratic legitimacy, and the separation of powers doctrine. *Southern California Interdisciplinary Law Journal, 23* (1), 67–106.

Shannon, L. M., Birdwhistell, S., Hulbig, S. K., Jones, A. J., Newell, J., & Payne, C. (2017). Examining implementation and preliminary performance indicators of veterans treatment courts: The Kentucky experience. *Evaluation and Program Planning, 63*, 54–66. https://doi.org/10.1016/j.evalprogplan.2017.03.003

Sivanich, A. (2021). *Military combat veterans, sentencing reform, and problem-solving courts*. Theses and Dissertations. 4192. https://commons.und.edu/theses/4192

Timko, C., Flatley, B., Tjemsland, A., McGuire, J., Clark, S., Blue-Howells, J., Blonigen, D. M., Rosenthal, J., & Finlay, A. (2016). A longitudinal examination of veterans treatment courts' characteristics and eligibility criteria. *Justice Research & Policy, 17*(2), 123–136. https://doi.org/10.1177/1525107117740087

Tsai, J., Finlay, A., Flatley, B., Kasprow, W. J., & Clark, S. (2018). A national study of veterans treatment court participants: Who benefits and who recidivates. *Administration and Policy in Mental Health and Mental Health Services Research, 45*(2), 236–244. https://doi.org/10.1007/s10488-017-0816-z

U.S. Department of Veterans Affairs. (2015). *Veterans employment toolkit.* https://www.va.gov/vetsinworkplace/docs/em_activeReserve.asp

U.S. Department of Veterans Affairs. (2021). *Fact sheet: Veterans treatment courts and other veteran-focused courts served by VA veterans justice outreach specialists.* https://www.va.gov/HOMELESS/docs/VJO/Veterans-Treatment-Court-Inventory-Update-Fact-Sheet-Jan-2021.pdf

Veterans Court Coordination Treatment Act of 2019, Pub. L. No. 116–153, 34 USC 10651a. (2019). https://uscode.house.gov/view.xhtml?req=granuleid:USC-prelim-title34-section10651a&num=0&edition=prelim

The Veterans Legal Clinic at the Legal Services Center of Harvard Law School. (2020). *Turned away: How VA unlawfully denies healthcare to veterans with bad paper discharges.* OUTVETS, Legal Services Center of Harvard Law School, and Veterans Legal Services. https://www.legalservicescenter.org/wp-content/uploads/Turn-Away-Report.pdf

Wilson, L. C. (2018). The prevalence of military sexual trauma: A meta-analysis. *Trauma, Violence, & Abuse, 19*(5), 584–597. https://doi.org/10.1177/1524838016683459

Winick, B. J. (2002). Therapeutic jurisprudence and problem solving courts. *Fordham Urban Law Journal, 30*(3), 1055–1090. https://ir.lawnet.fordham.edu/cgi/viewcontent.cgi?article=2087&context=ulj

No Veteran Left Behind? Perspectives on VTC Eligibility Criteria for Justice-Involved Veterans in Multiple Jurisdictions Across the United States

Don Hummer, James M. Byrne, Sabrina S. Rapisarda, Kelly M. Socia, and Kimberly R. Kras

ABSTRACT
The explosive growth of veterans treatment courts (VTCs) in the United States has raised questions concerning which justice-involved veterans (JIV) are eligible and ultimately selected for participation. For instance, should VTCs be more inclusive in their selection processes, and is it possible to do so within existing court parameters? Using data from 145 interviews of team members working in 20 VTCs across the country, this study explores the perceptions of those personnel on a range of factors impacting eligibility determinations of JIV. These include the decision-making processes of VTC teams, determinations of the nexus between a veteran's military service and their offending behavior, and the capacity of jurisdictions to provide treatment and services to all JIV, either through Veterans Affairs programs or community providers. Findings illustrate the variability of VTCs nationwide and suggest that specific midcourse alterations are necessary to fulfill stated court missions.

Introduction

Veterans treatment courts (VTCs) began in Buffalo in 2008 and since then have experienced dramatic growth (Douds & Ahlin, 2019). In 2011 there were 53 VTCs nationwide (Holbrook & Anderson, 2011); today, it is estimated that there are over 600 VTCs, serving at least 10,000 justice-involved veterans (JIV) across the country (DeVall et al., 2022). Their ranks increased steadily throughout the 2010s, but their growth accelerated markedly after H.R. 866 (2021) was signed into law in August of 2020 (Craddock, 2022), providing services and support for JIV facing charges. These veterans often suffer the symptoms of a mental health disorder, such as post-traumatic stress disorder (PTSD), cognitive impairment from a traumatic brain injury (TBI), substance use disorder (SUD), military sexual trauma (MST), or a combination thereof (see Clark et al., 2010; Council on Criminal Justice, 2022; Hartley & Baldwin, 2019; Justice for Vets, n.d.). A primary role of these courts is to connect the justice-involved former (or sometimes current) military member to available treatment and services, either within the Department of Veterans Affairs (VA) network or via community providers linked to VTCs. However, significant questions remain: which of these service members are eligible for participation in VTCs? How are eligibility determinations made?[1] What happens to those JIV who either refuse to participate in VTCs, or are not accepted if the JIV does not meet the established criteria of the court in the veteran's jurisdiction? The presiding judge in what is considered the first VTC in the United States, the Honorable Robert Russell, believed that VTCs should err on the side of inclusion when determining eligibility, and look for ways to bring more JIV into the courts:

> With respect to eligibility, the Buffalo court and many others accept all veterans with a clinical diagnosis of serious and persistent mental health disease, or drug or alcohol addiction. We believe all veterans should be eligible because all veterans deserve special consideration for their willingness to serve and defend their nation. (Russell, 2014, p. 395)

While not everyone agrees with this assessment, we think it is critical to ask the individuals who are working with JIV to offer their unique perspectives on who should – and who should not – be eligible to participate in VTCs. To accomplish this, we conducted a series of in-depth, semi-structured interviews with VTC team members in 20 jurisdictions across the country as part of a larger research project. During these interviews, we broached the topic of eligibility with those who felt knowledgeable enough to discuss how their VTC decides which veterans meet the necessary inclusion criteria. Previous research has demonstrated that clear, substantive differences exist in who is eligible and accepted into VTCs versus those excluded (Pomerance, 2019). We were interested in gaining team members' perspectives on how eligibility was determined in their VTC, as well as their views on how VTCs *should* make these decisions. While research suggests that these differences are due to a variety of influences, such as legislation detailing eligibility and individual court rules (see Timko et al., 2016), we wanted to hear the perspectives of VTC team members themselves. We found that while some VTCs are guided by state statutes outlining which JIV may be considered (Rapisarda et al., 2024), in practice, the substantial variability in eligibility criteria detailed by Timko et al. (2016) is apparent, and the subjectivity involved in making final decisions on which veterans are ultimately selected proves to be the rule, rather than the exception, in most of the courts included in our analysis. In the following article, we briefly highlight previous research on VTC eligibility issues, and then present our analysis of 145 interviews with a range of VTC team members: Judges, defense attorneys, prosecutors, veterans justice outreach (VJO) specialists, court coordinators or managers, community mental health providers, probation officers, social service providers, and mentor coordinators. Team members addressed critical issues related to the participation of JIV in VTCs; taken together, their combined voices offer a unique perspective on VTC eligibility that policy makers and the public should consider when assessing how best to respond to the problems and needs of JIV.

VTC eligibility criteria: a review of previous research

The VTC model evolved out of the larger treatment court movement, specifically drug courts and mental health courts, due to the number of veterans struggling with either or both (Douds & Hummer, 2019). VTCs developed in ad hoc fashion in individual jurisdictions based primarily on available court and community resources. As the VTC model spread nationally, a core set of requirements or principles – such as an honorable or general discharge, specific criminogenic needs, and willingness to participate in treatment court as a part of a goal-focused team – emerged that served as the basis for new courts for military veterans to be established. Many of these requirements have been subjected to little empirical scrutiny. It has been posited that certain policies and practices based on these requirements, including which JIV are eligible for VTCs, have the potential to be discriminatory (see Baldwin & Brooke, 2019). Though variations exist, the core components of the VTC model:

> combine a judge and a court team trained in mental health and substance abuse intervention, knowledgeable about veteran culture and military experience, a peer mentoring component that provides instrumental support and supports adaptive recovery, and the in-court presence of a U.S. Department of Veterans Affairs (VA) Veterans Health Administration (VHA) Veterans Justice Outreach (VJO) Specialist, who facilitates access to VA health care and other benefits. (Clark et al., 2014, p. 417)

In an analysis of the earliest implemented VTCs, Clark et al. (2010) document the differences in 24 courts on criteria – in addition to eligibility – such as the treatment court model on which the VTC is based, criminal charges allowed, VA staff role, and whether mentoring is a component of the court. In the early VTC era, eligibility was restricted to honorably discharged veterans who had mental health issues arising from service in a combat zone or hazardous duty area *and* had committed a nonviolent misdemeanor (Cavanaugh, 2011; Erickson, 2016). Later developments in the absence of a template, coupled with vague statutory guidance at the state level, resulted in jurisdictions determining eligibility for their VTCs based on factors such as the extent of local VA resources and community organizations that have developed initiatives to assist JIV (Council on Criminal Justice, 2022).

While eligibility criteria vary across jurisdictions (Baldwin, 2015; Baldwin et al., 2018; McGuire et al., 2013; Rapisarda et al., 2024; Tsai et al., 2018), all VTCs follow a similar framework and employ common elements to determine participant eligibility.[2] For example, in a statewide assessment of Pennsylvania's (PA) VTCs, Douds et al. (2017) identified eight common considerations for determining program eligibility: (a) military discharge status, (b) combat experience, (c) treatment needs and available treatment options, (d) relationship between military service and offense (the "nexus"), (e) current offense type, (f) criminal history, (g) victim input, and (h) plea requirements. Of the 17 VTCs assessed by Douds et al. (2017), none would accept veterans facing sex crimes or weapons charges, only a handful would consider those with homicide charges, and 14 of the 17 courts considered aggravated assault charges on a case-by-case basis. However, variations do exist among courts in the state. Over half of the PA VTCs would not consider a veteran who had been dishonorably discharged (10 of 17), and 12 of the 17 would consider other than honorably (OTH) discharged veterans on a case-by-case basis (Douds et al., 2017). PA is not out of step in comparison to other states (see Flatley et al., 2017). A national assessment conducted by Baldwin (2015) noted the ad hoc nature of determining eligibility in VTCs. While the majority of courts did *not* definitively exclude veterans with dishonorable or bad conduct discharges or require that the veterans be eligible for VA services, in practice, these veterans were routinely excluded. Additionally, 57% of these courts allowed veterans charged with violent felonies to be considered for participation (Baldwin, 2015).

There have been efforts in recent years to standardize eligibility and participation criteria in VTCs nationwide. The National Conference of Commissioners on Uniform State Laws drafted a model act allowing veterans to participate in treatment courts regardless of the character of discharge from the service (Lennon, 2020; National Conference of Commissioners on Uniform State Laws, 2017). A broad approach to eligibility nationwide would result in more inclusive courts, and potentially serve JIV with the most pressing service needs. Such inclusivity is not yet in consistent practice across the U.S. Currently, eligibility decisions are impacted by a multitude of factors at the federal, state, and local levels. For instance, the discharge granted at separation from service is a Department of Defense decision (see Siedor, 2020) that has significant consequences for veterans that encounter the criminal justice system. A 2016 review of discharge status by Harvard Law School's Veterans Legal Clinic revealed that 6.5% of all veterans who served since 2001 have been excluded from VA services due to their discharge status, which amounts to 125,000 veterans. During this period the rate of veterans released due to a dishonorable discharged has remained the same (about 1% of all discharges were for bad conduct). What *has* changed during this period is that an increasing number of veterans have received other than honorable (OTH) discharges. Between 2001 and 2013, 5.8% of all discharged veterans received other than honorable discharges.[3] Without full access to VA services, it is likely that these veterans are at a heightened-risk for involvement in crime; these justice-involved veterans with other than honorable discharges are also at-risk for denial of access to VTCs, because these jurisdictions have policies and practices in place that exclude these veterans (Veterans Legal Clinic, 2016). This is a double blow that the Harvard researchers viewed as undeserved, given the discretionary nature of this discharge determination. They found major variations in the use of OTH discharges by branch of service that is not related to the behavior of veterans. Instead, they found it was the product of discretionary decisions by commanders. They go on to note that "Congress specifically noted that the discretion given to commanders for administrative separations can result in unfair outcomes, and gave veterans the benefit of the doubt by only excluding those who received or deserved a Dishonorable discharge by court-martial. Because the VA's regulations have presumptively excluded all veterans with administrative Other Than Honorable discharges, the VA is failing to act in accordance with Congress's decision" (Veterans Legal Clinic, 2016, p. 13).

Individual state legislatures have passed statutes that both call for the creation of VTCs and provided guidelines for who should be served. These statutes also typically outline *exclusionary criteria* that disqualify a candidate from participating in the VTC (Rapisarda et al., 2024). These exclusionary criteria may focus specifically on a military member's discharge status to include only those who have been honorably discharged or may focus on the charged offense. For example, the Montgomery County (PA) VTC typifies the types of exclusionary offenses: murder or manslaughter, felony sex crimes, and drug distribution charges (Montgomery County PA Veterans Treatment Court, n.d.). Other VTCs also prohibit those charged with arson, gun crimes, or certain acts of violence from participating as well (Seamone et al., 2018). The types and severity of offenses that might be considered have expanded since the earliest courts, with VTCs often considering the totality of a veteran's background to determine if the specific VTC is equipped to serve their particular needs (see Douds & Ahlin, 2019; Hartley & Baldwin, 2019; Shannon et al., 2017). One assessment of the offenses that brought veterans into VTCs demonstrates that although a wide range of crimes are committed by participants, the most prevalent offense types were drug crimes, driving under the influence (DUI), and theft/fraud cases (Baldwin, 2017).

Aside from offense characteristics and discharge status, some state statutes, and individual VTCs, emphasize the establishment of the "nexus" – the link between an individual's experiences in the military and diagnosed traumatic effects, and a connection between that trauma and the subsequent behavior that resulted in the veteran becoming justice involved – as a prerequisite for inclusion (Rapisarda et al., 2024). From an eligibility standpoint, questions exist regarding *what* constitutes a nexus and *who* is best suited to make such a determination. Neither of these is an easy question to answer, nor is there evidence to suggest that a nexus must exist for participants to ultimately benefit from the treatment and services provided by VTCs. For instance, some individuals bring issues with them upon enlistment, and those issues (e.g., histories of sexual abuse and/or childhood physical abuse) are then exacerbated by experiences during their military service (Blosnich et al., 2014). In other scenarios, veterans are arrested for criminal charges that are entirely unrelated to their military service (Culp et al., 2013). Whether veterans' behavior is a function of their time spent in the military, or if they were simply a former member of the military who would benefit from services, is an administrative and philosophical debate. Veterans who have been arrested for their third DUI might benefit from treatment irrespective of their alcohol use disorder (AUD) arising before enlisting, during their service, or afterward, and whether the AUD emerged as a result of their service or not.

Similarly, many VTCs also require a diagnosis of PTSD, MST, TBI, or SUD[4] for the veteran to be eligible for participation, which is in alignment with research showing that the treatment court participants who benefit most are those who have the highest risk and/or the greatest needs (NPC Research, 2019; Yerramsetti et al., 2017). The past decade plus has seen an expansion of the types of veterans becoming involved in the justice process, and who may be served by VTCs.[5] Establishing a direct link between combat experience, trauma, and subsequent criminal offending can be a challenging task.[6] A decade ago, a quarter of veterans in state and federal prison (25%) reported that they had seen combat while in the military (Bronson et al., 2015). The most recent data on veterans in jails and prisons indicates this figure has not changed appreciably (28% of state prison inmates, 21% of federal prison inmates; see Maruschak et al., 2021). Further, there is an ongoing debate regarding who is best able to provide a clinical diagnosis for the issues delineated above, or for the nexus between a disorder and subsequent criminal offending. Should this assessment be performed exclusively by a forensic psychiatrist, or are other professionals (e.g., licensed clinical social worker, clinical psychologist, probation officer) able to complete such a task to help determine court eligibility?

The basis for diagnoses outlined above is not to be taken lightly if the VTC in question is legislatively mandated to include only those veterans with demonstrable trauma. In the more than 600 VTCs in the U.S., there are a broad range of criteria used to determine VTC participant eligibility (Douds et al., 2017; U.S. Department of Veterans Affairs, 2021). At present, 48 states have VTCs as a specialty court type (Connecticut & Vermont being the exceptions), and 34 states have *enacting* statutes establishing a basis for VTCs (Rapisarda et al., 2024). Of these 34 states, 22 also have *eligibility* statutes that set forth specific eligibility criteria for courts to follow when considering potential participants. Timko et al. (2016) indicated that a disjunction may exist between the needs of the veteran population in any given jurisdiction and how statutes define VTC-eligible veteran populations. In those states without enacting statutes – and even in some states with eligibility statutes – many jurisdictions have created VTCs by Court Rule or practice, without explicitly stated eligibility criteria (Lennon, 2020). In these cases, participants are often assessed for inclusion by VTC team members, with final decisions coming from district attorneys, judges, or both. As with most justice policy, factors at the state and local levels have the greatest influence in determining which participants are served by VTCs. While discharge decisions and which veterans qualify for VA services occur at a higher level (i.e., the DoD, the VA), funding and resources at the local level, coupled with the discretion of VTC team members and the local culture, drive both the number and type of veteran served by the VTC, within statutory parameters (Shah, 2014). Most of these statutes are broad enough in scope to allow for final decisions to be made by the individual courts. Relatedly, in those VTCs that are post-disposition, veterans may be declined admission to the VTC because an operational criterion of the court mandates that a guilty plea must be entered *prior* to participation (Erickson, 2016). An eligible veteran may decline to participate in treatment court with such a provision in place – for any number of reasons – and opt for disposition of their case in the traditional court process.

Documenting the variation in eligibility criteria across VTCs and linking them closely to evidence-based assessments and justice frameworks, is necessary for advancing an effective VTC model. Interviews of VTC court personnel have been conducted in case study format (see Shannon et al., 2017) as a means of gauging court practices in one jurisdiction. While a review of eligibility and operational criteria existing individually at state court or local levels is important in establishing a framework for consistent court structure, the current study's aim is on eligibility criteria at the ground level as perceived by key VTC team members. More specifically, we detail how key VTC personnel view eligibility criteria in their courts, how policies are applied to particular offense types in their jurisdictions, and the specifics of the decision-making processes underlying the flow of participants into their respective courts.

Methods

The current study originates from a larger project on VTC operations and service delivery. A complete detailing of the methodology, including participant recruitment, data collection procedures, and the analytic strategy is contained in an earlier article in this special issue (Byrne et al., 2024). For the current analysis, we focus on information coded in relation to eligibility policies, practices, and the history of participants who had begun the treatment court process and either successfully completed the program or failed to do so. These codes were queried in NVivo software and then focus-coded to discern more specific and nuanced themes pertaining to participant identification, eligibility and admittance to a VTC. Analytic memos were produced reflecting the larger themes emerging from this round of coding, which we collectively reviewed to produce the final iteration of findings. Researchers engaged in inter-rater agreement and member-checking strategies to verify the data veracity, analysis, and conclusions. Member-checking strategies involved providing analytic memos to our Advisory Board for review and commentary, which we later discussed in our monthly Advisory Board meeting. This process allowed us to refine the analysis and ensure we were capturing the most salient patterns. Most quotes are presented verbatim to preserve the tone and language of the participants, with a limited number of edits for readability or to preserve the confidentiality of interviewees and courts.

Findings

Interviewees provided valuable insights on the eligibility policies and practices of their respective VTCs. Team members discussed the process once prospective participants came under the purview of their court, usually via one of several avenues, including self-identification as a military veteran, defense counsel bringing their client's status to the court, information gleaned by local jails, or identification by community corrections personnel with whom the veteran may have had prior interactions. From our analysis, five primary themes emerged relative to team member perspectives on eligibility: (1) location of potential participants and initial engagement; (2) state statutory and court policy requirements; (3) the decision-making process and discretionary practices used by stakeholders to ascertain eligibility; (4) the nexus between a veteran's military service and offending behavior; and (5) capacity/available resources for providing services to VTC participants. Each theme is discussed below, and grounded by quotes that represent and contextualize the perceptions of VTC team members.

If you build it, they will come: locating and initiating engagement with JIV

Two of the initial lines of questioning were centered on how veterans became knowledgeable of the existence of VTCs in their jurisdiction, and relatedly, how team members became aware of newly arrested veterans who may be eligible to participate in a VTC. These questions revealed that in several jurisdictions, the individual veteran had to self-identify as a veteran, and if a veteran chose not to disclose, then this individual would not be considered for VTC programming even if they were potentially eligible. To address this problem, several jurisdictions had systems in place, such as relying on the Veterans Reentry Search Service (VRSS)[7] or through direct outreach to jails by VJOs, to independently identify veterans in the arrest and jail populations. Once identified, various methods were used by VTC team members to contact and engage with these veterans, as outlined in the excerpt below:

> [W]e can get referrals from not only the defense attorney but the VJO, sometimes they reach out if somebody's within the system, the state attorneys if they talk to the victim or somebody else is involved and says, "You know this person was in the military." Sometimes, a client might just hear about it from another friend or something, and they request it. – **Public Defender, Site #3**

Another approach to the identification process is to provide outreach to prosecutors and defense attorneys in these jurisdictions, highlighting the benefits and drawbacks of VTCs for JIV and their unique circumstances and needs. One defense attorney described the importance of vetting the VTC option for their client:

> I don't know of any vet that has come into our system that has not been made aware that veteran treatment court is an option. The defense bar is very quick to bring that up because generally the alternative to treatment court is less desirable. At every turn, particularly with veteran treatment court, I think the defense bar is trying to inquire of their particular clients if that's an option so they can explore it. Because it's better for them. Also, in our forming days, we had a police officer involved that was command staff and they adopted a principle of when they arrest someone, part of their arrest questionnaire is whether or not they've served in the military irrespective of their discharge. – **Defense Attorney, Site #5**

Finally, team members in several jurisdictions mentioned the myriad reasons why some veterans do not want to self-identify. Some of the more common reasons perceived by court actors include: fear of losing VA benefits; poor experiences with VA services in the past; misperceptions about the length of service necessary and/or release status required to be eligible; and/or not wanting associations with the military due to past traumas during service. The following excerpts represent some veterans' concerns with entering VTCs, as perceived by team members:

> Usually when we see a vet select a different court, it's because they don't necessarily identify [themselves] as a vet, or don't have that strong connection, that camaraderie, that the other vets we see do. – **Court Coordinator, Site #10**

> When it comes to referrals, I think some people are eager to try it out. Some people are apprehensive, but they'll defer to the attorney who says, hey, this will be great for you. Some people are just mistrusting. They've had bad experiences. – **Court Clerk, Site #20**

The ties that bind: state statutory and court policy requirements

Even in those states with enabling and eligibility statutes, individual courts typically have wide latitude in the cases they can consider for inclusion, particularly at the misdemeanor level. Eligibility frequently is determined by whether: 1) the charging offense is one for which probation is a possible sanction, and 2) whether state statute and/or court policy stipulates that a participating veteran have an honorable discharge. Logically, crimes that carry mandatory prison terms are not considered, as the JIV would be unable to participate in a non-institutional treatment regimen. Therefore, if the crime is probation-eligible, and the veteran meets other criteria for inclusion (e.g., discharge status), then their case is typically accepted so long as the veteran agrees to the conditions of treatment court:

> On the felony side, there's just a handful of things that are not probation eligible, so that narrows certain things down. There's not stuff that's specifically—on the misdemeanor side, there's nothing that's disqualifying defense-wise. The court cannot consider public safety because the legislature said participation increases public safety. The district attorney has no voice in our misdemeanor statute about who gets to participate or not. There's no gatekeeping on their part. It's a very, very broadly written statute. It's very good that way. – **Defense Counsel, Site #1**

> [T]he way we handle referrals is . . . there's a list of charges that are not accepted into veterans court. [T]hey're eligible if they're VA healthcare eligible and even if they're not. It's mainly based on their legal history, and if the state attorney approves them to enter the program based on what's allowed in the statute. I'd say the majority are eligible. – **VJO Specialist, Site #12**

While courts may have wide latitude under pertinent state statutes, they also must consider the requirements behind external funding sources that have certain guidelines as conditions for allocating resources. In these instances, eligibility decisions are determined as most contingent on the backgrounds of veterans and whether they are a complimentary fit to the parameters and requirements of the specific VTC program. Different treatment court models have been implemented across the U.S., and one model that is a hallmark of federal funding agencies is based on ensuring participant abstinence (see Bureau of Justice Assistance, 2023). Therefore, if the various treatment phases of the VTC require participants to be abstinent from drugs and alcohol as they move through the program, JIV with SUD may not be well-served or a good fit for those VTCs employing an abstinence approach. Team members described the challenge in striking a balance between abiding by the stipulations of funding sources while also simultaneously enrolling JIV whose needs have been largely unmet:

> We have a much longer history doing Veterans Treatment Court than the statute itself. The statute says pretty much anyone can come in, but we have to align our program with what are the requirements of the funders, right? We're a funded program, and we have to meet those criteria, so for example, I would say if the funder said, like they say today, 'They must abstain from all substance'–that's challenging because there are some individuals who are here not because they have substance abuse issues, but because they have mental health issues, and they rely on cannabis, for example, as part of their treatment. Does that mean that person can't be in Veterans Court? – **Judge, Site #1**

> I think the one issue is use of marijuana. Our grants are through SAMHSA [Substance Abuse and Mental Health Services Administration], so they're not supposed to be using marijuana, but in [STATE], marijuana's a ticket. It just really depends on the amount. I personally have no issue with it. If you have a note from a doctor that says you need this for your PTSD or you need this because it keeps you from having to be involuntarily detained on a mental health hold, then I don't have a problem with it. But because our grant money says it's an abstinence program, it becomes an issue. – **District Attorney, Site #1**

Bureaucratic requirements and restrictions (e.g., not having an honorable discharge) were another cause for frustration among interviewees, in that they felt hamstrung by subjective criteria along the decision-making chain, as well as a failure of the system to address needs while in service, that ultimately led to veterans being excluded from the VTC. This issue is doubly confounding when a resource or funding impediment exists as well:

> I feel like there are a lot of vets that got screwed over by their commands and maybe received an OTH or less than honorable discharge for mental health or drug issues. Instead of working with them to try to help them get better and get back to a deployable status, they were just kicked out, and then now they're not eligible for VA services. Now the great thing about the VA is that a few years ago, they opened up the door to allow some OTH discharges to receive mental health services, and then they can apply for disability. If they get approved for disability, then they can apply for an upgrade in their discharge status. That I'm happy about that that the VA saw that as an issue, and they took steps to make that right. I feel like there are a lot of vets with less than honorable discharges that need to be helped because that's the sole reason they got kicked out of the military. From a programmatic standpoint as the program coordinator, I understand why we do the things we do because we use the VA for treatment. We don't want them to have to pay for their treatment. They earned their VA treatment with their service. We use [the VA] for treatment, thus they have to be eligible for services at the VA, which is why we can't take those discharge statuses. Now I will say because the VA opened the door to some OTH discharges, we now look at OTHs on a case-by-case basis. If they have an OTH and they determine that the OTH was due to a mental health or substance use issue, which makes them eligible for VA services, then we will look at those on a case-by-case basis and we have started taking those but they're very few and far between. – **Treatment Program Director, Site #6**

In or out – who decides? Decision-making processes and discretionary practices

Once a potential participant is brought to the attention of the team, their case is examined for suitability for inclusion into the VTC. This determination may be determined by one court team member (usually the district attorney or judge), but often occurs in consultation with the entire VTC team. This decision is made on the basis of not only whether the veteran's case meets basic inclusion criteria, but also whether the veteran is a suitable fit for treatment court. Giving an overview of their process, a team member in one jurisdiction stated the following:

> It's a team effort, so I'm one of two prosecutors assigned to the Veterans Treatment Court. We have a second prosecutor who's a deputy city attorney. The city attorney handles misdemeanors within the city, and occasionally we'll get those, so we have to have the city attorney on, as well. As the prosecutor, it's kind of fluid. It's not a traditional adversarial system. It's a team effort. I will try and find cases to refer here. I will do trainings for prosecutors and also the private defense bar so that they know about us. I think my biggest role in the team is I'm the gatekeeper. With the exception of mentors, I'm the only one who's [a veteran] who's sitting at the table. Some of the treatment providers, but they aren't always at the meetings, so it's —you've got the gatekeeper to screen out the lingering war stories that don't add up, and for us we've got this big statute on point, but there are statutory requirements to be eligible for restorative relief. One, you've got to have prior military service, so a lot of times I can help kind of figure that out to determine who, what, when, where, and why. They've got to have a duty-related mental illness, and we've got a great treatment team that helps us with that. Finally, that duty-related mental illness must have resulted in the criminal offense. – **District Attorney, Site #16**

Court personnel in all 20 VTC jurisdictions alluded to some degree of subjectivity with respect to eligibility decisions even in those states that have eligibility statutes delineating specific eligibility for VTC participation. This degree of subjectivity in the decision-making process ranges substantially from jurisdiction to jurisdiction. The following excerpt represents a common response related to the discretion of the court in making eligibility determinations:

> Yeah, there is a process. They[the clinicians] do all the assessments, and then if they meet the criteria, generally they are in. Of course, if they—they may not make the criteria, then they wouldn't be considered but sometimes—it's a lot of—we do have a lot of discussions if it's not straightforward like, "Yes, they make it." Sometimes in our court we take individuals that have previously completed the Vet Court but then happen to get into trouble again later in the future. – **Court Coordinator, Site #20**

Within the parameters of treatment court statutes, individual courts have latitude to weigh the merits of specific cases and ascertain if they are viable VTC participants. While some jurisdictions may have exclusionary criteria based on specific offenses or discharge status, others have wide discretion on the types of cases and participant backgrounds that are considered for participation in the VTC:

> As you know, each judge is different. This particular judge is not a veteran, but he has a heart of gold for veterans. Sometimes the team says he's a little bit more lenient than he should be as it relates to eligibility as well as sanctions and incentives. How we determine eligibility is once whoever makes the referral, whether that referral comes from self-refer, the family, the criminal justice system, the attorneys, however it gets referred, it goes directly to the DA's office first. They want to make sure that individual is legally eligible prior to sending the information for

> the treatment [component] to then determine if they're eligible via a mental health and/or substance use issue. **–VJO Specialist, Site #4**

There are also diverging perspectives on whether veterans who are ineligible for VA services are in turn ineligible for inclusion in VTCs. Some jurisdictions unwaveringly restrict participation to *only* honorably discharged veterans who qualify for services through the VA, while others partner with community service providers already engaged via other specialty courts (e.g., drug courts, mental health courts) or nonprofit organizations that have experience working with veteran populations to serve those JIV not eligible for VA services:

> If someone had been part of the military, but they don't qualify for veterans benefits—generally, if they don't qualify—they haven't been in the armed services long enough to be able to qualify for benefits—then, even though they were part of the military, the veterans treatment court here will see if they can get services, and so they can become a member of the veterans treatment court. - **Public Defender, Site #2**

Much of this decision-making on which JIV are eligible to be served by a particular VTC is a function of the local context, and any one model cannot be transferred to a different setting without alteration. One team member eloquently detailed what many alluded to during their interviews - that VTCs can be discussed, planned, and developed as a framework before being implemented, but it is only once a court is established that the team gets a true sense of the population they are serving (e.g., their behaviors and treatment needs) within their specific jurisdiction and who may potentially be served by the resources available to the VTC:

> I think when you create a problem-solving court in a community, you first need to figure out—there's the philosophy and the theory about it, what do you want the program to look like? Then you have to go back and collect data and really figure out who do you actually have in the community that's going to benefit from this program. You can't invent those people. They either exist in your community or they don't. When we started vet court, our district attorney only wanted people in this program who really had very little criminal history to begin with. Then because of service-connected disability or combat trauma, or if they came out on the other end and started getting into trouble. He had this vision, this romantic notion, of what vet court should look like. Being a PO at the time, I knew right off the bat that the vast majority of people in [this] community that are going to be veterans and criminal justice-involved probably had some criminal history before they went into the service, and they were probably—their involvement was probably due to low-level domestic violence stuff and DUI. I did about six months' worth of research and got back to him and said, "Look, these are the people that we have in [this city], and we need to create a program that's going to target that population, not a population that really doesn't exist." They went along with it, and it was the right thing to do. Those are the people we serve. We take everybody. We take somebody that's been in the military for five minutes or five years. We take all kinds of discharges, and we take people that have absolutely no ties or are not eligible for VA services. Our litmus test was can you show us that you were enlisted or a commissioned officer for even a day. We do that because those are the people that we have in this community. - **Court Coordinator, Site #13**

Even in the collaborative environment of a treatment court, there is a hierarchy within the decision-making process. Discussions on individual cases bring all team members to the table, but disagreements necessitate a final determination being made by one team member, typically the judge or district attorney as the representative of the state. While such a gatekeeper is necessary even in cooperative process, it can lead to discomfort among other team members, and a perception that the court does not follow said goals, missions, or policies and procedures:

> One of the things [we need to work on], and I've had this discussion before, how I said the district attorney gets the say in whether or not we can bring people in. I don't think in some aspects that's fair. We've had this discussion before because if they met the criteria, which we put in our policies and procedures, then I think they should . . . be allowed to do the program. – **Court Coordinator, Site #8**

> It is the district attorney who is the gatekeeper. If we have a veteran and he applies for the program, obviously, they're brought up on charges. They stand before the district attorney. The district attorney says, "Hey, you're a good veteran. Thank you for your service. Sorry, you're not being admitted into this program." We, the judge, the team cannot overrule that. – **Mentor Coordinator, Site #8**

> We discuss as a team, and, at the end, the judge decides what we want to do. He does take into what we say, the team, and how we feel about the case. I will say the ones that we do get turned down are offenders that have multiple cases. Their criminal background is multiple of the same charges that they're up for. [T]hose would be the most that get turned down, especially the violent and the multiple offenses for the same charge that they're up for. As far as what we pick, again like I said, it's based out of the team's input, how everyone feels about it, and, at the end of the day, what the judge has to say about it. – **Probation Officer, Site #2**

As suggested in the above quotes, despite the collaborative model of decision making that underlies many VTCs, in the end, it is typically either the judge and/or district attorney that has the ultimate say in who is eligible to participate or not.

What happens in the military stays in the military – or does it? The nexus and eligibility decisions

Ascertaining a definitive link between a veteran's time in service, the trauma they experienced, and how these traumatic experiences are related to the offense that led to justice-involvement – the nexus – is one of the more controversial aspects of determining eligibility for VTCs. A 2015 national survey of 129 VTCs found that only 21% required a nexus between a veteran's military service and the criminal offense that brought them before the court (American University, 2016). In most cases, the connection between service-related trauma and offending behavior is not clear-cut, and instead is the result of an assessment by either a member of the VTC team or an outside consultant. This lack of clarity has led some courts to discount the need for establishing such a connection, and instead, they view any justice-involved military veteran in need of services as a candidate for treatment. The following was a common response across multiple jurisdictions:

> I don't think it's very difficult for anybody to link their trauma to their criminal behavior whether it'd be military trauma or not. Frankly, I personally don't care whether it's military trauma or other kind of trauma. We need to treat their trauma. I think it's morally reprehensible to say, "Oh, you can only have this kind of trauma for us to help you." That's unconscionable to me. I want to honor anybody who has any kind of trauma because they didn't ask for it. Do I want lift people up who have served our country? Absolutely. I want to lift anybody up who needs lifting up personally and to exclude somebody from services or from a criminal case disposition that's going to make it easier for them to find housing, to get a job, to have healthier relationships just because their trauma happened outside of a particular branch of the military, I find appalling. – **Court Coordinator, Site #18**

Establishing a clear causal link between a veteran's military service and the offense for which they are being considered for VTC enrollment is a nebulous undertaking. To date, there has been no consensus on which team member (clinician, forensic psychiatrist, probation officer) should make such a determination. The question also remains whether the genesis of factors that contributed to the veteran's offending behavior occurred prior to enlistment or during service. Further, if the service member had previously experienced trauma, did their military duty exacerbate these issues and contribute to their offending behavior? We found a variety of opinions regarding how the nexus is established, who can establish it, and its implications for VTC participation:

> I think there should be a connection. If you're going to apply to be in a specialty court specifically for veterans based on your military service, there needs to be a connection between your military service, the crime you committed and your mental health and or substance use issues related to your military service which cause you to commit this crime. Otherwise, why have a specialized program just that goes beyond regular probation? – **Treatment Program Director, Site #6**

> It's basically a double nexus between their mental health history, the legal charge, and their military background. That was the nexus that needed to be established to participate in the veteran's court, so who better to do that than a board-certified forensic psychiatrist? Now most of the other courts that were developing in [this state] at the time, they just said, "well, if you were in the military and you have PTSD, that was enough for them to welcome the folks into their court programs." We actually included with ours, a forensic assessment to establish that nexus, and to make a clinical recommendation for joining the court team, but also recommendations for the type of treatment that they in conjunction with their participation in the court program. – **VJO Specialist, Site #6**

> Who determines the nexus? Well, I think it's the staffing team. We'll talk about these cases, and we'll go over it. The court will have some background then. We can all talk about it and make some decisions. Sometimes, we'll have some input from the defense attorney also. That'll help out because they've been talking to their client, so we'll get enough input. Then, I think, through the interview process, we'll get enough information to be able to make that determination. – **District Attorney, Site #7**

Across sites, interview participants largely diminished the importance of the nexus as a primary criterion for court entry. One judge stated, "We take all comers really. At the beginning I think the nexus was much more important [in the past] than it is to us now" (Site #7). When state statute indicates that the nexus play a role in the decision-making process but does not provide clear guidance on what the nexus is, how it should be determined, and by whom, VTC team members are left to make determinations based on their court's available resources, as well as the perspectives of key team members such as judges and prosecutors. The decision-making process becomes one of determining if a specific participant meets the specific VTC model and existing treatment and service modalities of the court:

> There is a diversion statute in [this state] that does require a nexus, but it is not under either of the two that impact veterans. What the court has to be satisfied is that the person is eligible because they have a mental health substance abuse-related condition to a diagnosis that's tied to their military service, so in other words, your mental health condition has to be tied to the fact that you were in service and resulting from that as opposed to it resulted from the years prior to your service. That is usually when the court is satisfied with that element by receiving

documentation from either their government service record, by the person who's diagnosed them and has treated them. – **Judge, Site #1**

No room at the inn: capacity and available resources for providing services

Many interviewees indicated that the typical offense profiles of veterans within their VTCs were driving while intoxicated, domestic violence, non-domestic assaults, drug possession, and minor property and public order offenses. While these crimes may not be the most serious offenses for treatment courts to consider, there are logical factors that drive this trend. First, SUD is common diagnosis among JIV (Finlay et al., 2017), and these offenses are typical offending behaviors of substance users in general (Tsai et al., 2017). By bringing these cases into a VTC as relatively minor incidents, it allows veterans to be matched with services to address underlying issues driving their behavior *before* more serious offenses are committed. Second, in most jurisdictions these offenses are (or can be) probation-eligible, thus paving the way for entry into the VTC and subsequent community-based treatment. Third, both the VA and community providers have existing programs in place to address issues such as addiction and family relations (e.g., the VA's "Strength at Home" program), therefore it seems reasonable that VTCs focus on participants who would benefit from preexisting resources. Conversely, all but one of the 20 courts in our study prohibited participants accused of, or with a history involving, arson. This had less to do with the nature of the offense and more to do with the lack of available resources and services available to address the needs of such offenders:

> We just shy away from current sex offenses, convicted sex offenders, and those with an arson history because of the difficulty of placing them in a residential setting. I know that's something that is a common theme across a lot of treatment courts, but we certainly shy away from that as well. Again, it's a case-by-case basis. It has to do with the availability of treatment for those folks. – **Court Coordinator, Site #2**

Unlike sex offense cases, VTCs include another group of individuals that appear to challenge their general tendency to exclude violent offenses – veterans charged with domestic violence:

> For the most part, the domestic violence cases in [this county], at least, are normally [low-level] and misdemeanors. Those are all what I consider eligible. I think Veterans Court is a good avenue for those cases to go through because of the availability of services, counseling, treatment, so this is perfect for them. They go in – and what I normally notice – they come out a different person. As long as they're willing to do the program and do the services, get the treatment that's available, hopefully, it helps them. – **District Attorney, Site #7**

Services must be offered in an environment that adheres to the unique components of VTCs, such as meeting set milestones and proceeding through phases of the court as a team. Service providers in non-VA community settings may not have the capacity to offer treatment in a context unique and exclusive to a veteran population, thus negating a key element of VTCs. As a result, some courts opt to not admit those veterans ineligible for VA services because their available resources are incompatible with the assumptions of the VTC model:

> If they have mental health issues at all, we can't accept them. It's just—we don't have the resources to help. If they're just substance abuse, we have [one program available], which is a contract. It's pretty good. If they've got mental health issues, they're not getting any help. – **Mentor Coordinator, Site #3**

The focus on JIV identified as high risk/high need may be rendering some ineligible for VTCs if they do not have access to VA services, because there may not be community resources available for this group. Most of the interviewees who discussed the target population for their VTCs indicated that their courts were structured to service high risk/high need offenders, however they would not have the resources to provide needed services without the VA providing for those JIV eligible for their services, grants from federal, state, and/or local government, or partnerships with nonprofits to serve JIV eligible for the VTC but not for VA services. Interviewees did not indicate that their courts sought out, for example, OTH (other than honorable) cases with high risk/high need JIV to receive treatment and services in the community. Even assuming the bulk of high risk/high need offenders will receive services through the VA, this focus may be counterproductive to reducing veteran offending, as the types of offenses for which veterans commonly find themselves in the justice process include acts such as driving while intoxicated, domestic conflicts, drug possession, and simple assault, which are not necessarily considered high risk/high need offenses:

> The judge ultimately makes the decision. You don't have to be high risk/high need. That is the target audience, but our treatment court judge makes exceptions. I don't like the idea of just excluding someone because they're [not] high risk/high need. I also know that there's capacity in terms of we can't let everybody in just because they think this offer is a good offer. – **District Attorney, Site #5**

Discussion

Rowen (2020) states that the raison-d'etre of veterans treatment courts is simply that veterans have distinct social and medical needs that are best addressed by a treatment court tailored specifically to those needs. However, the rapid growth of VTCs has resulted in a number of unintended consequences. While examining the eligibility criteria of 20 VTCs across the U.S., several themes emerged, including (1) location of potential participants and initial engagement, (2) state statutory and individual court requirements for inclusion, (3) offense characteristics and background of the veteran that drive VTC team decisions, (4) the nexus between a veteran's service time/experiences and their offending behavior, and (5) the capacity of treatment/service resources available to the court. The uniqueness of the eligibility decision-making process is particularly acute in states that have only enacting statutes for VTCs, or those states that have no statutory guidelines at all. In the latter context, VTCs are often based on preexistent guidelines for other specialty courts, such as drug treatment courts. The most common strategy for determining eligibility in such states is for the VTC team to assess each JIV and collectively determine which cases are a fit for that specific VTC.

In terms of eligibility, criteria have been developed and adopted as policy, even without an evidence base that these criteria have any bearing on which veterans are best suited to the VTC regimen (Timko et al., 2016). This infers that it is the veteran who should be the focus of consideration, not the act which drew them into the justice process. At worst, this may lead to the perception that eligibility decisions are arbitrary or biased, given that there is already variation in eligibility criteria across VTCs and no evidence base exists to validate strategies currently in place. Following this line of reasoning, another argument exists that the proliferation of VTCs – and the eligibility decision-making surrounding who can enter VTCs – are guided by perceptions of military veterans being both *deserving* and *worthy* of specialized intervention when they become justice-involved (Rowen, 2020), based on the personal sacrifices they've made in service to their country. Viewed through this lens, the philosophy of punishment is altered and delineates the restorative mission of the court and distinguishes it from the more retributive aspects of the traditional justice process (Huskey, 2015). Further, court practices and personnel engage in distinguishing between worthy and unworthy veterans (Rowen, 2020). This categorization can fundamentally impact the guiding principles of a court and which veterans are deemed eligible to participate. In turn, without clear and standardized eligibility criteria, questions of fairness and disparate treatment have been called to question (Arno, 2015).

This issue comes into even sharper focus when considering the etiology of criminal behavior for military veterans being less of a "choice" or a by-product of a "criminal lifestyle," and more of an outcome of trauma suffered while in service to the country (see Huskey, 2015). When such a perspective on offending is shared with the public, the notion of who the offender *is* transmogrifies and elicits greater empathy from the general public toward veterans and the issues with which they are struggling. This in turn may result in VTC personnel being more inclined toward inclusivity in eligibility considerations, particularly if there is a belief that the *totality* of veterans' backgrounds (including the discharge decision) is a function of military-experienced trauma, the absence of which would perhaps have led to a host of different life outcomes for the veteran.

What is certain is that VTCs are emblematic of the notion that rapid growth results in less structural consistency[8] VTCs in the U.S. are the philosophical offspring of the first VTC in Buffalo, and of the overall drug/specialty court movement. But each court exists individually in a form shaped locally by law, policy, ideology, and available resources. The current study's findings demonstrate the allegiance VTC team members have for the court model, but also give voice to the frustration that many team members have for their inability to assist all JIV who could benefit, and what could be improved to prevent some from falling through the cracks (see Council on Criminal Justice, 2023).

The establishment of a VTC in a community to serve the justice-involved population is shown to be just an initial component of "therapeutic jurisprudence" (see Perlin, 2013) for JIV. An entire infrastructure needs to be in place to serve the entirety of the population, and greater coordination between federal, state, and local governments is necessary for courts to function optimally. Most of the hundreds of VTCs currently operating are new enough to easily implement midcourse alterations, and revise standards to increase the pool of eligible JIV. Impediments to VTC participation are both real and perceived. For example, some courts simply do not have non-VA treatment resources in their jurisdictions, therefore making veterans without access to VA benefits, who would otherwise be eligible for VTC participation, a poor fit for these courts. Alternatively, some veterans not presently eligible for VA benefits due to their discharge status could avail themselves of cooperative efforts between the Departments of Defense and VA that help facilitate upgrading discharge statuses. However, this process is hampered – even after being streamlined – by the perception that it is too onerous (Axelrod et al., 2023).

Regardless of factors external to VTCs, moving forward, courts will need to meet their justice-involved populations where they are at, tailoring a treatment court that is responsive to the needs of their specific population. The courts cannot simply implement an established model that does not match what an individual court has already been practicing on the ground. The information we gleaned from interviews with team members from various VTCs across the country demonstrates that there is not a one-size-fits-all approach to establishing eligibility for VTCs, nor is such a unilateral method desired. When courts have the discretion to apply eligibility criteria that maximize connecting veterans to treatment and services, those who do participate will have a greater probability of success than if courts attempt to fit "square pegs in round holes." For example, one of our study jurisdictions was located in an urban center with multiple treatment options available for both VA-eligible and non-VA-eligible veterans. It also had a strong relationship and consistent funding from a community partner to provide services for less than honorably discharged veterans. Therefore, this court's model for determining eligibility differed considerably from another jurisdiction housed in a rural setting, further away from a VA facility, and with no other treatment resources other than those with basic funding at the county level. No specialty court exists in a vacuum, and as our findings demonstrate, VTC team members work within the parameters they have been given. However, parameters can, and should, change based on the experiences of those working and participating in the courts, so that those who enter VTCs in the future will benefit from the experiences of their fellow service members who've gone before them.

Notes

1. The definition of who is a "veteran" remains variable, and can change. For example, in late 2106, President Barack Obama signed the Miller-Blumenthal Veterans Health Care and Benefits Act that sought to increase access to a host of veterans' benefits for previously excluded reservists and national guard members. With the passage of this act, a new pool of service members became eligible for VTCs in many states.
2. Basic eligibility criteria of the 20 courts in our study are presented in tabular form in the earlier article in this volume detailing the study's protocol (Byrne et al., 2024). Half of the VTCs had no eligibility exclusions based on a veteran's discharge, 19 excluded veterans charged with homicide, sex offenses, arson, and/or other violent crimes, and 9 courts had at least a stated requirement of a "nexus" between a veteran's military career and subsequent criminal offending.
3. The Veteran's Legal Clinic (2016, p. 12) report highlighted the discretionary nature of discharge status across the branches of the military: "What is more, significant disparities exist among the administrative separation practices of the various service branches. The Army, Navy, Air Force, and Marine Corps each has its own separation regulations and policies. Moreover, within each branch, different units and commands may implement those regulations and policies in a different manner. Thus, service members who engage in similar misconduct may receive disparate treatment: one may be retained, another may be discharged under General conditions, another discharged under Other Than Honorable conditions."
4. For a discussion of these issues and how they impact veterans, see Council on Criminal Justice (2022).
5. In the first VTCs, which were outgrowths of the larger drug court movement, the majority of participants were honorably discharged, male veterans charged with misdemeanors, typically

drug possession (Clark et al., 2010). More recently, the target population has been expanded, both in terms of offense types and with respect to veterans' backgrounds (see Baldwin, 2017).

6. In 2017, the Department of Defense provided more comprehensive guidance for considering how MH issues from military service contributed to offending behavior, and to have this information presented to military discharge and review boards for possible reconsideration of negative discharge decisions (see Kurta, 2017).
7. VRSS is a secure website that enables correctional and other criminal justice system entities to identify inmates or defendants who have served in the U.S. military (U.S. Department of Veterans Affairs, n.d.).
8. The rapid growth in all of Illinois' problem-solving courts (PSCs) led the state's Supreme Court to propose uniform standards for the practices, procedures, and operations of all PSCs in the state (see Illinois Criminal Justice Information Authority, 2017).

Disclosure statement

Community Participatory Research on Veterans in Specialized Programming. Funded under the Justice Community Opioid Innovation Network (JCOIN) Coordination and Translation Center (CTC) (U2CDA050097, MPI Taxman/Rudes). The contents of this publication are solely the responsibility of the authors and do not necessarily represent the official views of the National Institutes of Health (NIH), National Institute on Drug Abuse (NIDA) and the Bureau of Justice Assistance (BJA), or the participating sites.

Funding

The work was supported by the Justice Community Opioid Innovation Network (JCOIN) Coordination and Translation Center (CTC).

ORCID

Don Hummer http://orcid.org/0000-0003-3026-0287
James M. Byrne http://orcid.org/0000-0001-9216-9871
Sabrina S. Rapisarda http://orcid.org/0000-0001-5148-8630
Kelly M. Socia http://orcid.org/0000-0003-0560-3399
Kimberly R. Kras http://orcid.org/0000-0002-0592-0418

References

American University. (2016) . *Veterans treatment courts: 2015 Survey results*. American University, School of Public Affairs, Justice Programs Office.

Arno, C. (2015). Proportional response: The need for more—and more standardized—veterans' courts. *University of Michigan Journal of Law Reform*, *48*(4/5), 1039–1072. https://doi.org/10.36646/mjlr.48.4.proportional

Axelrod, J., Kegu, J., & Milton, P. (2023). Military veterans kicked out for being gay still fighting for honorable discharges. *CBS News Com*. https://www.cbsnews.com/news/military-veterans-don't-don'tdont-tell-honorable-discharges/

Baldwin, J. M. (2015). Investigating the programmatic attack: A national survey of veterans treatment courts. *Journal of Criminal Law and Criminology*, *105*(3), 705–751.

Baldwin, J. M. (2017). Whom do they serve? A national examination of veterans treatment court participants and their challenges. *Criminal Justice Policy Review*, *28*(6), 515–554. https://doi.org/10.1177/0887403415606184

Baldwin, J. M., & Brooke, E. J. (2019). Pausing in the wake of rapid adoption: A call to critically examine the veterans treatment court concept. *Journal of Offender Rehabilitation*, *58*(1), 1–29. https://doi.org/10.1080/10509674.2018.1549181

Baldwin, J. M., Hartley, R., & Brooke, E. J. (2018). Identifying those who served: Modeling potential participant identification in veterans treatment courts. *Drug Court Review 1*, 11–32. https://ntcrc.org/drug-court-review/dcr-archive

Blosnich, J. R., Dichter, M. E., Cerulli, C., Batten, S. V., & Bossarte, R. M. (2014). Disparities in adverse childhood experiences among individuals with a history of military service. *JAMA Psychiatry*, *71*(9), 1041–1048. https://doi.org/10.1001/jamapsychiatry.2014.724

Bronson, J., Carson, E. A., Noonan, M. & Berzofsky, M. (2015). Veterans in prison and jail, 2011–12 (NCJ 249144). Retrieved from Bureau of Justice Statistics: https://www.bjs.gov/content/pub/pdf/vpj1112

Bureau of Justice Assistance. (2023). BJA FY 2023 veterans treatment court discretionary grant program. In *Office of justice programs, bureau of justice assistance*. US Department of Justice . BJA FY 2023 Veterans Treatment Court Discretionary Grant Program (ojp.gov). https://bja.ojp.gov/funding/opportunities/o-bja-2023-171536

Byrne, J., Kras, K. R., Hummer, D., Socia, K., & Rapisarda, S. S. (2024). Community participatory research on veterans in specialized programming; project overview and initial findings. *Victims & Offenders*, this volume.

Cavanaugh, J. M. (2011). Helping those who serve: Veterans treatment courts foster rehabilitation and reduce recidivism for offending combat veterans. *New England Law Review*, *45*(2), 463–488.

Clark, S., McGuire, J., & Blue-Howells, J. (2010). Development of veterans treatment courts: Local and legislative initiatives. *Drug Court Review*, *7*(1), 171–208.

Clark, S., McGuire, J., & Blue-Howells, J. (2014). What can family courts learn from veterans treatment courts? *Family Court Review*, *52*(3), 417–424. https://doi.org/10.1111/fcre.12101

Council on Criminal Justice. (2022). *From service through reentry: A preliminary assessment of veterans in the criminal justice system*. Council on Criminal Justice, Veterans Justice Commission. https://counciloncj.org/veterans-justice-commission/

Council on Criminal Justice. (2023). *Honoring service, advancing safety: Supporting veterans from arrest through sentencing*. Council on Criminal Justice, Veterans Justice Commission. https://counciloncj.foleon.com/veterans-commission/report-1/

Craddock, T. B. (2022). Veteran's treatment courts: Will more be necessary now that the 20-year war on terror has concluded for US soldiers? *Journal of Veterans Studies*, *8*(2), 8–20. https://doi.org/10.21061/jvs.v8i2.359

Culp, R., Youstin, T. J., Englander, K., & Lynch, J. (2013). From war to prison: Examining the relationship between military service and criminal activity. *Justice Quarterly*, *30*(4), 651–680. https://doi.org/10.1080/07418825.2011.615755

DeVall, K., Lanier, C., & Baker, L. J. (2022). *Painting the current picture: A national report on treatment courts in the United States*. National Drug Court Research Center. https://perma.cc/Y7F7-9KHT

Douds, A. S., & Ahlin, E. M. (2019). *The veterans treatment court movement: Striving to serve those who served*. Routledge.

Douds, A. S., Ahlin, E. M., Howard, D., & Stigerwalt, S. (2017). Varieties of veterans' courts: A statewide assessment of veterans' treatment court components. *Criminal Justice Policy Review*, *28*(8), 740–769. https://doi.org/10.1177/0887403415620633

Douds, A. S., & Hummer, D. (2019). When a veterans' treatment court fails: Lessons learned from a qualitative evaluation. *Victims & Offenders*, *14*(3), 322–343. https://doi.org/10.1080/15564886.2019.1595248

Erickson, J. W. (2016). Veterans treatment courts: A case study of their efficacy for 'veterans' needs. *International Journal of Law and Psychiatry*, *49*(Part B), 221–225. https://doi.org/10.1016/j.ijlp.2016.10.009

Finlay, A. K., Stimmel, M., Blue-Howells, J., Rosenthal, J., McGuire, J., Binswanger, I., Smelson, D., Harris, A. H. S., Frayne, S. M., Bowe, T., & Timko, C. (2017). Use of veterans health administration mental health and substance use disorder treatment after exiting prison: The health care for reentry veterans program. *Administration and Policy in Mental Health and Mental Health Services Research*, *44*(2), 177–187. https://doi.org/10.1007/s10488-015-0708-z

Flatley, B., Clark, S., Rosenthal, J., & Blue-Howells, J. (2017). *Veterans court inventory 2016 update: Characteristics of and VA involvement in veterans treatment courts and other veteran-focused court programs from the veterans justice outreach specialist perspective*. U.S. Department of Veterans Affairs. https://www.va.gov/HOMELESS/nchav/resources/docs/justice-involved/incarcerated/2016-Veterans-Court-Inventory-Update-VJO-Fact-Sheet-508.pdf

Hartley, R. D., & Baldwin, J. M. (2019). Waging war on recidivism among JIVs: An impact evaluation of a large urban veterans treatment court. *Criminal Justice Policy Review*, *30*(1), 52–78. https://doi.org/10.1177/0887403416650490

Holbrook, J., & Anderson, S. (2011). Veterans courts: Early outcomes and key indicators for success. *Widener University School of Law: Widener Law School Legal Studies Research Paper Series*, 11–25. http://papers.ssrn.com/sol3/papers.cfm?abstract_id=1912655

H.R. 886–116th Congress (2019–2020). (2021). *Veteran treatment court coordination act of 2019, H.R. 200, 116th congress*. https://www.congress.gov/bill/116th-congress/house-bill/886

Huskey, K. A. (2015). Reconceptualizing "the crime" in veterans treatment courts. *Federal Sentencing Reporter*, *27*(3), 178–186. https://doi.org/10.1525/fsr.2015.27.3.178

Illinois Criminal Justice Information Authority. (2017). *An overview of problem-solving courts and implications for practice*. https://icjia.illinois.gov/researchhub/articles/an-overview-of-problem-solving-courts-and-implications-for-practice

Justice for Vets. (n.d.). *What is a Veterans treatment court?* https://justiceforvets.org/what-is-a-veterans-treatment-court/

Kurta, A. M. (2017). *Memorandum for secretaries of the military departments clarifying guidance to military discharge review boards and boards for correction of military/naval records considering requests by veterans for modification of their discharge due to mental health conditions, sexual assault, or sexual harassment*. US Department of Defense, Office of the Undersecretary of Defense. Clarifying-Guidance-to-Military-Discharge-Review-Boards.pdf (defense.gov).

Lennon, C. (2020). The growth and need for veterans treatment courts. *Touro Law Review*, *35*(4), 1171–1194.

Maruschak, L. M., Bronson, J., & Alper, M. (2021). *Veterans in prison: Survey of prison inmates, 2016*. U.S. Department of Justice, Office of Justice Programs, Bureau of Justice Statistics. https://bjs.ojp.gov/content/pub/pdf/vpspi16st.pdf

McGuire, J., Clark, S., Blue-Howells, J., & Coe, C. (2013). *An inventory of VA involvement in veterans courts, dockets and tracks* (White paper). https://justiceforvets.org/wp-content/uploads/An%20Inventory%20of%20VA%20involvement%20in%20Veterans%20Courts.pdf

Montgomery County (PA) Veterans Treatment Court. (n.d.). *Policy and procedure manual*. https://www.montcopa.org/DocumentCenter/View/740/Veterans-Treatment-Court-Policy-and-Procedure-Manual?bidId=

National Conference of Commissioners on Uniform State Laws. (2017). *Model veterans treatment court act and model veterans court Treatment Court Rules*. https://www.uniformlaws.org/viewdocument/final-act-153?CommunityKey=3c91a212-1d3d-4768-9adf-ce809a43f66b&tab=librarydocuments

NPC Research. (2019). *How to implement a multi-track model in your treatment court*. NPC Research. How-To-Manual_Multi-track-Treatment-Court-Final.pdf (ndci.org).

Perlin, M. L. (2013). 'John Brown went off to war': Considering veterans' courts as problem-solving courts. *Nova Law Review*, *37*(3), 445–477.

Pomerance, B. (2019). Rational justice: Equal protection problems amid veterans treatment court eligibility categorizations. *Oregon Law Review*, *97*(2), 425–476.

Rapisarda, S. S., Kras, K. R., LeMoyne, G., Hummer, D., Socia, K., & Byrne, J. (2024). Veterans' treatment courts: A nationwide review of U.S. enacting and eligibility state statutes. *Victims & Offenders*, this volume.

Rowen, J. (2020). Worthy of justice: A veterans treatment court in practice. *Law & Policy*, *42*(1), 78–100. https://doi.org/10.1111/lapo.12142

Russell, R. T. (2014). Veterans treatment courts. *Touro Law Review*, *31*(3), 385–401.

Seamone, E. R., Brooks Holliday, S., & Sreenivasan, S. (2018). Veteran non grata: Veteran sex offenders with service-related mental health conditions and the need to mitigate risk. *Virginia Journal of Criminal Law*, *6*(1), 182–237.

Shah, S. (2014). Authorization required: Veterans treatment courts, the need for democratic legitimacy, and the separation of powers doctrine. *Southern California Interdisciplinary Law Journal*, *23* (1), 67–106.

Shannon, L. M., Birdwhistell, S., Hulbig, S. K., Jones, A. J., Newell, J., & Payne, C. (2017). Examining implementation and preliminary performance indicators of veterans treatment courts: The Kentucky experience. *Evaluation and Program Planning*, *63*, 54–66. https://doi.org/10.1016/j.evalprogplan.2017.03.003

Siedor, M. (2020). Towards an end to Veteran homelessness and suicide: Recommended changes to the Va's character of discharge determination process. *Testimony before the subcommittee on disability assistance & memorial affairs, house veterans affairs committee, July 8, 2020*. https://www.congress.gov/116/meeting/house/110852/witnesses/HHRG-116-VR09-Bio-SiedorM-20200708.pdf

Timko, C., Flatley, B., Tjemsland, A., McGuire, J., Clark, S., Blue-Howells, J., Blonigen, D. M., Rosenthal, J., & Finlay, A. (2016). A longitudinal examination of veterans treatment courts' characteristics and eligibility criteria. *Justice Research & Policy*, *17*(2), 123–136. https://doi.org/10.1155/2016/6793907

Tsai, J., Finlay, A., Flatley, B., Kasprow, W. J., & Clark, S. (2018). A national study of veterans treatment court participants: Who benefits and who recidivates. *Administration and Policy in Mental Health and Mental Health Services Research*, *45*(2), 236–244. https://doi.org/10.1007/s10488-017-0816-z

Tsai, J., Flatley, B., Kasprow, W. J., Clark, S., & Finlay, A. (2017). Diversion of veterans with criminal justice involvement to treatment courts: Participant characteristics and outcomes. *Psychiatric Services*, *68*(4), 375–383. https://doi.org/10.1176/appi.ps.201600233

U.S. Department of Veterans Affairs. (2021). *Fact sheet: Veterans treatment courts and other veteran-focused courts served by VA veterans justice outreach specialists*. https://www.va.gov/HOMELESS/docs/VJO/Veterans-Treatment-Court-InventoryUpdate-Fact-Sheet-Jan-2021.pdf

U.S. Department of Veterans Affairs. (n.d.). *Welcome to the veterans re-entry search services*. https://vrss.va.gov/

Veterans Legal Clinic at the Legal Services Center of Harvard Law School. (2016). *Underserved. How the VA wrongfully excludes veterans with bad paper*. https://www.nvlsp.org/images/uploads/NVLSP__Swords_to_Plowshares_Underserved.pdf

Yerramsetti, A. P., Simons, D. D., Coonan, L., & Stolar, A. (2017). Veteran treatment courts: A promising solution. *Behavioral Sciences & the Law*, *35*(5–6), 512–522. https://doi.org/10.1002/bsl.2308

SNAFU, Situation Normal All Forces United in Veterans Court: From the Perspective of a California Court of Appeal Justice and Mentor

Eileen C. Moore

ABSTRACT

This article by a California Court of Appeal justice presents her perspectives and experiences in a Veterans Treatment Court (VTC). She volunteered as a mentor in a Veterans Treatment Court every week for nine years. From her unique perspective, she compares what happens in a VTC with what goes on in a typical criminal court. Her experience as a mentor demonstrates the lack of connection between mentors and the collaborative team. The author describes the VTC process, how laws dictate much of what happens within a VTC, how veteran/defendants react to the process, and what still needs to be done.

Introduction

As Veterans Treatment Courts (VTCs) grow in number across the United States, a question emerges about various aspects of their operation and experience related to eligibility criteria, admission, assessment, court staff, and mentoring. While research has been conducted regarding these topics, there is an important side of the story to tell – from the people who have lived and worked in VTCs. The voices of these stakeholders are necessary for understanding how VTCs are implemented and how people are experiencing them from the standpoint of people interacting directly with the criminal justice system and with veterans enrolled in VTC programs. In this article, I will engage with these topic areas from the viewpoint of someone who is a veteran, a mentor, and a judge. I bring these three lenses together to offer a dynamic look from various roles serving veterans in VTCs.

A changing country

Let me give you a little background about why I am writing about Veterans Treatment Courts (VTCs). I served as a combat nurse in Vietnam where I was Lieutenant Moore. But when I came home and saw that the Women's Liberation Movement was part of the many social causes changing our country, I grabbed for that brass ring, got myself into the University of California, and never looked back to Vietnam.

I went on to law school at Pepperdine University and then to the University of Virginia for a masters degree in the judicial process. In 1989, I was appointed to the California

Superior Court and became Judge Moore. In 2000, the Governor elevated me to the California Court of Appeal, where I still sit. I am now Justice Moore.

It was sometime in the mid to late 1990s that the local chapter of Vietnam Veterans of America asked to speak at a special event at the Richard Nixon Presidential Library. When I arrived at the Library, a Vietnam vet using a cane was waiting to escort me inside. His name was Greg. Greg had lived on the streets for 15 years and had somehow pulled himself up and was in his last year of college when I met him.

Inside the auditorium, off to the side, sat three rows of disheveled-looking men wearing tattered fatigues and appearing lost. I said to myself, "Vietnam vets, homeless, self-medicated." After I spoke, those men completely surrounded me. A few had tears in their eyes. Each had to touch me somewhere. I think they wanted to connect with something soft. One vet brushed his pointer finger over and over the back of my hand. Others stroked my shoulder or arm. That's when the lightbulb went off in my head. These men probably had no good memories about Vietnam . . . except the nurses. They brought back to me thoughts of soldiers opening their eyes in the hospital, just tents and Quonset huts, and seeing an American girl standing next to them. You could see in their eyes they had no idea where they were, but wherever it was, they felt safe. They often reached up to touch our faces, just to make sure we were really there. I realized back then how the very thought of America kept our boys going.

Back to Greg. He went on to graduate from college and I thought he was doing well. But about five years later, I spoke at his funeral. His Vietnam demons would not release him and he died from alcoholism.

My speaking event experience at the Nixon Library caused me to reflect on post-Vietnam times when some chapters of the American Legion and Veterans of Foreign Wars refused to accept Vietnam vets as members (Vietnam Veterans of America, n.d.). That's why Vietnam Veterans of America (VVA) was formed – to provide support and advocacy to a generation of military veterans largely forgotten by prior service members (Vietnam Veterans of America, n.d.). I have been involved with veteran activities ever since that event. I joined the local chapter and became a life member of VVA. I decided to adopt VVA's motto and incorporate it into my own life: "Never again will one generation of veterans abandon another."

When I realized around 2008 how many Iraq and Afghanistan veterans were experiencing homelessness, I also realized this country was doing the same thing it had done to Vietnam veterans, and that our more current veterans who were not making a successful transition into civilian life were going to spend their lives with tin cups at the entrances and exits of highways and freeways, just like homeless Vietnam vets.

I saw this as a call to action to make sure California courts did what they were able to do. I managed to launch a Veterans and Military Families subcommittee for all California courts within the Judicial Council, the governing body for California courts, in 2008. I have been its chair since then.

That same year, California established its first VTC, started by Judge Wendy Lindley. Knowing I was a Vietnam vet, Judge Lindley asked me to gather up some of the "guys" to act as mentors in her new court. I did, and that's how Vietnam vets became volunteer mentors in California's first VTC. For nine years, I ran over to that VTC every Tuesday afternoon to act as a mentor, primarily to women veterans. California now has 48 Veterans Treatment Courts.

Thus, I have been involved with California's VTCs from two perspectives. First, I founded and currently chair the Judicial Council's statewide Veterans and Military Families subcommittee, where we provide education, monitor legislation, author rules and forms and provide guidance to all California courts., n.d.Second, I volunteered as a mentor in California's first VTC. This article will discuss my involvement in California's first VTC. Acting as a mentor, I experienced the VTC from the perspective of a woman veteran and a judicial officer.

Background

VTCs began in Buffalo, New York in Judge Robert Russell's courtroom in 2008 (American Psychological Association, 2012). Judge Russell followed the drug court treatment model but made it veteran-centered. Other VTCs opened across the country. The VTC in Orange County, California was either the second or third. It was in that one that I volunteered as a mentor.

One of the primary goals of VTCs is to help our veterans heal, while avoiding incarceration, if possible. Different jurisdictions have different rules and procedures. VTCs are collaborative courts (California Courts, n.d.; Cavanaugh, 2010). What that means is that a group of professionals, headed by the judge, collaborate about each veteran appearing in court. Usually, the collaborative team consists of the judge, an administrator, a deputy district attorney, a deputy public defender, a probation officer, a county mental health professional, a person from the Department of Veterans Affairs (VA), sometimes a member of a volunteer agency, and perhaps a few others. The team decides who will be admitted into the VTC and once admitted discusses the person's progress, and plans how best to proceed, reviewing each case just prior to beginning each court session.

The admission process changed over the years of my involvement as a mentor. Early on, the California statute that authorized VTCs restricted participants to those who served in combat (CA Penal Code § 1170.9. 1965). A veteran whose job it was to unload coffins from airplanes sent from Vietnam was denied entry despite the fact that he was diagnosed with Post-traumatic Stress Disorder. That experience drove home to me the importance of the wording of a statute. Since then, the combat requirement has been deleted.

Once admitted a veteran progressed through four phases. As the veteran advanced to the next stage, the number of court appearances decreased. If successful in the process, the veteran would graduate from the VTC in 18 to 24 months.[1]

From what I observed, there are four main attributes of a VTC. First, the defendants are usually inexperienced with the criminal justice system in that they had no previous criminal record. Second, there is a representative of the VA on the collaborative team. Third, to a certain extent, there is an emphasis on symbols, phrases, structures, and cultural norms that are emblematic of military life. And fourth, and I think most important, each veteran is assigned a mentor. Just like the defendant, the volunteer mentor is a military veteran.

Different VTCs operate in various ways. Most have some sort of phasing process, where the veteran moves forward to the next phase of the treatment program. If successful, and most are, the veteran graduates. If the veteran had to suffer a conviction, the court usually either seals or vacates it so the veteran can apply for a job without the baggage of a criminal conviction.

After the court session begins, those who have complied with all the court's requirements are recognized. Applause from the courtroom audience is common. Some courts even have a drawing for gift cards. Then those in noncompliance are called up one by one. Whatever rule or order the veteran violated is discussed by the judge and the veteran. By the end of the court session, each veteran is called before the court.

VTCs are constantly changing, depending on what they learn from experience. The use of sanctions is a good example of how VTCs have adjusted their procedures. Early on, a veteran who was non-compliant with the conditions of court spent a night or two in jail as a consequence. But experience has taught the courts that these jail stays involve the humiliation of being treated like a criminal and the embarrassment of having to tell families and employers about their failures, which is very destructive to the healing process. Currently, it's common to avoid sending a non-compliant veteran to jail. Instead, community service, writing essays, or more frequent court appearances are ordered in lieu of jail. Avoiding overnighters lessens the shame that veterans may experience from incarceration.

How veterans treatment courts differ from traditional courts

Prior research on collaborative and therapeutic courts highlights how the problem solving and collaborative approach can contribute to improved outcomes for defendants who go through them (Gottfredson et al., 2003; Marlowe, 2011; Winick, 2003). VTCs are even more specialized in their approach, operations, and functioning in ways that are unique to the veteran experience (Douds & Ahlin, 2018; Rowen, 2020; Russell, 2015). Here, I will elaborate on three important ways that were central to my experience: espirit de corps, judicial discretion, and mentors.

Esprit de corps

We've all seen films showing courtroom events. There's the individual defendant and perhaps some family members who care about that defendant, but everyone else in the courtroom has other concerns. Under ordinary circumstances, one criminal defendant is absorbed with his or her case and not particularly interested in the cases of the other defendants. In a VTC, the courtroom dynamics are different. The first time I walked into a VTC, I realized that every single person in that courtroom wanted all the veterans to succeed, from the judge to the court clerk, to the bailiff to the prosecutor and defense attorney, everyone in the audience, the mentors, the collaborative team, and especially the other veterans who were also defendants in the VTC. The esprit de corps, or feeling of pride, fellowship, and common loyalty shared by the members of the military (Oxford Reference, n.d.), is palpable in a VTC.

As the judge discusses the non-compliant veteran's case, the other veterans pay close attention. When the non-compliant veteran returns to the audience, others reach out and whisper something like, "sorry man." There is a community spirit that encourages the non-compliant veteran to do better next time. It's subtle, but it's there. And when a veteran gets promoted to the next phase of the program, there is often cheering and applause, smiles, "attaboys" and encouraging pats on the back. Branch cheers such as the "oorah" of the Marines can be heard.

And the community is not only inside that courtroom. It's outside the courtroom doors while waiting for those doors to open. Outside the courtroom, there are veteran defendants, veteran mentors and family members of veterans. There is a strong sense of esprit de corps there as well, a feeling of all for one and one for all.

The reality that VTCs are a group venture especially hit home for me one time while I was a mentor. One of those veterans died by suicide. The collaborative team had to decide how to inform the rest of the veterans in the VTC that he was gone. The judge ordered all the veterans to return to court at the regular time on Tuesday afternoon, and the mental health professionals were all there. The judge explained what happened and the team was there for the vets. Some cried. Some swore. Most remained silent. Everyone grieved together. As I looked over the faces of the veterans, I worried how many others might be contemplating doing just what their former comrade had done. The espirit de corps is revealed in shared sorrow, not just success, further cementing the collective experience among these individuals.

Judicial discretion

A judge exercises discretion with every ruling and order. I served as a trial court judge for almost 12 years. I permitted counsel to argue and when arguments were complete, I made my order. That was it. No one second-guessed me. Perhaps 18 months or so later, I might have heard from a higher court that my ruling was wrong, but in the moment, my order was the final word.

Collaborative courts are not the same. It involves a team of professionals who have decided how to proceed with a particular defendant. While the judge still has the final word, the underlying forces are different. There was an agreement among the team about how to proceed in each veteran's case before the court session began. Thus, the judge's orders for each veteran are largely based on the informed input from mental health professionals on the collaborative team.

It's not common that one judge has the opportunity to observe other judges in action. But I got to observe many during the years I acted as a mentor. Thus, it was sometimes fascinating for me to watch judges make decisions in open court. I will tell you about a few incidents.

While most defendants in the court I mentored in were veterans of Iraq or Afghanistan, a Vietnam vet's case was called on one occasion. Looking scrubbed and happy, the Vietnam vet displayed an A+ grade on his college paper to both the judge and the whole courtroom. With tears in his eyes, he thanked Judge Lindley for giving him a chance.

At that point, some rattling could be heard from the holding cell in the courtroom. An in-custody defendant on a non-VTC matter, who just happened to be another Vietnam vet, was shaking the cell door. The caged Vietnam vet looked filthy, pitiful, and bedraggled. He was clinging to the cage, seemingly desperate to be admitted to the VTC. As Judge Lindley talked with him, it appeared she was looking over to the collaborative team for reactions. Some of the team members were shaking their heads. The judge told him the team already decided not to permit him into the VTC due to his many decades of crimes and drug use. After he pleaded with her to change her mind, she relented and said she would give him the opportunity. I think I heard some clearing of throats from team members, and I believe I saw Judge Lindley's face redden as she ruled contrary to the team's decision. He was in.

At the recess, I asked the bailiff if I could approach the holding cell and speak with him. I told the man I had been a nurse in Vietnam and that I had seen many Vietnam vets succeed, and I hoped he would as well. He assured me he could do it. The next time I saw him in court, about two months later, he looked like a college professor, wearing a corduroy blazer with patches on the sleeves. His hair was shampooed and in a ponytail. The last time I saw him was at his VTC graduation. One of the things he said in his remarks was, "I couldn't let that nurse down." I don't think he had any idea I was a judge.

On another occasion, one of my mentees was a beautiful young woman whose urine test was abnormal in that it was diluted. It seems that some people try to skew drug and alcohol test results by drinking large amounts of water. She explained to me that it was all a big mistake in that she is very health conscious and always drinks a lot of water. I didn't believe her because I noticed she had been a bit jittery and acting differently.

Sitting in the audience when her case was called, I listened to her explain her situation to the court. The judge was a man sitting in for Judge Lindley. Standing at the podium and looking profoundly sincere, the young woman carefully explained her health routine. She sounded quite convincing.

From the judge's face, I gleaned he wanted to give her a break. Then he put his head down into his cupped hands. When he looked up, his eyes went around to the team members scattered throughout the courtroom. The judge shook his head as if he was clearing it out. Pretty soon, my mentee was hooked up and taken to jail.

I supposed what happened was that the judge was considering just giving her a stern lecture and sending her on her way. But then he remembered the team had decided she should spend a night in jail, and he didn't want to buck the team's decision, even though he had the power to do so. That incident illustrates that collaborative teams felt that immediate consequences are more effective than the traditional routine of bringing a defendant back in 90 days to see how she was doing. Of course, since that time, as I mentioned earlier, court procedures changed, and overnighters are avoided if possible.

Mentors

Someone once said to me that mentors are the "secret sauce" in VTCs.

The majority of mentors have no affiliation with the VA (for a review of VTC mentors see Lucas, 2018). VTCs conduct outreach to the community that volunteers are needed, and veterans who want to help other veterans come forward. Different courts assign a particular veteran mentor to a particular veteran defendant in different ways. Many courts, however, have a person who is an administrator to or supervisor of the mentors. That head mentor position may or may not be a paid position. However, courts often do not have the financial means to pay for a head mentor, so, along with all the other mentors, the administrators of the mentors tend to be volunteers. Whoever does the pairing of the mentor and defendant tries to find two persons with similar backgrounds. If possible, both will have served in the same branch of service.

Everyone with whom the veteran defendant deals in the court process, from the probation officer to the VA representative to the mental health practitioner to the lawyer, is taking notes, giving orders, or preaching to the defendant. Most of them have no military experience. The veteran mentor, on the other hand, has experienced some of what the veteran defendant has. At some point, the mentor was in the military and later transitioned back into the civilian world. Thus, the mentor serves as an example of how the veteran defendant can successfully overcome what may seem insurmountable. The mere fact the mentor succeeded in that transition subtly provides guidance and encouragement for the veteran defendant to do the same thing.

Probably the most important function of the mentor/defendant relationship, however, is that the mentor is usually not taking notes or recording anything. The mentor is there for one reason only: to help the veteran defendant. Quite simply, the mentor is a source of constant support and encouragement, an important step toward getting the veteran back on the good citizen track.

Mentors try to be in court with their mentees, but between court dates, each relationship depends on the two individuals. Some communicate by telephone, text or e-mail from time to time. I would occasionally meet for coffee or lunch with my mentees. Mentors do not attempt to provide any treatment, just camaraderie. Some mentors continue to provide encouragement, even after graduation.

There seems to be a correlation between what happens in court and how much the mentee leans on the mentor. At the early stage, veteran defendants sometimes have an attitude that the whole process is a waste of time. But after receiving some sort of sanction, veteran defendants tend to want to interact more with the mentor and take the whole matter more seriously. The mentor is there to go with the flow. Mentors react to the needs of the veteran by giving reassurance and boosting the veteran's morale. In effect, the mentor is like an individual coach who provides encouragement. The mentor can communicate with the veteran defendant in ways only another veteran can. They both understand the mentee prefers to suffer in silence because in the military they were taught to "embrace the suck." The mentor is available to engage when the mentee is ready to make the transition from compliance with the court rules to actual engagement with the healing process.

One of my mentees had numerous tattoos and wild hair colors, sometimes pink or orange. Her appearance drew negative attention to her, and she might as well have had "arrest me" written across her forehead. I never asked her, but from some of the things she volunteered, I was of the impression she had been sexually assaulted in the military. I suspected she was trying to make herself unattractive so she wouldn't be attacked again.

Early one Sunday morning, she drove two blocks to a relative's house, still wearing her pajamas. A police officer pulled her over and she was arrested for being under the influence. Before court, she swore to me that she had not taken heroin or any other drug for 54 days. She explained she was scared and nervous when the officer questioned her. During the court session, the prosecutor read from the police report that when she was arrested, she was speaking very rapidly, her pulse was 125 and her eyeballs were shaking. It looked as if she was going to jail, even though the drug test results had not yet made it to court. During the break in the proceedings, I told her I didn't know how things were going to work out, but that I believed her. And I did. About 20 minutes later, court was back in session and the judge announced they were able to locate the test results. No drugs had been found in her system!

The next day, I opened an e-mail from her that had been written after midnight: "Eileen, I just wanted to tell you, thank you for going to court with me and being there and believing me." That young woman went on to graduate from the VTC and gain employment.

Laws governing veterans treatment courts

Most VTCs operate under a statutory scheme or statewide court rules (Douds et al., 2017; Timko et al., 2016). Then each court adds its own local flavor, so, each VTC is unique. Various states have their own eligibility requirements. Some allow people convicted of felonies and misdemeanors, while others permit only those who commit misdemeanors into VTCs. Many exclude anyone who used violence.[2] Even when a state accepts those who commit felonies, I have never seen a VTC accept people convicted of child molestation, sexual assault, or murder.

To give you an idea of how differences can be significant, I compare two states' approaches: California and Minnesota. Of course, I am familiar with California law, and I had an opportunity to study VTCs in Minnesota while working on a project recently. In this comparison, I examine causation, investment of veterans, identification of veterans, and some creative aspects of the two states.

Linking military experiences to crime after service

Causation refers to the direct or indirect connection of military service with the crime. There are different aspects to causation in the VTC context:

(1) Was or is the veteran defendant in the military?
(2) Does the veteran defendant have a qualifying condition [military sexual trauma, traumatic brain injury, post-traumatic stress disorder, substance use abuse, mental health problems]?
(3) Does the condition stem from military service?
(4) Was the crime committed as a result of the condition?

There's a substantive difference in what is required for a defendant to be eligible to enter a VTC in the two states (see Table 1). California only requires that the defendant was or is in the military and "may be" suffering from a qualifying condition as a result of that service.

Table 1. Comparing VTC eligibility statutes in California and Minnesota.

California	Minnesota
The court must make a determination whether the person was, or currently is, a member of the United States military and whether the defendant *may be* suffering from one of the conditions as a result of the service. [CA Penal Code § 1170.9 (a)]	The court *must determine by clear and convincing evidence*, whether the defendant suffers from one of the conditions, stemming from service, and whether the offense was committed as a result of the condition. [Minn. Stat. § 609.1056 Subd. 2(c)]

Emphasis added.

But Minnesota additionally requires that the offense was committed as a result of that condition, and all that must be shown by "clear and convincing evidence." Clear and convincing evidence is somewhere between more probable than not, the standard required in civil cases, and beyond a reasonable doubt, the standard required in criminal cases, so it's a high requirement (California Evidence Code § 115).

Obtaining clear and convincing evidence, as required by the Minnesota statute (2022), can be challenging for veteran defendants. Both the VA and the military are notoriously slow in responding to document requests. It can take months or years to have the VA perform a requested medical examination, and hiring a civilian health professional, assuming there is someone available who is familiar with the maladies of war, is very expensive Not only are expert witnesses expensive, but the statutory requirements can also be onerous. In Minnesota, the statute requires specific qualifications of knowledge, skill, experience, training, or education (50 M.S.A., Rules of Evid., Rule 702). The requirement for clear and convincing evidence means the expert's opinion is highly probable, which is more than is required in civil cases, but less than the requirement to find someone guilty in criminal cases (*State v. Jones* (2008) 753 N.W.2d 677). So, satisfying that clear and convincing standard may be very difficult.

Investment of veterans

What the veteran defendant has to invest, or what is required of a veteran, in order to reap the benefits of a VTC in the two states is quite different.

When someone is diverted, it means the person is able to avoid prosecution altogether. The person is arrested, goes to court, and the court orders the person into a diversion option, which is usually linked with some healing program.

In California, the veteran who is charged with a felony must suffer the conviction to be eligible for entry into a VTC. Once in the VTC, the veteran works to earn the way back to a clean criminal record, which could happen by the court's vacating the conviction or sealing the record of conviction. It's only the veterans who commit misdemeanors who are diverted from prosecution (see Table 2).

Thus, a veteran in California may decide that it's more expeditious to plead guilty and be placed on probation, if probation is available for that crime, than to spend 18 to 24 months in a VTC. And that's a major issue since it requires veterans to remain crime-free without intense treatment for their condition. But in Minnesota, even those accused of felony-level offenses are eligible for diversion. Thus, once a veteran gets into a Minnesota VTC, he/she may never suffer a conviction.

Based on this comparison, it is much more difficult to be eligible and admitted into a VTC in Minnesota than it is in California. But once in a VTC, it can be much easier to complete the program in Minnesota than it is in California. The long-lasting effects on recidivism remain to be seen.

Table 2. Comparing diversion options in California and Minnesota statute.

California	Minnesota
California has two statutes. One is post-conviction, and the veteran defendant must earn the way back to clearing the conviction. [CA Penal Code § 1170.9] The other is a diversion statute, for misdemeanors only. [CA Penal Code § 1001.80]	Minnesota's VTCs are all pre-conviction, diversion-type courts. [Minn. Stat. § 609.1056 Subd. 2]

Table 3. Comparing veteran defendant identification in California and Minnesota statutes.

California	Minnesota
At arraignment of all defendants, the court in California must inform all defendants that certain provisions of the law benefit veterans and offer them a court form that explains those benefits. [CA Penal Code §858 (d)]	Minnesota's statute mandates early identification and prompt placement of eligible participants in its program, but no identification process is set forth. [Minn. Stat. § 609.1056 Subd. 1 (3 iii)]

Identification of veterans

Courts have struggled to consistently identify which criminal defendants are veterans. The VA does have an identification process, but it's not available to most who try to access it. It's called VRSS or Veterans Reentry Search Service. Even though it's there, however, it's not known to be accurate or up to date, and many who had less than honorable discharges are not on the list. Courts are at a loss as to how to identify veterans (see Table 3).

California has a process to inform defendants there are certain benefits available to them if they have veteran status, but it's up to the veteran to self-identify. California does not mandate identification of veterans out of concern for privacy, so identifying as a veteran is optional. How Minnesota identifies its veterans is not set forth in its statutes, which likely means it's left up to veterans to self-identify if they so choose. Courts tend to rely on the police and jails to ask arrestees whether or not they are veterans. Some ask; some don't. Even when the question is asked, veterans are not always forthright with their responses. Some assume they lost their veteran status when they were arrested. Others are ashamed to admit they are veterans. Because definitions of who is a veteran vary, some mistakenly believe the length of service or access to benefits from the VA dictates whether or not they are veterans. Definitions differ from one state to another. As a result, individuals are unsure whether or not they qualify to call themselves veterans. More and more, the question that is asked is not whether the person arrested is a veteran, but whether or not the person ever served in the military These strategies aim to increase the number of individuals who have veteran status in receipt for specialized services that are offered by the VA, however, much more needs to be done (see Baldwin, 2015; Seamone, 2023).

Creative aspects of some statutes

In different states, there are creative and individual aspects to help veterans succeed in a VTC or after graduation from a VTC.

California's creativity relates to employment after graduation from a VTC (see Table 4). When the veteran is applying for a job, information about an arrest or conviction or VTC-involvement need not be provided, even if the veteran is required to answer such questions under oath. Under some circumstances, non-veterans with criminal convictions may come

Table 4. Comparing creative aspects of VTC statutes in California and Minnesota.

California	Minnesota
Except when applying for a job as a peace officer, the defendant is not obligated to disclose the arrest or conviction when such information is requested to be given under oath, affirmation, or otherwise. [CA Penal Code § 1170.9 (h)(4)(C)]	Minnesota includes the veteran defendant's family members who agree to be involved in the treatment and services provided to the participant under the program. [Minn. Stat. § 609.1056 Subd. 1 (3)(xi)]

back to court after the end of probation or incarceration and ask that their convictions be sealed (CA Penal Code 851.91 and 851.92) or expunged (CA Penal Code 1203.4), but those laws do not permit the person to misrepresent to a potential employer.

Minnesota's creativity relates to the healing process. Especially in the domestic violence context, it is a wonderful approach to include the veteran's family members, if they agree to be included. Military families are known to be very supportive of their military member. Including them in treatment is helpful to the whole family.

The many statutory differences among the states are likely a big reason for the lack of nationwide research articles about VTCs. It's almost always a comparison of apples and oranges.

Problems that continue for veterans treatment courts

VTCs have been operating for 15 years. But there are still kinks that need to be worked out.

Identifying eligible veterans for VTCs

By far, identifying those who are the veterans in courts is the major problem. As discussed above, there are some attempts, such as California's requirement that arraignment magistrates inform *all* criminal defendants there are certain statutes that benefit veterans, and then leave it up to the veteran to self-identify. But many veterans in courts remain unidentified as veterans.

In my opinion, identification of veterans who appear in criminal courts is a major problem. The Veterans Justice Commission, a group of 15 members, of which I am one, headed by two former Secretaries of Defense, Chuck Hagel and Leon Panetta, was launched by the Council on Criminal Justice in 2022 (Veterans Justice Commission, 2022b). The very first recommendation the Commission reported to Congress was:

> To improve identification of veterans when they come in contact with the justice system, Congress should authorize a study to evaluate the effectiveness of databases that capture veteran status, order, necessary improvements, and incentivize their use by local and state agencies. Addressing a related problem, the Commission urged Congress and state legislatures to codify a uniform definition of the term "veteran." As detailed in a report to the Commission, the federal government, states, criminal justice agencies, and community programs all differ in the specific criteria they use to determine who is, and who isn't, a veteran, creating confusion and barriers to services. (Council on Criminal Justice, 2023, para. 4)

Female veterans

Historically, of course, the military has had primarily male troops. So, it makes sense that VTCs have also been predominantly male. However, the number of female veterans is increasing, and women's issues are often different from those of men (Department of Defense Sexual Assault and Response Annual Report, 2022; Street et al., n.d.). Local courts do the best they can to serve the needs of their communities in a world where a legislature authorizes VTCs but provides little or no extra money to fund them. So, VTCs designed to serve male veterans is sometimes all that is available. I have little doubt that judges would also like treatment courts specially designed for women vets.

Of the women vets I mentored over those nine years, I estimate 90 to 95% of them had been sexually assaulted. That's only anecdotal. No one really knows how many women are assaulted in the military because most don't report the incidents for fear of retaliation and bullying. But the Department of Defense reports there was a 23% increase in sexual assault reports between 2015 and 2020, and 13,000 military women were sexually assaulted or raped in 2018 ("Facts on Military Sexual Violence," 2021). Many VTCs are not meeting women's needs.

There was a sad incident with one young woman I mentored. She was very small in stature and was charged with some kind of drug crime. I didn't ask her if she had been sexually assaulted in the military, but I suspected she had been. The judge ordered her into group therapy at the VA. She asked the court to order her to an all-female group, but the court couldn't do that because the VA was only providing therapy to mixed gender groups. Instead of complying with the court order, the young woman opted to be sentenced to jail. She told me: "I'll feel safer in jail than I will in a room full of military men."

Over the years I volunteered as a mentor, I noticed other failures to consider the needs of female veterans. One time, I sat next to my mentee while we waited for the courtroom doors to open. She had previously told me she had been sexually assaulted in the military. A group of male mentors, all vets, were chatting with their male veteran mentees. Their conversation went to a discussion of a certain woman's breast size. I could feel my mentee tense, and I thought I saw her eyes fill up.

Another time, one of my mentees had her babysitter cancel just before she was to leave for a probation appointment. She called every other babysitter on her list but found no one was available. As she had no relatives in California, she took her children with her to the appointment. The probation officer was not happy she brought the kids. She was ordered to write an essay on setting the right priorities.

Lastly, the rules of the VTC required 17 hours a week of productive use of time, in addition to all the court sessions and court-ordered appointment with VA representatives, mental health professionals and probation officers. Most veterans satisfied this requirement through time spent at employment or going to college. My mentee had small children and spent much of her time taking the kids to and from various medical and dental appointments, pre-schools, and play dates. She was told that time did not count as productive use of her time.

Since I was a mere mentor, I was not part of the collaborative team and felt like I could not intervene. My communications were limited to the head mentor and he was the one who had led the conversation about a woman's body. Without a direct link to the team, I could not change the way that particular court was conducted. But I have been able to include these examples in different educational presentations to judges to recognize these gendered issues.

Diversion courts

Diversion courts for veterans vary a great deal, and one of the major problems is that probation departments are sometimes opting out of involvement, probably due to funding issues. Without that community supervision "stick," the "carrot" of avoiding prosecution doesn't work as well. That is, if the veteran does not have to report to either the court or a law enforcement representative, the consequences of not complying are not as apparent, despite advisements to the veteran by the court when diversion is ordered. Without ongoing law enforcement involvement, the veteran simply attends treatment classes. But the significance of noncooperation could mean being returned to court for prosecution. Unless the state's statute requires the involvement of the probation department, this will remain a problem.

Domestic violence

According to the Council on Criminal Justice, veterans with multiple deployments are three times more likely than service members who were not previously deployed to develop PTSD (Veterans Justice Commission, 2022a). Veterans with PTSD have been found to perpetuate intimate partner violence at rates two to three times the national average (Veterans Justice Commission, 2022a).

The nation's domestic violence laws were enacted during the early days of the Women's Liberation Movement, after judgments in two class actions, one in Oakland and the other in NYC, required police and prosecutors to treat the victims of domestic violence the same way they treat other crime victims (*Scott v. Hart*, 1976; *Bruno v. Codd*, 1979). By the 1990's, states across the country adopted domestic violence laws based on power and control dynamics, as illustrated in the Duluth Power and Control Wheel (n.d. www.duluth-model.org). Domestic violence laws usually require courts to separate families with protective orders for the safety of the families.

From what I have observed, it appears to me that our current veterans often commit domestic violence, not often as a result of power and control issues, but perhaps as a result of conditions they developed in the military. As noted above, veterans with PTSD have been found to perpetuate intimate partner violence at rates two to three times the national average (Veterans Justice Commission, 2022a)., and those I saw in the VTC all had either PTSD, traumatic brain injury or had experienced sexual trauma. Often, it's best for the families to be able to work together toward healing, so long as the victims want to do that. That's why Minnesota's law, as discussed above, that includes the veteran's family in the healing process, is so forward thinking.

Less than honorable discharges from the military

The VA is an integral part of VTCs. But loss of veteran health care benefits often goes hand in hand with a less than honorable discharge. As reported by the Veterans Justice Commission (2022a), "bad-paper veterans may lose access to all VA benefits and programs" (p. 6). Accordingly, in a VTC, the VA will not provide the therapy veterans need if they have this discharge status. That leaves these veterans who developed one of the collaborative court qualifying conditions while serving in the military without the treatment they need to heal. Often a state or county health department will step in and provide the needed treatment, but not all local public entities are financially capable of doing so. Much more needs to be done to assure those who are less than honorably discharged receive the services they need.

Graduating from a VTC with a clean record

Even when a veteran can have a conviction stricken or avoid prosecution altogether through diversion, word of the legal issue often gets out. A typical scenario is that there's a news story about the crime and it ends up on the internet.

Or a veteran might successfully graduate from a VTC and apply for a job. The potential employer assigns its investigating service to do a background check. Even though the court ordered the conviction expunged from the record, it's possible an overworked court clerk couldn't carry out the order before the investigator discovered the conviction. Such problems would likely be solved if state legislatures would supply courts with sufficient funding to perform needed administrative tasks.

Conclusion

VTCs across the country are successfully meeting their primary goal, helping our veterans heal, while avoiding incarceration. But much more is needed. The Veterans Justice Commission (Council on Criminal Justice, 2023) notes that one in three of the nation's 19 million veterans report having been arrested at least once in their lifetime, and at last count, an estimated 181,500 veterans were incarcerated in local, state, or federal facilities. The Commission recommends that the federal government establish a National Center on Veterans Justice to fund research and identify effective program interventions (Council on Criminal Justice, 2023). Many challenges remain, but at least we're doing a better job for our current vets than we did for our Vietnam vets.

Notes

1. For more information on court operations, see the Orange County Superior Court Veterans Treatment Court Participant Handbook (2014).
2. Some courts differentiate between intimate partner violence/domestic violence and other violent crimes. A clear protocol does not exist regarding eligibility for entry into VTCs for violent offenders. See Kravetz (2012) for a critique.

Disclosure statement

No potential conflict of interest was reported by the author(s).

References

American Psychological Association. (2012). A history of treatment courts. *Monitor on Psychology*, *43*, 3. https://www.apa.org/monitor/2012/03/treatment

Annual Report on Sexual Assault in the Military. (2022). *Department of defense sexual assault and response*. https://www.sapr.mil/sites/default/files/public/docs/reports/AR/FY22/FY22_Annual_Report_Slick_Sheet_Reference_Copy.pdf

Baldwin, J. M. (2015). Investigating the programmatic attack: A national survey of veterans treatment courts. *Journal of Criminal Law & Criminology*, *105*(3), 705–751.

Bruno v. Codd, 393 N.E.2d 976, 977 (N.Y. Ct. App. 1979). United States Supreme Court.

California Courts. (n.d.). *Collaborative justice models*. https://www.courts.ca.gov/programs-collabjustice.htm

California Evidence Code, 299 $ 115. 1965. https://leginfo.legislature.ca.gov/faces/codes_displaySection.xhtml?sectionNum=115.&lawCode=EVID

California Penal Code § 1170.9 (h)(4)(C). 2012.

Cavanaugh, J. M. (2010). Helping those who serve: Veterans treatment courts foster rehabilitation and reduce recidivism for offending combat veterans. *The New England Law Review, 45*(2), 463–488.

Council on Criminal Justice. (2023). *Press release: National panel says justice system fails to consistently identify veterans and steer them away from incarceration.* https://counciloncj.foleon.com/veterans-commission/report-1/about-the-council#Press-Release

Douds, A. S., & Ahlin, E. M. (2018). *The veterans treatment court movement: Striving to serve those who served.* Routledge.

Douds, A. S., Ahlin, E. M., Howard, D., & Stigerwalt, S. (2017). Varieties of veterans' courts: A statewide assessment of veterans' treatment court components. *Criminal Justice Policy Review, 28*(8), 740–769. https://doi.org/10.1177/0887403415620633

Duluth Power and Control Wheel. (n.d.). *Domestic abuse intervention programs.* www.duluth-model.org

"Facts on U.S. Military Sexual Violence." (2021). *Statistics from the 2016 – 2020.* Department of Defense. https://www.protectourdefenders.com/wp-content/uploads/2021/05/MSA-Fact-Sheet-2021.pdf

Gottfredson, D. C., Najaka, S. S., & Kearley, B. (2003). Effectiveness of drug treatment courts: Evidence from a randomized trial. *Criminology & Public Policy, 2*(2), 171–196.

Kravetz, P. (2012). Way off base: An argument against intimate partner violence cases in veterans treatment courts. *Veterans Law Review, 4*, 162–205.

Lucas, P. A. (2018). An exploratory study of veterans treatment court peer mentors: Roles, experiences, and expectations. *Drug Court Review, 1*, 59–68.

Marlowe, D. B. (2011). The verdict on drug courts and other problem-solving courts. *Chap Journal Criminal Justice, 2*(1), 52–92.

Minnesota Statute § 609.1056 Subd. 1 (3)(xi). (2022). https://www.revisor.mn.gov/statutes/cite/609.1056

Orange County Superior Court Veterans Treatment Court Participant Handbook. (2014). *Ninth judicial circuit.* https://ninthcircuit.org/sites/default/files/Orange%20County%20Veterans%20Court.pdf

Oxford Reference. (n.d.). *spirit de corps.* https://www.oxfordreference.com/display/10.1093/oi/authority.20110803095758104;jsessionid=9FD508760FE18D5B44046B2DCAFE5F63

Rowen, J. (2020). Worthy of justice: A veterans treatment court in practice. *Law & Policy, 42*(1), 78–100. https://doi.org/10.1111/lapo.12142

Russell, R. T. (2015). Veterans treatment courts. *Touro Law Review, 31*(3), 385. https://digitalcommons.tourolaw.edu/lawreview/vol31/iss3/8

Scott v. Hart, No. C-7-2395 (N.D. Cal. Filed Oct. 28, 1976). United States Supreme Court.

Seamone, E. R. (2023). *Who's a veteran? Challenges in defining and identifying veteran status.* Council on Criminal Justice. https://counciloncj.org/wp-content/uploads/2023/02/Whos_A_Veteran_Final.pdf

Street, A., Skidmore, C., Gyuro, L., & Bell, M. (n.d.). Military Sexual Trauma. US Department of Veterans Affairs. https://www.ptsd.va.gov/professional/treat/type/sexual_trauma_military.asp

Timko, C., Flatley, B., Tjemsland, A., McGuire, J., Clark, S., Blue-Howells, J., Blonigen, D. M., Rosenthal, J., & Finlay, A. (2016). A longitudinal examination of veterans treatment courts' characteristics and eligibility criteria. *Justice Research & Policy, 17*(2), 123–136. https://doi.org/10.1155/2016/6793907

Veterans Justice Commission. (2022a). *From service through reentry, a preliminary assessment of veterans in the criminal justice system.* Council on Criminal Justice. https://counciloncj.org/vjc-preliminary-assessment/

Veterans Justice Commission. (2022b). *Honoring service, advancing safety: Supporting veterans from arrest through sentencing.* Council on Criminal Justice. https://counciloncj.foleon.com/veterans-commission/report-1/

Vietnam Veterans of America. (n.d.). *About Us.* https://vva.org/who-we-are/about-us-history/

Winick, B. J. (2003). Therapeutic jurisprudence and problem solving courts. *Fordham Urban Law Journal, 30*(3), 1055–1103. https://ir.lawnet.fordham.edu/ulj/vol30/iss3/14

At Risk and Underserved: Veterans Treatment Court Team Member Perspectives on Service Delivery Challenges

Kimberly R. Kras, Sabrina S. Rapisarda, Kelly M. Socia, Don Hummer, and James M. Byrne

ABSTRACT

As Veterans Treatment Courts (VTC) proliferate across the United States, questions have been raised about their capacity to provide critical services and support for justice-involved veterans. The current study examines the key decisions made by core VTC team members as justice-involved veterans move through each stage in the VTC process. This study presents in-depth interviews with 145 VTC team members from 20 court jurisdictions across the United States. Interviews revealed common challenges in meeting the service needs of VTC participants coalescing around five intercepts addressing challenges related to pre-entry, eligibility, service coordination and access, and veteran engagement. VTC team members' views about how best to provide services and support to justice-involved veterans are also highlighted. This study provides the unique perspectives of VTC team members on how to address these challenges in ways that will enhance their ability to offer services and provide support for justice-involved veterans.

VTCs provide a pathway for legal system-involved individuals who are current or former members of the United States military to receive services related to areas of need in a therapeutic court model. The underlying assumption of the VTC model is that justice-involved veterans have unique problems and needs arising from their military service that require a specialized court response developed in conjunction with the Department of Veterans Affairs (VA) (Russell, 2009). VTCs utilize a collaborative approach amongst VTC team members, which include court administrators, judges, prosecutors, defense attorneys, probation officers, mental health professionals, mentor coordinators, and Veterans Justice Outreach (VJO) Specialists and treatment/service providers from the VA. These VTC team members pool resources and expertise to address the problems and serve the needs of justice-involved veterans, focusing on mental health, substance use disorders, housing, employment, and social connectedness.

While a growing body of literature exists documenting the needs and experiences of veterans who are participating in VTCs, less scholarship reflects the perspectives of its team members about 1) what needs veterans present with, and 2) how the court or current VA and community-based services attend to these needs. Viewpoints of VTC team members like judges, attorneys, probation officers and VJO Specialists can offer insight into the inner workings of the VTC, its collaboration and coordination efforts with services, and ultimately where the gaps in those services exist.

Background review

Existing research documents many unique and often compounded needs of veterans, especially when compared to their non-veteran counterparts, that may lead to deviant or criminal behavior (e.g., Finlay et al., 2019). Veteran needs following military discharge are often direct corollaries to their service *and* future contact and involvement within the criminal-legal system (e.g., arrest and incarceration), and include mental disorders such as serious mental illness and post-traumatic stress disorder, substance use disorders, social reintegration difficulties, and socioeconomically deprived housing circumstances (e.g., Bennett et al., 2018; Elbogen et al., 2022; Hyde et al., 2022; Lucas et al., 2022; Short et al., 2018; Taylor et al., 2020; Timko et al., 2020). While efforts have been made to meet the needs of veterans post-discharge, veteran populations remain susceptible to risk factors that lend themselves to criminal-legal system contact.

Although there have been recent calls for true legal system diversion for low-level offense types,[1] alternative approaches like court-based diversion and treatment programming provide post-arrest intercepts for legal system-involved populations (such as veterans) with existing mental and substance use disorders that link to services to meet their psychiatric, medical, and social needs. A vital component of connecting legal-system involved veterans to services that address their needs within VTCs involves collaboration between the VA's Veterans Justice Programs, via VJO Specialists, and the specialized court (Blue-Howells et al., 2013; Foley & Rowen, 2022; Rosenthal & Finlay, 2022). VJOs are certified as licensed clinical social workers, psychologists, or clinicians and often take on numerous roles within their respective courts, including identifying legal-system involved veterans, primarily through jail identification; assessing their needs; making referrals and linking them to care; assisting in bridging gaps or removing barriers to services; and providing longer-term case management (Blue-Howells et al., 2013).[2] Together the VJO, court/correctional staff, and other mental health professionals collaborate to ensure that VTC court participants are properly evaluated, receive individualized plans to address their needs, and are connected to the necessary health and social services for program and future success.

VTC participant needs and operational challenges

In much of the prior research, VTC participants' perceptions and experiences were reported to be positive and supportive of the model (e.g., Guyden, 2020; Herzog et al., 2019, Shannon et al. 2017; Watson, 2016). Despite this, service accessibility issues were also documented. In a process evaluation carried out by Shannon et al. (2019), veteran participants recounted travel and transportation challenges and the lack of available services associated with certain military discharge statuses (e.g., "other than honorable" discharge status results in an inability to utilize VA healthcare; see also Watson, 2016).

A growing body of literature examines key VTC team members' perspectives on various VTC-related topics, including veterans' service needs and operational challenges. Luna and Redlich's (2021) survey of 284 VTC team members, including judges, coordinators, and

VJOs, found support for including individuals convicted of intimate partner violence and manslaughter crimes. The underlying reason given for this support was that the VTC could be the conduit for services related to substance use or mental health issues. Their study focused solely on court eligibility, which is inherently tied to veteran's future access to much needed services through VTCs (Luna & Redlich, 2021).

In a mixed methods process evaluation of two VTCs in Kentucky, Shannon et al. (2017) revealed areas of strength and in need of improvement. The study emphasized the accomplishments of these two programs, namely the ability to connect veterans with the referrals and services that they need, the existence of accountability while also giving veterans a second chance, and that success was fostered through a shared sense of camaraderie. Challenges within these courts included communication and coordination issues (especially between providers), gaps in streamlining protocols, specific issues with VTC programming identified by veterans, transportation challenges, and the lack of services for those who had "other than honorable" military discharge designations (Shannon et al., 2017). Thompson (2021) found that the positive collaboration between VTC team members stemmed from the shared principle of service to system-impacted veterans but noted that the adversarial relationships between some groups (prosecution vs. defense) sometimes inhibited such collaboration. Despite this framing, interviewees spoke positively about collaborating with their colleagues in this VTC. However, this study did not focus on the delivery of health and social services to veterans (Thompson, 2021).

Process models

To conceptualize where to focus efforts and resources, the field has turned to process models. One useful framework that has been applied to veteran populations is the Sequential Intercept Model (SIM), which depicts precisely how individuals with mental and/or substances use disorders encounter and move through the criminal-legal system. The SIM is often used as a community strategic planning tool to assess available resources, determine gaps in services, and plan for community change (Policy Research Associates, 2018). The SIM portrays how service delivery within VTCs, and in tandem with the VA, can be conceptualized and situated in the broader legal-system context. While the SIM approach successfully identifies the pathway someone takes through the system and highlights process gaps or points of diversion away from formal system processing, it does less to identify gaps or deficits in service provision, especially in the VTC context.[3] By considering the existing literature on team members' experiences and perspectives, additional research can take the core principles of SIM and apply it in new ways.

Current study

The current study explores team members' perceptions of VTC operations and the barriers in providing services to veterans. Knowing about veteran service needs and operational challenges from the perspective of core VTC team members offers an array of viewpoints related to service gaps and recommendations in improving the VTC and outcomes. Using 145 interviews with key team members, including attorneys, judges, probation officers, other court team members, and clinical personnel, this study developed a framework for considering veterans' needs across various intercepts before, within, and after legal system involvement. Our study also builds on prior work by using process and intercept models to conceptualize the areas of service needs that veterans experience, and provides VTCs with a framework for identifying where to target their resources and efforts.

Methods

The current study stems from a larger project on VTC operations and service delivery that is described in detail by Byrne and colleagues (this issue). We take a qualitative approach to uncovering VTC processes and relationships and focus on in-depth interviews with 145 VTC team members from 20 courts across the U.S.

Analytic strategy

All interview transcripts were imported into NVivo for coding and analysis. We adopted a thematic analysis approach, which is a strategy for coding and analyzing qualitative data that uses deductive and inductive approaches and is theoretically flexible, meaning researchers can engage in analysis steps that are tightly tied to specific theoretical propositions or enter the analysis phase *a priori* (Braun & Clarke, 2006).

For the current analysis, we focus on information coded in relation to service provision and service gaps. These codes were queried in NVivo, and the first and second authors engaged in an iterative, focused coding process to accommodate inductive codes via to discern more specific and nuanced themes (Locke et al., 2022). In the iterative rounds of coding, we identified additional codes specific to *types of services* and *service quality*, as well as aspects of participant experiences and their perceptions of client experiences, such as about the *VA*, *VTC staff*, and *VTC peers*. We produced analytic memos reflecting the larger themes from this round of coding, which were collectively reviewed by the entire research team to produce the final iteration of the findings. This consensus approach to distilling our findings allowed for sufficient probing of the data and development of new conceptual framing about service delivery. We also engaged in a version of member checking by presenting our findings to the larger study's Advisory Board,[4] who provided rich and detailed feedback on the veracity of our conclusions (Kornbluh, 2015).

Findings

Interviews with VTC team members revealed common challenges in meeting the service needs of VTC participants, as well as some areas for improvement that are specific to the conditions of particular court jurisdictions. These coalesced around various intercepts before, during, and after engagement in the legal system. Using an intercept framework to organize themes related to service provision facilitates a process-based approach to understanding how, why, and at what stage a VTC client may need services and the barriers to receiving them (Blue-Howells et al., 2013). In our model of identifying service delivery gaps among legal system-involved veterans, we expand intercept framing by blending thematic elements related to the context and nature of barriers to services as they relate to legal-system activities rather than time points. We depict these stages in Figure 1. Beginning at the *Pre-Entering* stage to the VTC or with VA services, we move through

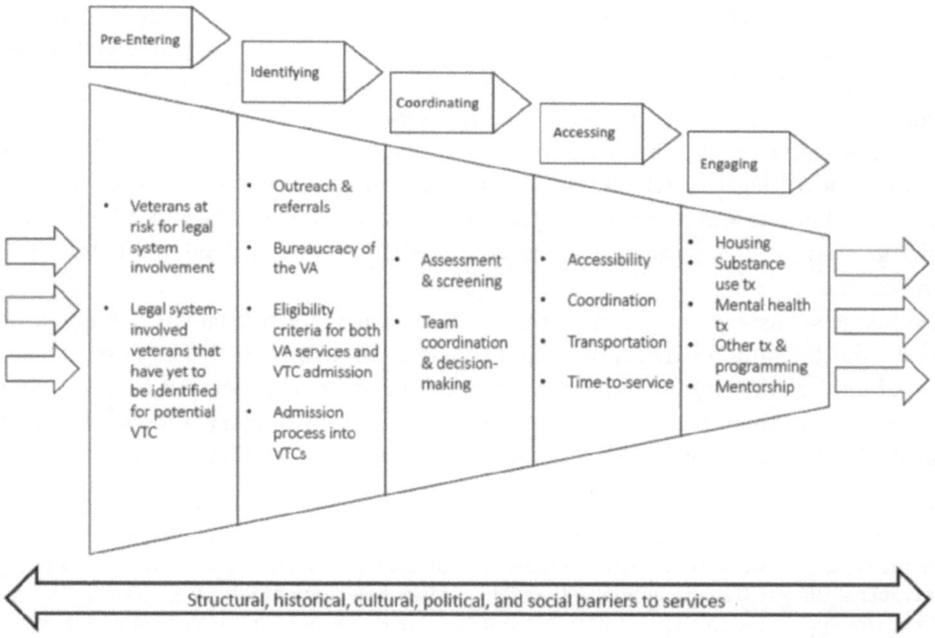

Figure 1. A framework for assessing service delivery gaps for legal-system involved veterans.

the process of *Identifying*, *Coordinating*, and *Accessing* services, ending with descriptions and perspectives of the nature of *Engaging* in programming. Throughout, we distinguish where areas of service needs were discussed collectively, or where they were specified as referring to services provided by community-based or VA-based providers.

Our model is visualized as a funnel that veterans progress through after being discharged from the military. We initially constructed our model beginning at the point of admission to the VTC, but study participants acknowledged that *prior* to that, veterans may face unaddressed trauma and other mental health issues, substance use disorders (SUD), and an array of other challenges related to their military service and transition into civilian life. The model also is further contextualized by two overarching elements. First, we conceptualize this model as moving fluidly across stages, where a set of tasks and activities might occur in multiple stages depending on the nature of those tasks or the circumstances of a particular case or jurisdiction. While the model is not necessarily linear; it also maps onto the sequence of activities occurring in the VTC program. Second, as reflected across the bottom of the figure, across all the stages are sociological, cultural, political, and structural components that influence the experience of being in and separating from the military. These themes affect all stages: stigma related to mental health concerns, access to services, discharge status, and military culture (Mobbs & Bonanno, 2018; Owens, 2022).

Stage 1: pre-entering the VTC – transition from the military and legal system-involvement

Team members acknowledged that any assessment of VTCs should begin by considering the contexts in which veterans are encountering the legal system. Since discharge status impacts availability of VA-supported services, team members suggested that this should be the starting point for any discussion of service provision in VTCs. Among out sample, 50% of sites required VA service eligibility, which is directly tied to discharge status. Some team members suggested that ineligibility for VA services due to dishonorable or other discharge status places these veterans at a heightened risk for criminal-legal system involvement by potentially leaving the most vulnerable veterans without access to services.[5] That is, the very needs that led to a bad conduct discharge may be the same needs associated with criminal behavior after discharge from service.

Discharge status and confusion around other military service-related eligibility criteria were the most common barriers to getting people connected to the VTC. Team members reflected on the difficulty they experienced in linking veterans to services because "people just don't know" about the intricacies of separating from the military, and how to become connected to services provided by the VA. As described by one social worker:

> The different VAs have different protocols . . . and some of those get bad mouthed [which] goes through the whole veteran community. I think that having the VAs . . . to have points of contact or maybe even—we have transitional advocates in ours, so having them contact the service member as they're transitioning out, like, "Hey, this is how you enroll in VA services. This is what you do." You don't really think that you have other options, so learning how to do self-advocacy, I think, is a huge thing too. - Social Worker, Site 16

In some ways, this lack of knowledge resulted in tensions or misconceptions about the VA itself. Team members described the negative sentiments harbored by veterans about wanting to dissociate with the military due to past traumas from service, which could translate to a failure to connect veterans to future services:

> I think that that's a big part of it because some of them didn't serve very long or they got kicked out, so they don't have very good feelings, very good memories. Then we have a lot of people who have experienced a lot of trauma in the military and they wanna separate from that. - Court Coordinator, Site 18

Despite knowledge gaps about VA eligibility, some court team members reported making concerted efforts to repair the mistrust between veterans who were discharged on poor terms and the VA. A prosecutor speaks to this process and accentuates the significance of legal system contact in many of these cases, especially for veterans who would otherwise have continued to be disconnected from VA services:

> We are able to have the folks who maybe are not [VA] service eligible but could become service eligible. We've actually gotten some people service-connected with the VA that would've never done it absent being in our court. I know, having been a part of the process of kickin' people out of the military, how it is completely focused on "you did this bad thing." Get out. There is no rehabilitation. There's no treatment. You're not supposed to say that you have a problem. You're not supposed to say that you need help. - Prosecutor, Site 10

Stage 2: identifying who needs or is eligible for services

Team members revealed that identifying the target population (high-risk/need for services or recidivism) in their local settings presented challenges. First, identifying the veterans involved in the legal system was difficult. Second, even after being identified, determining whether they are eligible for VA services or the VTC program proved more complex than anticipated. A VJO Specialist conveyed uncertainty in their jurisdiction's ability to identify veterans incarcerated in the local jail, describing it as "bureaucratic" and experiencing a high degree of turnover in leadership:

> I do not feel like we're hitting most veterans in [this county], and part of that is the jail, quite honestly. They do not screen for veteran status, or if they do screen for veteran status, they don't pass that information along to other people to help get more veterans engaged. I really do think there's a huge missing piece there. I've tried to navigate that system for years, and it's full of bureaucracy, and it's just that's a bottleneck, the jail and getting veterans identified. - VJO Specialist, Site 5

A major barrier to identifying system-involved veterans in need of services was the veterans' own perceptions about the VA bureaucracy limiting access to care. Some of the perceived bureaucratic barriers included excess paperwork, coordination issues, distance to the funded VA location, and perceived quality of treatment. Even when eligible for VA services, paperwork can hinder the process and timing of applying and tapping into benefits and accessing services. When asked about barriers, one DA stated:

> ... Not having access to healthcare. A lot of them are VA eligible, but the paperwork, the bureaucracy—and I think that's what's so important about VTC. ... people aren't linked up to their [VA] services ... It's people that are eligible but have never signed their paperwork. They don't have their ID. It's just like the DMV. You need to have all your paperwork together to get these services. If you're missing one piece, you're not getting any service. - District Attorney, Site 1

This perception reveals an important discrepancy between policy and perception. When applying for VA benefits, a veteran only needs a DD-214 (US Department of Defense, n.d.). However, the *perception* of the district attorney in this VTC reflects conversations and experiences provided by VTC participants who felt stymied in the process.

An important gap highlighted by this team member is their lack of knowledge or understanding of the VA's programs, like *Community Care Network*, that provides reimbursement to community-based providers if distance is an issue in accessing services (Department of Veterans Affairs, n.d.). Despite the VA's efforts at remedying this issue, misperceptions grounded in historical practices persist. Team members discussed the underlying tension between clinical practice to provide treatment to voluntary clients, and the court's authority to order treatment, regardless of client willingness. Interviewees described that some VA-eligible veterans have personally "denied a need" for treatment during initial screenings at the VA, resulting in VA providers refusing services. Although this is a clinically appropriate response by VA providers, some court actors expressed the negative implications of these cases when the court had ordered participation in treatment programs:

> Because our vets get VA treatment, which is supposed to alleviate certain funds that we'd be spending on our private treatment provider, I find it to be the opposite. Most of our treatment comes from our private treatment provider because what I'm being told is they go to the VA. They do their assessment. Well, if they get in the assessment and say, "I don't have anything wrong with me. There's nothin.' I'm just here 'cause the judge made me come," then the VA says, "Okay, you don't need any treatment." Then they don't get any treatment. That initially blew my mind. I just didn't understand. If we're sendin' "em to you—if they're there—they need treatment. I understand what's coming out of their mouths. It's because they have

> a criminal charge, so they're just tryin" to get past that. It's puttin' a strain 'cause the state pays for most of the treatment that my private provider provides, and they will only give you so much money for that. As our program continues to grow, we're continuously running out of funds at the end of year because some of the treatment that my treatment provider's providing could be done at the VA. - Court Coordinator, Site 4

The above scenario shared by a court coordinator reveals that despite being eligible for services through the VA, the onus of treatment had been displaced onto the court, which staffs private, community-based providers who were initially intended for veterans ineligible for treatment through the VA. A judge in this same court expressed the challenge of ordering and delivering treatment when participants deny the need:

> [In] the VA everything is volunteer . . . If the vet didn't wanna, do it, even if I order it, the vet doesn't have to do it. I really don't like that. I've been trying for four years to be able to talk to somebody at the top, the VA, to see if they can work together with us so that when that vet comes there, the vet knows he's not there voluntarily. He's there because of a court order, and that they will . . . They will not do that. They say it's all volunteer, and they can't do that. I wish we had a better relationship because they have a lot of services that could help the vets, but if it's only voluntary, that does no good. We have to use a lot of avenues to get the same treatment that the vet—I don't wanna say is entitled to—through the VA, but they won't take advantage of, because if they don't have to do it, they won't do it. They'll leave or whatever. I wish we had a better relationship where they could basically implement a court order. They don't have that authority to do so. - Judge, Site 4

These tensions may also be exacerbated by any negative perception veterans hold about the VA, influencing attempts to avoid further involvement. When asked about programming via the VA and why veterans may want to seek treatment elsewhere, one provider weighed in:

> There are some that just say, "Hey, I don't want anything to do with the VA," versus some of them that have claims in and they wanna make sure that they're not causing any harm to the claims that they have. I feel as if with the VA, if they were more engaging with their veterans, I feel as if they probably would have a better turnout in individuals more willing to partake in those services. - Community-Based Treatment Provider, Site 4

This quote reflects the dichotomy between those who wanted nothing to do with the VA and those who had submitted claims but were concerned about involvement in the VTC would be detrimental to their claims. For this provider, the solution was situated in the VA being more flexible and open in their approach connecting services to veterans.

Some team members also noted that engaging with services can be stymied by the military cultural norms that reflect individual perseverance and independence, such that treatment isn't needed, or veterans can be successful without support. In light of this, one district attorney (Site 1) stated, *"Part of it is the culture of the military where [they say], 'I'm fine, everything's okay, push forward.' It's more of a hurdle to have the participants really understand they do need help, and they do need support."*

Alluding to similar attitudes held by some veterans, an assistant director of this county's VA shared that in these cases, veterans may not seek services until it is too late (i.e., they are sick or receive a terminal diagnosis):

> Even though they [the veterans] knew we [the VA] were here, they're very prideful, and they don't like to reach out. It's a generation that—we'll get through this. We don't need help. We don't ask for help until it gets to the point where, they're ill, they've possibly been diagnosed, like I said, with one of those presumptive illnesses related to their exposure. – Assistant Director of [County's] Veterans Affairs, Site 8

Navigating specific eligibility criteria for VA services and the VTC

Team members across various courts identified limitations to existing VA resources, referring to substantial issues with time-to-treatment and continuity of care, as compared to existing community-based resources:

> The wait list for inpatient residential at the VA through this pandemic has been horrific. The wait list is long. We've had to find alternatives for a lot of people instead of going to inpatient residential through the VA, just simply because the wait is too long. I've found that their step-down plans do not involve as long of an intensive outpatient, outpatient sober living. I feel like they tend to just cut people lose a little bit more afterwards, and it leads to a lot of rapid relapses. Treatment at the VA is still virtual. I can't get any programming at the VA in person right now, it's very frustrating, but everything else has returned to in person, the VA is not. – Judge, Site 10

In contrast, team members from other jurisdictions expressed large differentials in service delivery between VA and community-based services, favoring VA-services. Multiple team members within one court emphasized the stark difference between these service types, and the adverse impacts on non-VA eligible court participants compared to their VA eligible counterparts:

> It's not even comparable. The veterans' services are just so much better than anything else, any other program. If you qualify for housing assistance, that changes my client's world. Those are the things that are some reasons why veterans court is just one of the only ones I may even recommend depending on your needs and how motivated you are. If you aren't eligible, you get nothing, absolutely nothing. There's not even a contact, a current—our other treatment provider is [local provider] and I think that they are worthless. It doesn't compare. – Public Defender, Site 12

Despite the Department of Defense determining eligibility criteria for VA benefits (U.S. Department of Defense, 2023), team members often misperceived the VA as responsible for these decisions.[6] Regardless of where these changes originate from, team members described the ever-changing nature of VA social and health services eligibility based on discharge status. One mentor coordinator describes these changes and its impact on service coverage:

> I think the VA's always changing who's eligible for what. We just heard just recently that other than honorable (OTH) vets are eligible for HUD-VASH (Veterans Affairs Supportive Housing) or certain vets that don't have VA healthcare are eligible for emergency mental health services. We're constantly trying to figure that out, what is the vet? Then, a lot of times what happens is, maybe a vet has an OTH discharge, they come into Veterans Court, and you know, we connect people with the [Veterans Service Organizations], who helps them with their service connection pension. Maybe applying for one. We'll see vets that go from being OTH vets with no service connection pension, to being 100 percent service connected and then they actually transfer to our caseload, and we help them navigate through the VA. – Mentor Coordinator, Site 18

Finally, a highlighted service gap in identifying the population of veterans who are eligible for VTCs relates to court requirements for specific discharge statuses and the existence of a "nexus." Some VTCs require that a "nexus" is established — the criminal offense committed is connected in some way to military service *and* a diagnosed mental health condition that resulted from, or in connection to, this service — and consider this eligibility criterion to hold considerable weight in determining program admittance (citation redacted for review). Among our sample, 45% had a nexus requirement, though some members within courts disagreed about whether they enforce it. First, the requirement or reliance on the nexus determination between the current offense and a condition related to the individual's military experiences (e.g., PTSD from combat experience is directly related to the criminal offense committed) potentially excludes individuals from participation in the VTC. Second, the variations in accepting certain discharge types, and if accepted, the additional service accessibility challenges based on discharge type, emerged as a distinct service gap of VTCs. One team member highlighted the clashing of discharge status (and therefore non-VA eligible), despite an established need for treatment:

> That's one thing [that] I really get angry at the VA because we get a lotta young men, I've got one right now that yeah, he was in combat. I think he had two tours in Iraq. He saw a lotta different things. He started usin' drugs or what have you. Then he gets a dishonorable discharge.[7] Now the service put him in a position to act up, we'll say, to be dishonorably discharged. Then the VA turns their back on him. He's entitled to no services, which angers me. You're the guys that screwed him up. You gotta take some responsibility for straightenin' him out, but they don't. - Mentor Coordinator, Site 20

Stage 3: coordinating – determining what services & programming to provide

The next stage in our model for identifying VTC service gaps relates to making determinations about what services to provide veterans, often occurring through assessment and review processes by both the VA and the VTC. Once a veteran is admitted to the VTC program, the next steps involve conducting further assessments to better specify needs and identify appropriate services to attend to those needs. In this stage, the primary activity where gaps emerge is in coordination between the VTC and other agencies to supply services. While many team members identified positive and successful working relationships with the VA and community-based organizations, there was room for improvement in coordination of service referral and delivery with other agencies. Some issues in coordination were related to process, such as paperwork or referral authority (as described in Stage 2); but others were related to providing specific types of services to court participants, such as residential mental health treatment. These concerns also included coordination between the VA and the court where, despite working together in the VTC docket on a weekly basis, there were process gaps in sharing information, as well as service coordination gaps in connecting veterans to much-needed mental health and other services. However, as the judge below describes, developing a system of communication alleviated the delays in service delivery and coordination:

> Well, I know early on we were having some difficulties with the VA being responsive to us. So, a few of us went up to meet with the VA to explain to them what we're doing here so that when we have people who are really at high risk, and we want them to be in the PTSD program, for

> example, that they really should try to work with us and try to get somebody into that program ASAP. Because if we're seeing them on a weekly basis and our participant, we know that they're really, really at high risk, and the VA's giving pushback about where they want to treat the person, I think they become more responsive after that meeting. - Judge, Site 20

Other issues in the coordination of services between agencies were related to balancing the availability of certain types of treatment and the length of time-to-treatment (waitlists), such as in the case of long-term substance use or mental health treatment options. The case manager in one court speaks to this coordination challenge for VTCs:

> Most of that has been our vets who recognize that they need some help. Our judge is really adamant about if you have to self-refer yourself in and so that's the quickest way, versus bein' on the waiting list is to do the self-referral in. He will still count the time. He will not hold it against you as you're progressing through this program. We've had a couple of vets do that. They've done self-referrals, and they've gone in for whatever time needed to get more stabilizing mental—that mental health piece of it. We do have, like I said, community partners are the ones that we really focus in on more so. If [the court participants] do have the benefit to pay, they pay. If not, then the court is picking up the cost. That's the way we try to handle that. Yeah, it's still a waiting period. Our judge tries to pull as many resources as he can and try to get those beds as quickly as we can, but sometimes we do have to—some of our vets have to sit in jail until those beds are available. - Case Manager, Site 4

Team members described the various methods employed by VTCs to meet the myriad needs of veterans, including those who might not hold VA service eligibility. Team members conveyed how the differing needs of veterans can shape which services are provided and by whom:

> I'm sure there's always a way to get around things. I'll give you an example. If somebody has PTSD, but it's not related to the military, it could be childhood that may have caused, or it may be the effect of a mental health issue, then that person can be brought in. However, the court counselor can work with them on the PTSD . . . The VA will not work with them with the PTSD 'cause it's not military-related. - VJO Specialist, Site 4

While some courts, like those above, have the resources available to meet the needs of their court participants, other VTCs with fewer community-based resources reported struggling to provide these services to their veterans, especially if a nexus between a need and one's military experience could not be established.

Court team members also discussed how resource constraints, via external funding sources, shaped the types and extent of services provided to veterans in VTCs, in addition to the breadth of personnel courts could hire to maintain the court's proper functioning. A VJO Specialist remarked on how a potential lack of funding could adversely impact the court:

> We really try to provide those wraparound services so they don't come back, and what is [the state]'s investment in that? Well, we don't have residential [treatment]. We don't have affordable housing. Our veteran services office is not the best. There's a lot of stuff working against us, and if the funding were not to be renewed, our program would run 'cause I'm a state job. The two case managers are a state job, but the peer recovery specialist and the community liaison are grant [funded]. If the state didn't pick those up, those would go and we wouldn't have the screening tools to use for our [de]tox screens, the remote breathalyzer, anything like that and we would not be able run the program successfully. - VJO Specialist, Site 14

Another VJO Specialist from a different VTC spoke to the inconsistent nature of funding by the VA, and consequently, the uneven distribution of resources dependent on what the VA deems worthy of focus:

> It's really interesting within the VA. The funding can be so specific. It's what's the flavor of the day? Is it homelessness? Is it suicide prevention? That infiltrates how that funding lands. You can have a clinic that's drowning because there's not enough providers. There's another clinic that's just getting fresh employees, just getting a lotta new hires, a lotta new hires. Then you're over here looking at this one clinic that's got nothing. It's really an unbalanced approach. - VJO Specialist, Site 11

Stage 4: accessing services

Beyond service assessments, referrals, and coordination, the accessibility of services for veterans appears in the fourth stage of our model. Service accessibility issues emerged in a variety of forms, from direct access issues to the processes presenting barriers to accessing treatment. At the forefront of accessibility issues are those related to directly engaging with the treatment programming, and one prime example is access to and capabilities in using technology. In the excerpt below, one VJO specialist describes the challenges for veterans, especially those with multiple needs, in maintaining a cell phone. This issue was particularly acute among older veterans and amidst COVID-19 changes by the court and providers that relied heavily on technology for engagement. The VJO stated,

> If I had a wish list, as far as resources . . . Just the real incidentals that people don't think about. A lot of my vets struggle with maintaining a phone, so things like that. There are phones that I can access through the VA, but you can imagine what the bureaucracy is like. I want somebody to just give me a dozen phones, so if I see a vet who needs one, I can give 'em one, so I don't have to put in a request and wait two weeks. Now with COVID, there's all sorts of pains around that. - VJO Specialist, Site 17

This VJO posits that developing systems and readily available resources will help veterans not only access services but have more consistent engagement. These technology access and capacity issues expanded to the methods by which veterans received treatment services. Identified as primarily an outgrowth of the system response to the COVID-19 pandemic, many service providers engaged in treatment virtually. While more programs were returning to in-person services at the time of this research, study participants emphasized that many VTC veterans did not understand how to use the technology effectively (if at all), as well as concerns for the ability of web-based treatment services to provide the same quality of intervention as in-person services. One district attorney articulated the gaps in treatment that can result from different treatment modalities:

> I know it's really hard to find psychiatrists and psychologists because it's just the pandemic. Everyone's fleeing. A lot of the vets wanna do in person, and because of the pandemic having to do Zoom AA and Zoom group doesn't work for everyone. Some of them don't even understand the technology. - District Attorney, Site 1

Distance to travel for court or services was identified as another treatment access concern, especially in large jurisdictions, or places where the public transit system was limited or non-existent, such as in rural settings. Team members also noted the intersections between lack of transportation and impediments to employment or treatment schedules, and access to VA services:

> I think transportation is huge. If we could have our own van specifically for our folks to get them even to probation, for example. To have somebody go on a bus for three hours, one way, to get to where they need to get, and then you expect 'em to go to work at four o'clock in the afternoon, and then be at court for three hours. You know what I mean? It's just so many—so transportation is huge. I don't think it's enough to just give them a bus pass, although that would be amazing too, or Uber, or whatever, that would be amazing. Transportation is a big, big piece. - VJO Specialist, Site 16

A team member discussed another implication of long commutes to access services in rural settings: an overreliance on community-based resources due to closer proximity, and an under reliance on VA-based services, which sometimes required substantial commuting times. When asked what percentage of cases in the Site region were being handled by a local provider rather than the VA, one VJO Specialist stated:

> Almost all of them [are handled at the community-based outpatient clinic]. [The treatment provider] is able to provide services right next to the probation office, and they also do their UAs right now, so for ease of access, it's better for the veteran because if it's a day, random UA is two to three times a week, and they're doing treatment, and they have to check in with their PO, and if they can all do that within a three-block radius [in lieu of commuting 40+ miles to the nearest VA facility], that's much better for them. - VJO Specialist, Site 19

Another concern posed by team members was the time lapse between entering the court, establishing the need for services, and accessing those services. In their view, the delays in accessing treatment meant an increased risk for relapse as well as other forms of instability:

> Sometimes those programs, because they wait so long, the veteran really falters. They have relapses. They get in real difficulty—it's disheartening to see that happen to them. Like I was saying, we do have a high success rate after we do go through this with them. Most of "em straighten out their lives to a good extent, which is rewarding. Some of them are still struggling, and some of them keep on pushin" on. We support 'em. - Mentor Coordinator, Site 20

Some team members noted the length of time to receive treatment differentially impacts those who are ineligible for VA services. Where the VJO can provide direct links to services offered by the VA, in some courts, options are limited for those not receiving services through the VA. This gap in mental health services revealed the contextual concerns of the community in which each VTC is situated. When asked about how to improve treatment engagement, one court coordinator said:

> I think just removing some of those barriers to treatment in the community for those folks that aren't VA eligible. Because like I said, the waitlist of 8 or 12 weeks really doesn't work for the treatment court model. If we're tryin' to get someone into an IOP (intensive outpatient program), we need it now because they just failed three drug screens, and they're at risk for overdosing. We're told that an IOP doesn't start for another three weeks, that doesn't really help. Residential beds are fairly difficult to come by. For those folks that aren't attending treatment through the VA, that's where we'd see a communication gap. Obviously, we have them sign two-way releases with their community treatment provider so that we can verify treatment attendance. It's certainly not as seamless as it is by having someone right on our team. That would be the disparity–the ability to confirm treatment. - Court Coordinator, Site 20

Despite the smoother access to treatment through VA services, some participants remarked that delays can occur due to the "bureaucratic lockstep" of the VTC and VA, where waiting for paperwork to process and decisions to be made (including discharge status), team members identified some very real consequences of veterans being unable to engage in treatment. One excerpt conveys this service challenge:

> It's just a burden for them that when they first come, they don't have anything so they're all in limbo. In a sense, a good deal of the time [VTC team members are] the ones who get them enrolled in [state health insurance]. Though in the interim, they're without services .... Don't make em go through a bureaucratic lockstep to get to the treatment they really need. Admit right up that they need to go to an in-house facility. They really need to have more counseling, more therapy, more hands-on. Another problem I have, too, is "we're tryin and it's difficult," but we would like to have the VA become more friendly to help us to upgrade their discharges.[8]
> – Mentor Coordinator, Site 20

Mental health stigma was another concern expressed by team members related to access to care. As stigma related to mental health diagnoses and treatment is common among the general public (Pescosolido et al., 2021), it is not surprising that veterans also presented concerns about stigma (Goode & Swift, 2019). Layered within mental health stigma for veterans is both the juxtaposition of: (1) self-stigma, referring to individuals' negative self-perceptions related to seeking mental health treatment (e.g., a common belief among military personnel related to the machismo culture in the military is that they are weak if they seek mental health care), and (2) the concern of non-veteran providers being unable to truly understand the veteran experience (Held & Owens, 2013). When asked about how to improve mental health treatment engagement, one team member said:

> Maybe [engagement] comes with breaking the stigma of mental health, too. I know the military is finally doing a good job about that. I've done in-services for active-duty units, for leadership, to help understand what PTSD is and how it impacts us. Through that, they're able to speak to their junior Marines, soldiers, sailors, airmen, which, then, they can see the signs earlier and maybe be that advocate, like, "Hey, maybe we need to force you to—" you know, in the military, "Force you or strongly encourage you to go seek help before it gets too late." ... One thing that a lot of service members come with is, like, "I'm not gonna talk to a non-veteran. They won't understand what it's like." – Social Worker, Site 16

When discussing gaps and barriers to connecting veterans to treatment, a central component identified by court team members was the value and benefits of having mentors as part of the VTC. While the presence, quantity, and organization of mentors varied across jurisdictions, team members noted the importance of, and potential for, mentors in creating an informal access to programming and ability to overcome stigma. Whether via general social support for an individual to pursue treatment or direct connections to support and programming (e.g., transportation), mentors are an underdeveloped asset of the VTC model according to a variety of team members:

> The other kind of weak link that we have is the most important part of our program are our mentors. Our mentors are the secret sauce if there is such a thing. They are so hard to come by. They're volunteers. It's a stressful job, and you really gotta put your heart into it. I also think it's a very rewarding experience for everybody who's involved, but recruiting mentors, even—we struggle to get mentors. It's hard, and most of the mentors we have, we've got a fair amount who are still in the workforce working. I would say the majority, though, are retirees and Vietnam-Era vets. They do a bang-up job. – VJO Specialist, Site 16

Stage 5: engaging with VTC services and the VA

In the final stage of the service gaps model, we present themes related to the quality, nature, and context of engaging with specific services provided in jurisdictions. Team members highlighted common concerns about programs addressing homelessness, substance use, and mental health, and identified the deficits in specific types of programming. Across the interviews, we captured an array of service needs that remain unfulfilled or require greater resources.

Housing & homelessness

Team members conveyed the common experience of homelessness among veterans in their VTCs and the need for more housing programs. While housing insecurity is pervasive across jurisdictions (United States Interagency Council on Homelessness, 2015), it was viewed by participants as an insurmountable task, and one that acutely impacts veterans. One district attorney described the nature of the housing crisis among veterans and how the VA has tried to address it:

> [We need] more housing in areas where the vets feel safe, more long-term housing ... Really, if we could house every vet that wanted housing, I think that would solve a lot of issues because most of these crimes stem from homelessness. A lot of people use substances to stay warm at night, and that's a basic thing. A lot of people don't realize that, so I feel like if we could address the homelessness population and really give them services and support and methadone treatment, whatever they need to get through their withdrawal, I think it would be life changing ... I do feel like the VA does address a lot of it. Like I said, I haven't seen so many people placed in any other court. The VA gets it done, but it's just not enough because the population is so great. – District Attorney, Site 1

The dearth of community-based programming that is vet-centered, and in some jurisdictions, the related shift from veteran-specific to general service provision was identified as a key gap in fostering engagement with services among court participants. This differentially impacted VTC participants who were ineligible for or opted out of VA services, as described by one court coordinator:

> Well, here what we found happened is we moved our homeless population being mixed in with our veteran population, and the sober people being mixed in with people who are still using. We saw a tremendous change in our [veterans] in the residential treatment program 'cause they were not getting the support and the group support that they used to get. [...] We need better, stronger residential treatment places we can put people so they can get their life straightened out. Not just sober but begin the process of meeting with other veterans who have many of the same problems. There's only so many residential beds, and they've been decreased [here]. – Court Coordinator, Site 16

The team member identified that when the city moved to the "housing first" model to address homelessness in the city, it meant the remaining veteran-only housing program began accepting non-veterans in need of housing. While veterans still had access to housing (such as through HUD-VASH programs[9]), this particular facility, which once was a community for those with veteran status only, began to also house civilians experiencing homelessness.

Substance misuse treatment approaches

Team members identified the challenge of not having enough substance use disorder treatment programs serviced by the VA or within the community, especially those that are long-term, intensive, dual diagnosis (i.e., coexistent mental health and substance use disorder diagnoses), and/or residential:

> If I could change one thing, I would allow for [longer treatment], the inpatient program is anywhere from three to six months. The individuals that have gone through and been able to access that inpatient program, afterwards, it's a year, two years of sobriety. The success stories coming out are just absolutely amazing. Usually, what they're able to do is they're able to parlay that into a PTSD [diagnosis] and patients stay. I would lengthen that stay, and I would hope that we would have a similar program [here] that we could utilize for people that would create a longer period of stabilization 'cause I think that's often what people are asking for. I hear a lot, "Thirty days doesn't work for me. I don't want a 30-day program. It needs to be longer than 30 days," and that's just not something that is available for most people. – Clinician, Site 17

Team members discussed the need to tailor substance use treatment to the needs of their client population, as well as highlighted the tensions between existing evidence-based treatment programs and the court or jurisdiction's apprehension about – or resistance to – adopting these interventions. For instance, in certain jurisdictions, the use of medical marijuana prescribed by a medical doctor, or in tandem with other forms of treatment (such as mental health), runs counter to the parameters outlined by VTC funding sources regarding substance use:

> I pretty much think we're all on the same page. I think the one issue is use of marijuana. Our grants are through SAMHSA, so they're not supposed to be using marijuana, but [here], marijuana's a ticket. It just really depends on the amount. I personally have no issue with it. If you have a note from a doctor that says you need this for your PTSD or you need this because it keeps you from going [into involuntary detention], then I don't have a problem with it. Because our grant money says it's an abstinence program, it becomes an issue. We have participants that are completely functional, and they remain in a phase [of the VTC program] because they have marijuana in their system. They're doing everything else that's required. They're doing well . . . . [but]but we still wanna respect the funding source and what they require and what their program needs. – District Attorney, Site 1

Mental health services

Mental health related services are a common treatment provision for clients of VTCs. Study participants reflected on the need for more mental health professionals and streamlining continuity of care. Team members emphasized the potential for and importance of having dedicated mental health professionals on the VTC team to support assessment, diagnosis, and other treatment-related practices. One team member explicitly suggested the need for a psychologist or psychiatrist on the VTC team:

> What we really need back on the team is we need a psychologist. Ideally, we'd have a psychiatrist, too, whether they're sitting with us at the table, or they're simply on call. Once upon a time we did have a clinical psychologist with us at every weekly meeting and every court session, and she was also treating our participants, and she was priceless, but resources are what they are, and obviously the demand is we come to take care of patients and veterans as opposed to spending their days in court, but it was very valuable to us. Having a complete treatment team is one of our gaps. It's not fatal. We make do, but that would be very helpful. – Social Worker, Site 16

In this excerpt, the social worker offers that having a trained psychiatrist or psychologist who is dedicated to the VTC and routinely part of the process would better support their ability to provide mental health related services to court participants.

Amidst the general concern for more treatment staff, the issue of breaks in the continuum of care emerged, offering insight into the nature of gaps in service that exist, even among locales that have robust treatment provider relationships. Team members shared the view that disruptions in treatment were a direct corollary to the high turnover afflicting the mental healthcare profession at present. The frequent changes in treatment providers translated to stunted relationships and therapeutic development. When asked about what services were needed, one judge stated:

> I would say mental health counseling. It's hard to actually get people even if with full benefits from the VA to get them stable, high-level psychological help. Most of the people that need counseling end up with a psych fellow, so somebody who's not permanent, and as a result, they put in the work to establish a relationship, if we're lucky enough to get them to put in the work, and then the person leaves. That in itself is a traumatic experience for the vet. – Judge, Site 18

Other treatment services

Team members remarked on existing gaps within other types of treatment services for veterans. These services reflect both the types of offending which veterans had engaged in as well as the needs presented by veterans in VTCs. Team members expressed the need for more domestic violence (DV) specific services, especially offered by the VA.

> It's crazy when you think about it, the vast majority of vets have a DV offense or they're coming into these programs or on probation for DV offenses, but the VA doesn't have a DV treatment modality. They never have. I just can't wrap my head around that. It's the same for DUI stuff. – Court Coordinator, Site 13

The misperceptions about the VA's DV treatment programming reveal the ongoing discrepancies in knowledge among VTC team members. As many of the VTC participants have been charged with or identify past issues with domestic violence, the need for DV programming offered by the VA is central, such as expanding the *Strength at Home* program, which has been found to be effective in preventing DV among veterans or active military members and their partners (Taft et al., 2016).

Another existing gap for VTCs is the dearth of gender-specific services. This is not surprising given the challenges of providing gender-based services across the legal system, and that the VTCs in our study reported few women enrolled at any given time. Gender-specific services are expected to support more comprehensive, trauma-informed approaches to serving women, as described by one team member:

> Yeah. I mean, I think we tend to wanna be as like, trauma-informed care as possible .... and then, you know, as far as developing treatment plans, I'd say especially for women, the VA, it's very male-centric. I'll work with, you know, people don't have to receive their care at the VA. If they've got a community provider that they're connected to that's a positive support, I can build that into their treatment plan. – Mentor Coordinator, Site 18

Team members noted another VA-specific service gap as being a lack of family counseling and family-related services offered for the family members, especially spouses/partners of legal system-involved veterans. One case manager spoke to this issue:

> I think that the VA should have a family component for any veteran because, like I said, I truly believe . . . The family goes with them. As they served our country, the family serves with. I truly believe that the family serves. As they go through this criminal justice system, veteran or not, the family goes with you. The family goes with you. With all the requirements of our particular program, the family has definitely gotta come on board. – Case Manager, Site 4

Participants conveyed the need for more attention to the aftercare period following successful completion of intensive treatment programming and while in the VTC program. While some of the interruptions in aftercare were attributed to COVID-19 protocols, study participants noted that the issues remain in ensuring that veterans who receive and complete intensive treatment services are in environments that sustain the positive impacts of VTC programming. When describing the need for better aftercare coordination, one probation officer stated:

> Everything's looking upbeat for 'em. There's light at the end of the tunnel. The issue is the isolation. 'Cause when you're in [a particular program], there's a team. What we've identified is, when they leave [the program], they have to have not just aftercare 'cause we're in a different world with COVID. Everything is on Zoom. You can still be participating virtually and not engaged at all. That's the issue we're running into now is that with the aftercare, there's a gap. We need that same connection in the aftercare that they had when they were in the residential treatment program. – Probation Officer, Site 16

Discussion

The current study offers the unique perspectives of team members working with legal system-involved veterans in 20 VTCs across the country. While these jurisdictions operate VTCs that differ in a number of key areas (e.g., target population, selection criteria, program design and length), team members involved in these programs voiced similar concerns about the challenges they face as they attempt to address the service needs of veterans. Building on SIM-based approaches, we expand the concept of intercepts to further identify various activities where gaps in meeting these service needs emerge. We have grouped these challenges across five stages: (1) Military discharge and *Pre-entering* the VTC; (2) *Determining* eligibility for VTCs; (3) *Coordinating* assessments and services, (4) *Accessing* services, and (5) *Engaging* the veteran in the VTC and programming. Across this process model, and within the array of activities discussed by team members, we can begin to pinpoint specific areas and intercepts where VTCs might attend to service gaps in their jurisdictions.

The first challenge identified by team members is that for many veterans transitioning from military to civilian life, support services were either not available or not accessible by returning veterans (Council on Criminal Justice, 2022; Mobbs & Bonanno, 2018). Team members pointed out that a veteran's discharge status directly affected their access to VA support services. Further, it is well-documented that veterans without access to these services are more likely to self-harm and manifest untreated mental health and substance use problems that may result in criminal legal system involvement (Gradus et al., 2017). A focus on the needs of veterans during this initial transition period would — in the view of our team members — reduce the underlying need for VTCs. Stated simply: team members argue that we need to pre-act, not react, because waiting only increased the likelihood of harm to veterans, their families, and the communities in which they reside. This recommendation is supported by members of our study sample who are working with veterans as they transition from military to civilian life.

Team members also pointed out that it would be misleading to simply lay the blame for service provision shortfalls at the feet of the DOD and the VA, because there are other factors to consider. Team members pointed out that some veterans have responded to the various types of traumas they experienced in the military — PTSD, military sexual abuse, racism, sexism — by disassociating from the military altogether. These individuals — regardless of discharge status — were not looking for, or willing to accept, VA support services even if they were available. Other veterans reject help because they view help-seeking as anathema to the military culture they still embrace, even as civilians. It should be noted that these veterans will not likely self-report mental health or substance use concerns to the military as they prepare to leave, which makes accurate discharge assessment and follow-up support a challenge (i.e., you can ask, but do not expect me to tell).

Team members proposed that better education of veterans, by the military, about service availability and contacts in their community may result in more veterans getting the services and support they need during this initial transition period. Efforts to improve this outreach are already occurring through the VA's *Solid Start* program, where VA representatives attempt contact with newly separated veterans three times within the first year.[10] Programs like this, with a focus on veterans who may have high risks or needs, will be instrumental in preventing legal system involvement when transitioning from the military.

Beyond initial mistrust of the VA post-discharge, additional gaps emerged related to determining eligibility for the program. Team members discussed that current eligibility requirements for participation in VTCs may exclude a sizable subgroup of veterans that need the most help and support. First, dishonorably discharged and other than honorably (OTH) discharged veterans may be excluded from participation because they are ineligible for VA services (Clark et al., 2010; citation redacted). According to one national review, about one in 3 VTCs surveyed did not accept veterans who were ineligible for VA services (Timko et al., 2016). Second, veterans charged with violent crimes are typically excluded from VTCs (Clark et al., 2010). Third, current screening procedures that rely on veterans self-reporting their veteran status are missing those veterans who do not report their status due to their distrust of the military and/or the VA, their fear that such disclosure could impact their veterans' benefits, and/or their view that military culture norms preclude looking for any special form of help. Fourth, by requiring that veterans have a direct link - or nexus - between mental health records identified in their military records and the crime they committed, it will exclude many veterans who have mental health concerns or diagnoses but could not establish the nexus. To address the needs of this subgroup of veterans who are currently falling through the eligibility cracks, team members offered recommendations for improved screening mechanisms, and expanding the target populations included in VTCs.

The Coordinating stage revealed the importance, and limitations, of service coordination between community-based service providers, the VA, and VTC. While team members in each of our twenty jurisdictions offered an overall positive assessment of support for service coordination, they emphasized that it will not be successful without information sharing and service availability. Information sharing is a continuing challenge, in large part due to the siloing of client data across two large bureaucracies — the court and the VA — which renders any assessment of program fidelity incomplete. In terms of service availability, team members noted the lack of residential mental health services available in their jurisdictions, and particularly from VAs, resulted in long waiting lists for justice-involved veterans. It is unsurprising that VA national funding priorities may sometimes not match local needs and context. In these instances, VTC program coordinators attempt to bridge this gap by identifying funding streams and service providers outside the VA network.

The fourth stage identified in our data is most aptly described in the following adage: do not confuse service *availability* with service *access*. Given the timing of our interviews, team members were quick to point out that COVID-19 fundamentally changed service access, because both court hearings and mental health treatment moved from in-person to virtual settings. Remote meeting access was a challenge for veterans in each of the twenty jurisdictions where we conducted interviews, but not just because of the limited technology access of veterans to both computers and cell phones. In fact, team members in several jurisdictions reported increased attendance at these remote hearings; but they observed that remote access does not necessarily replicate the VTC court in-person experience. While it remains to be seen whether virtual treatment is here to stay, team members pointed out that it does address — in the short term at least — the problems associated with getting veterans to court for hearings and to treatment providers for services. Another issue related to treatment access identified by VTC team members was the self-stigma associated with mental health problems, which leads some veterans not to access available services when the service provider is not a veteran and/or the treatment group includes both veterans and non-veterans.

As noted in earlier stages of the process model, delays in access to treatment exist and increase the likelihood of returning to substance use (Brignone et al., 2017; Reger et al., 2015; Veterans Legal Clinic, 2016). This was a problem mentioned by team members in many jurisdictions, and the reason for delayed time to treatment was two-fold: bureaucratic lockstep and continuity in trained mental health personnel. Team members noted that when direct access to treatment providers is not available or delayed, the importance of mentors as informal service providers is more pronounced. To several team members, mentors represented the "secret sauce" that is a key factor in the success of VTCs as service providers.

The fifth and final stage in our process model emerges from our findings that veterans require a multi-pronged engagement strategy that addresses veteran needs in physical health, mental health, substance use, housing, and family support. Team members emphasized the need for veteran-focused community-based strategies in each of these areas. They recommended developing veterans-centered services for critical care (e.g., housing and substance abuse). They also noted that mental health assessments should be conducted by psychologists and psychiatrists, who would then actively participate in the VTC team case planning process. There were several service need areas that require expansion to maximize engagement, including (1) increased access to gender-specific services, (2) more domestic violence-specific services, (3) increased family engagement and other family support services, and (4) more attention to engagement of veterans in the aftercare component of VTCs.

The current study adds to the field's knowledge about the perceived gaps in providing services to VTC involved veterans in the US. Our data provides richness to this growing conversation by highlighting the myriad perspectives of those working within the VTC. While a strength of our study is the breadth and depth of voices captured, we are missing one significant voice — the veterans'. Future research should consider these service gap issues, in addition to others not seen by team members with veterans who participate in VTCs and those who do not. This is necessary for bringing voice to those groups referred to, but not seen very often in our team members' perspectives, including people of color and genders other than male. Our data also provide important knowledge and context for VTC operation, but not necessarily how these ideas are directly tied to outcomes. Future projects performing outcome or impact analyses will address this gap.

Our model for identifying the location, timing, and activities related to gaps in service for legal system-involved veterans provides VTCs with a necessary framework to attend to existing and emerging issues in VTC court operation. Across our data, team members pulled back the curtain on how these issues can compound in veterans needs not being addressed, reinforcing mistrust and misperceptions in the VA and military, and excluding from programming some of the very servicemembers who need this support the most. The components are in place; a few strategic alterations to the service delivery process would go a long way toward realizing the stated objectives of VTCs first outlined a decade and a half ago.

Notes

1. For an overview of police-focused diversion programs targeting justice-involved veterans, see Mok et al. (2018); for a review of prosecution-focused diversion programs see Wright and Levine (2021).
2. Approximately 400 VJOs serve VTCs as program coordinators, clinical service providers, or both nationwide (U.S. Government Accountability Office, 2021).
3. See emerging work from the National Institute of Corrections on the V-SIM (https://nicic.gov/).
4. The Advisory Board consists of scholars, legal actors, and VA staff who routinely contributed to our understanding and analysis of the data through monthly meetings.
5. Team member perceptions of these transition challenges are supported by the available research. Owens (2022) estimated that half of the 250,000 veterans discharged from service each year are not immediately connected "with available resources, benefits, and services. Without support, more complex behavioral concerns might emerge." https://www.samhsa.gov/blog/supporting-behavioral-health-needs-our-nations-veterans.
6. There are eight different military discharge types. The military makes the determination of the discharge type — and the Department of Defense sets the guidelines for VA healthcare eligibility based on military discharge status.
7. A dishonorable discharge is the result of a conviction for a serious offense at a court-martial. The speaker may have meant an OTH discharge, but a dishonorable discharge would have different implications for a court process.
8. An important clarification is that the VA does not have the ability to upgrade a veteran's discharge status itself, but can and does offer support in the process.
9. It is important to note that this program requires that housing options being fully paid by the voucher; that is, the voucher cannot be used toward rent, it must fully cover the rent. In many jurisdictions this left individuals with subpar housing options due to increased housing costs. Team members reflected that many VTC participants opted out of the housing voucher program.
10. See https://benefits.va.gov/transition/solid-start.asp.

Acknowledgments

The authors would like to thank the members of our Community Advisory Board for their invaluable feedback on an earlier draft of this article.

Disclosure statement

No potential conflict of interest was reported by the author(s).

Funding

Funded by the National Institute on Drug Abuse (NIDA), in conjunction with the Bureau of Justice Assistance (BJA). This study was funded under the Justice Community Opioid Innovation Network (JCOIN) Coordination and Translation Center (CTC) (U2CDA050097, MPI Taxman/Rudes). The contents of this publication are solely the responsibility of the authors and do not necessarily represent the official views of the NIH, or the participating sites.

ORCID

Kimberly R. Kras http://orcid.org/0000-0002-0592-0418
Sabrina S. Rapisarda http://orcid.org/0000-0001-5148-8630
Don Hummer http://orcid.org/0000-0003-3026-0287
James M. Byrne http://orcid.org/0000-0001-9216-9871

References

Bennett, D. C., Morris, D. H., Sexton, M. B., Bonar, E. E., & Chermack, S. T. (2018). Associations between posttraumatic stress and legal charges among substance using veterans. *Law and Human Behavior*, *42*(2), 135–144.

Blue-Howells, J. H., Clark, S. C., van den Berk-Clark, C., & McGuire, J. F. (2013). The US department of veterans affairs veterans justice programs and the sequential intercept model: Case examples in national dissemination of intervention for justice-involved veterans. *Psychological Services*, *10*(1), 48–53.

Braun, V., & Clarke, V. (2006). Using thematic analysis in psychology. *Qualitative Research in Psychology*, *3*(2), 77–101. https://doi.org/10.1191/1478088706qp063oa

Brignone, E., Fargo, J. D., Blais, R. K., Carter, M. E., Samore, M. H., & Gundlapalli, A. V. (2017). Non-routine discharge from military service: Mental illness, substance use disorders, and suicidality. *American Journal of Preventive Medicine*, *52*(5), 557–565.

Clark, S. C., McGuire, J. F., & Blue-Howells, J. H. (2010). Development of veterans treatment courts: Local and legislative initiatives. *Drug Court Review*, *7*(1), 171–208.

Council on Criminal Justice. (2022). *From service to reentry: A preliminary assessment through the system*. Veterans Justice Commission. https://secure.counciloncj.org/np/viewDocument?orgId=counciloncj&id=2c918082829f83c70182b7c346ea0177

Elbogen, E. B., Amuan, M., Kennedy, E., Blakey, S. M., Graziano, R. C., Hooshyar, D., Tsai, J., Nelson, R. E., Vanneman, M. E., Jones, A. L., & Jo Pugh, M. (2022). Criminal legal involvement among recently separated veterans: Findings from the LIMBIC study. *Law and Human Behavior*, *46*(5), 385–394.

Finlay, A. K., Owens, M. D., Taylor, E., Nash, A., Capdarest-Arest, N., Rosenthal, J., Blue-Howells, J., Clark, S., & Timko, C. (2019). A scoping review of military veterans involved in the criminal justice system and their health and healthcare. *Health & Justice*, *7*(1), 1–18.

Foley, R., & Rowen, J. (2022). Putting the "VA" in VTCs: How facilitating VA access can make veterans treatment courts more effective. *Wake Forest JL & Pol'y*, *12*(1), 61–102.

Goode, J., & Swift, J. K. (2019). An empirical examination of stigma toward mental health problems and psychotherapy use in veterans and active duty service members. *Military Psychology*, *31*(4), 335–345.

Gradus, J. L., Leatherman, S., Curreri, A., Myers, L. G., Ferguson, R., & Miller, M. (2017). Gender differences in substance abuse, PTSD and intentional self-harm among veterans health administration patients. *Drug and Alcohol Dependence*, *171*, 66–69. https://doi.org/10.1016/j.drugalcdep.2016.11.012

Guyden, A. (2020). *The effectiveness of veterans treatment courts as perceived by veterans* [Doctoral dissertation, Northcentral University]. ProQuest Dissertations and Theses Global.

Held, P., & Owens, G. P. (2013). Stigmas and attitudes toward seeking mental health treatment in a sample of veterans and active duty service members. *Traumatology*, *19*(2), 136–143.

Herzog, J. R., Ferdik, F., Scott, D., Denney, A., & Conklin, S. (2019). Participants' perceptions of veterans treatment courts: A qualitative assessment and systems model. *Journal of Veterans Studies*, *4*(2), 78–93.

Hyde, J., Bolton, R., Kim, B., Yakovchenko, V., Petrakis, B. A., Visher, C., & McInnes, K. (2022). "I've just never done that:" The influence of transitional anxiety on post-incarceration reentry and reintegration experiences among veterans. *Health & Social Care in the Community*, *30*(4), 1504–1513.

Kornbluh, M. (2015). Combatting challenges to establishing trustworthiness in qualitative research. *Qualitative Research in Psychology*, *12*(4), 397–414.

Locke, K., Feldman, M., & Golden Biddle, K. (2022). Coding practices and iterativity: Beyond templates for analyzing qualitative data. *Organizational Research Methods*, *25*(2), 262–284.

Lucas, K. T., Marcum, C. D., Lucas, P. A., & Blalock, J. (2022). Military veteran involvement with the criminal justice system: A systematic review. *Aggression & Violent Behavior*, *66*. https://doi.org/10.1016/j.avb.2022.101721

Luna, S., & Redlich, A. D. (2021). A national survey of veterans treatment court actors. *Criminal Justice Policy Review*, *32*(2), 132–161.

Mobbs, M. C., & Bonanno, G. A. (2018). Beyond war and PTSD: The crucial role of transition stress in the lives of military veterans. *Clinical Psychology Review*, *59*, 137–144. https://doi.org/10.1016/j.cpr.2017.11.007

Mok, C., Weaver, C., Rosenthal, J., Pettis, T., & Wickham, R. (2018). Augmenting veterans affairs police mental health response: Piloting diversion to health care as risk reduction. *Journal of Threat Assessment and Management*, *5*(4), 227–237.

Owens, S. (2022). *Supporting the behavioral health needs of our nation's veterans*. Substance Abuse and Mental Health Services Association. https://www.samhsa.gov/blog/supporting-behavioral-health-needs-our-nations-veterans

Pescosolido, B. A., Halpern-Manners, A., Luo, L., & Perry, B. (2021). Trends in public stigma of mental illness in the US, 1996-2018. *JAMA Network Open*, *4*(12), e2140202.

Policy Research Associates. (2018). *The sequential intercept model: Advancing community-based solutions for justice-involved people with mental and substance use disorders*. https://www.prainc.com/wp-content/uploads/2018/06/PRA-SIM-Letter-Paper-2018.pdf

Reger, M. A., Smolenski, D. J., Skopp, N. A., Metzger-Abamukang, M. J., Kang, H. K., Bullman, T. A., Perdue, S., & Gahm, G. A. (2015). Risk of suicide among US military service members following operation enduring freedom or operation Iraqi freedom deployment and separation from the US military. *JAMA Psychiatry*, *72*(6), 561–569.

Rosenthal, J., & Finlay, A. K. (2022). Expanding the scope of forensic and other services for justice-involved veterans. *The Journal of the American Academy of Psychiatry and the Law*. https://doi.org/10.29158/JAAPL.210047-21

Russell, R. T. (2009). Veterans treatment court: A proactive approach. *New England Journal on Criminal & Civil Confinement*, *35*(2), 357–361.

Shannon, L. M., Birdwhistell, S., Hulbig, S. K., Jackson Jones, A., Newell, J., & Payne, C. (2017). Examining implementation and preliminary performance indicators of veterans treatment courts:

The Kentucky experience. *Evaluation and Program Planning*, *63*(2), 54–66. http://dx.doi.org/10.1016/j.evalprogplan.2017.03.003

Shannon, L. M., Birdwhistell, S., Hulbig, S. K., Jones, A. J., Newell, J., & Payne, C. (2017). Examining implementation and preliminary performance indicators of veterans treatment courts: The Kentucky experience. *Evaluation and Program Planning*, *63*, 54–66.

Short, R., Dickson, H., Greenberg, N., & MacManus, D. (2018). Offending behaviour, health and wellbeing of military veterans in the criminal justice system. *PLoS one*, *13*(11), e0207282.

Taft, C. T., Creech, S. K., Gallagher, M. W., Macdonald, A., Murphy, C. M., & Monson, C. M. (2016). Strength at home couples program to prevent military partner violence: A randomized controlled trial. *Journal of Consulting & Clinical Psychology*, *84*(11), 935.

Taylor, E. N., Timko, C., Nash, A., Owens, M. D., Harris, A. H., & Finlay, A. K. (2020). Posttraumatic stress disorder and justice involvement among military veterans: A systematic review and meta-analysis. *Journal of Traumatic Stress*, *33*(5), 804–812.

Thompson, C. S. (2021). *Veterans treatment court stakeholder's experience of community collaboration serving gulf coast veterans* [PhD dissertation]. Capella University.

Timko, C., Flatley, B., Tjemsland, A., McGuire, J., Clark, S., Blue-Howells, J., Blonigen, D. M., Rosenthal, J., & Finlay, A. (2016). A longitudinal examination of veterans treatment courts' characteristics and eligibility criteria. *Justice Research & Policy*, *17*(2), 123–136.

Timko, C., Nash, A., Owens, M. D., Taylor, E., & Finlay, A. K. (2020). Systematic review of criminal and legal involvement after substance use and mental health treatment among veterans: Building toward needed research. *Substance Abuse: Research & Treatment*, *14*. https://doi.org/10.1177/1178221819901281

U.S. Department of Defense. (2023). *Military/civilian records, deers and DoD ID cards: Requests for upgrade of discharge characterization*. https://www.defense.gov/Contact/Help-Center/Article/Article/2742507/requests-for-upgrade-of-discharge-characterization/

US Department of Defense. (n.d). *Requesting military records including DD-214*.

U.S. Department of Veterans Affairs. (n.d.). *Justice and reentry-related services*. https://www.va.gov/boston-health-care/health-services/homeless-veteran-care/

U.S. Government Accountability Office. (2021). *Veterans justice outreach program: Further actions to identify and address barriers to participation would promote access to services – fast facts*. https://www.gao.gov/products/gao-21-564#:~:text=The%20program%20relies%20on%20about,as%20a%20gateway%20to%20services.

U.S. Interagency Council on Homelessness. (2015). *Ending homelessness for people living in encampments: Advancing the dialogue*. http://usich.gov/resources/uploads/asset_library/Ending_Homelessness_for_People_Living_in_Encampments_Aug2015.pdf

Veterans Legal Clinic. (2016). *Underserved: How the VA wrongfully excludes veterans with bad paper*. Legal Services Center, Harvard Law School.

Watson, T. (2016). *A phenomenological study of justice-involved veteran experiences of veterans court* [Doctoral dissertation, University of Northern Colorado]. ProQuest Dissertations and Theses Global.

Wright, R. F., & Levine, K. L. (2021). Models of prosecutor-led diversion programs in the United States and beyond. *Annual Review of Criminology*, *4*, 331–351. https://doi.org/10.1146/annurev-criminol-061020-022236

OPEN ACCESS

"God, I Hope It Doesn't Fade Out": Team Member Perspectives on the Future of Veterans Treatment Courts

Kelly M. Socia, Sabrina S. Rapisarda, Kimberly R. Kras, Don Hummer, and James M. Byrne

ABSTRACT

Despite their rapid spread over the last 15 years, little research has explored the perceptions of Veterans Treatment Courts (VTCs) team members regarding the viability and longevity of VTCs. The present qualitative study explores the perceptions of 145 VTC team members from 20 VTCs around the United States regarding the future of their own VTC and VTCs in general. Our analysis revealed four overarching themes about team members' expectations and hopes for VTCs in the future: the need for continued funding and increased resources; desires to expand participation in VTCs; hope and uncertainty about the future of VTCs; and depending on specific people to ensure the future of VTCs. While interviewees in general felt quite hopeful and optimistic that VTCs *would* continue to exist and may even expand, there was unease about exactly *how* this would occur. These concerns included securing stable funding sources, maintaining "buy in" from key individuals, and resource needs for expanding the participation and eligibility criteria of VTCs. Given the important role that VTCs can play in effectively supporting justice-involved veterans, and offering more benefits compared to a traditional justice-system response, it seems vital to ensure that VTCs are able to continue operating in the future.

The first Veterans Treatment Court (VTC) began operations in Buffalo, NY in 2008 as a policy response to "growing concern that US veterans have unique needs that are not being met by the criminal justice system" (Rowen, 2020, p. 78). Since then, VTCs have spread rapidly, and there are currently over 600 VTCs operating in the United States (U.S. Department of Veterans Affairs, 2021). A form of specialty court, VTCs provide services in a therapeutic court setting to individuals who are current or former members of the United States military who have been charged with eligible offenses. Various team members, including court personnel, mental health professionals, and representatives of the Department of Veterans Affairs (e.g., Veterans Justice Outreach Specialists, or VJOs) collaborate to address the criminogenic needs of veterans, while also meeting their housing, employment, social, medical, mental health needs (Shah, 2014).

Not all VTCs operate in the same manner. VTCs can differ from jurisdiction to jurisdiction in a variety of ways, including eligibility criteria; sobriety requirements; treatment services offered; the requirement of a "nexus" between military service experiences, clinical diagnoses, and/or the charged offense; the involvement of veteran mentors in the VTC program; statutory authorization and/or regulations; sources of funding; and more.[1] While these differences can lead to unique opportunities and challenges for a given VTC in serving the local population of justice-involved veterans (JIV), it also can influence how VTC team member perceive the future of both their own VTC *and* the future of VTCs in general.

While research on specialty treatment courts to date suggests that " ... unlike other correctional fads of the past (e.g., boot camp prisons, or scared straight programs), specialty courts do not seem to be showing any signs of going away or of even slowing down" (Pratt & Turanovic, 2019, p. 379), despite ongoing debates on their effectiveness. There is minimal empirical research currently available evaluating the effectiveness of VTCs specifically. To address this issue, NIJ has recently funded a large-scale multi-site evaluation of VTCs, but the results of this evaluation will not be available for several years. In the interim, it appears that discussions of best practices in the design and development of Veterans Treatment Courts are based on the available research on the implementation and effectiveness of *other* specialty courts, most notably drug courts. Little research has been carried out that explores the viability and longevity of VTCs moving forward, or the perceptions of VTC team members on these issues. The present study explores how VTC team members from 20 VTCs around the United States perceived the future of VTCs in the short and long term, both in terms of their own VTC and VTCs in general.

Literature review

The limited research on VTCs suggest a high success rate for participants, with recidivism rates found to be as low as 11% in some programs (Hartley & Baldwin, 2019; Tsai et al., 2018).[2] Additionally, VTCs have been linked to improvements in housing stability, connection to VA services, and mental health, substance use, and quality of life outcomes among veterans (see Herzog et al., 2019; Johnson et al., 2016; Knudsen & Wingenfeld, 2016; Tsai et al., 2016, 2018).

Irrespective of empirical research demonstrating the positive outcomes of VTCs, some scholars and team members endorse and justify the continuance of this veteran-exclusive programming for other reasons. For instance, some justify VTCs solely due to the *ethical* implications they represent (i.e., veterans deserve differential treatment in the criminal legal system and diversion from traditional punishment because their military service may have yielded lasting adverse consequences that contributed to their involvement with the law; Yerramsetti et al., 2017). Others posit that VTCs will sustain themselves because they serve an important *administrative* purpose beyond rehabilitation and reductions in recidivism: efficiency. Illustrating the latter point, Pratt and Turanovic (2019, p. 379) state the following:

> So the bottom line is that, yes, there was an ideological component to the development of specialized courts for drug offenders, but the influence of ideology was dwarfed by the desire for system efficiency. And as different kinds of specialized courts came onto the scene—veterans' courts, domestic violence courts, mental health courts, and so on—it is clear that the primary job of such courts was to serve administrative purposes (the convenience of

> efficient processing) and that all other concerns (effective rehabilitation, reducing reoffending) would be secondary at best. (Casey, 2004)

Despite their successes and the various justifications for their continuance, VTCs face a variety of challenges that may adversely impact their future. For example, critics of VTCs suggest that eligibility criteria are too restrictive (i.e., requiring certain military discharge statuses, combat experience, establishment of the nexus, VA healthcare benefits, less severe mental health diagnoses), such that those justice-involved veterans who warrant the most support are also those most likely to be prohibited from program entry (Holliday et al., 2023; Johnson et al., 2016; Yerramsetti et al., 2017). An implication of selective program eligibility, lengthier and more intensive/rigorous court supervision compared to traditional court case processing, and the potential for harsher sentencing if unable to successfully complete the programming (Yerramsetti et al., 2017), is that veterans may be prohibited or deterred from voluntarily participating in VTCs. Consequently, program sizes may dwindle, potentially decreasing the need and demand for VTC programming in the longer term.

Another factor influencing the sustainability of VTCs is maintaining sufficient funding from stable sources. VTC personnel have noted difficulty in securing sufficient resources to sustain their programs and to meet the needs of their participants, such as the cost of mandated treatment services (Easter et al., 2021). While some VTCs may receive federal grant monies to provide their veteran participants with medications for opioid use disorder (MOUD) and other essential services, the vast majority of these funding streams are time limited, and even with such funding, court participants may be required to take on a portion of the treatment costs (Easter et al., 2021). Some federal reforms have been instituted to provide more permanent funding sources, including Congress enacting the Veterans Court Coordination Treatment Act of 2019 to facilitate the organization and dissemination of federal funds in pursuit of expanding VTC programming (Veterans Court Coordination Treatment Act of 2019, 2020). According to survey participants attending a conference and training event for treatment court professionals, state-level policy reforms that prioritize Medicaid expansion and continued state investments are important contributions to the sustainability of specialty courts, including VTCs (Easter et al., 2021). While the majority of respondents believed the programs were effective and important alternatives to incarceration and other punitive approaches within the criminal legal system, the deficits in funding (especially regarding health-related services for veteran participants) was the greatest barrier to continued operations and reduced recidivism within VTCs (Easter et al., 2021).

However, beyond issues of funding, VTCs are also often limited in terms of the availability, breadth (i.e., medical, mental health, substance use), and nature of the services they provide (i.e., lacking veteran-centered services), which influence factors like time-to-treatment and how court participants perceive treatment effectiveness and the quality of VTC programming (Kras et al., in press; Shannon et al., 2017). Given that veterans are more likely than non-veterans in the criminal legal system to present with trauma disorders and are at high risk for substance abuse (Landolfi & LeClair, 1976; Stacer & Solinas-Saunders, 2020; Yerramsetti et al., 2017), often produced by prolonged exposure to repeated deployments (Burns, 2010; Tanielian, 2008), efficient and effective treatment options are essential to the success of VTC programming. However, the specialized treatment services provided by VTCs are often limited (e.g.,

MOUD, intensive outpatient treatment), especially for veterans with complex needs like severe mental illness substance use disorders, and/or co-occurring disorders (DeMatteo et al., 2013; Easter et al., 2021). According to Easter et al. (2021, p. 1473), "Respondents cited problems of insufficient provider capacity and quality. Many specialized services – MAT [medication assisted treatment], intensive outpatient, residential services, co-occurring disorders programs, and programs that address criminogenic needs – are in very short supply and unevenly distributed in nonmetropolitan areas."

Further, treatment engagement among veterans may be predicated on whether veteran-centered services are readily available for VTC participants (Kras et al., in press). Prior research suggests that few VTCs emphasize programming that considers the contexts of military service and socialization, despite the seemingly positive impact on veterans engaging in and completing treatment programming (Ahlin & Douds, 2016; Kras et al., in press). This challenge is compounded for veterans who are ineligible for VA benefits, such as those with "other than honorable" (OTH) or dishonorable discharges (Yerramsetti et al., 2017). According to Tayyeb and Greenburg (2017), an increasing number of veterans since 9/11 are being discharged from the military with statuses that disqualify them from receiving Veterans Affairs (VA) benefits that entail healthcare, education and housing support, and other resources. Some VTCs will exclude veterans whose discharge status prohibits VA healthcare coverage, especially those that rely almost exclusively on VA funding (and not community-based resources) to service their veteran participants and sustain their programming. This effectively reduces the reach and size of these programs, potentially negatively impacting their future sustainability.

Another consideration for the expansion and sustainability of VTCs is the existence of statutory mandates. On one hand, statutes may be especially prohibitive for some programs in certain states. For example, statutory language that explicitly requires all VTC participants to have been honorably discharged may make programming highly restrictive and exclusive (see Rapisarda et al., in press). On the other hand, specialized court programming is designed to divert participants away from incarceration, accentuating therapy and rehabilitation over strict "crime control," which in turn allows judges and other court team members to reclaim some of the discretion otherwise lost to mandatory sentencing structures (Burns, 2010). Consequently, VTC programs may expand their reach and have more flexibility in not only who enters, but also how interventions and sanctions are administered (Burns, 2010). To this end, the Council on Criminal Justice (2023a, 2023b) recommends not only improving the definitions and the process of identifying JIVs to expand and sustain VTC programming, but also to have veteran status considered in sentencing outcomes even when they are ineligible for VTC and related programs due to discharge status.

Finally, like the success of any program, its expansion and longevity rely on the personnel that run them. Research to date has documented increased workloads due to the very existence of VTCs, compounded by issues of staff turnover (Shannon et al., 2017), which directly impacts the bandwidth and growth of these programs. Indeed, while staff turnover impacts *all* court processes, it can be especially detrimental to the identification and referral processes, which may restrict the size, growth, and longevity of these VTCs (Baldwin et al., 2018). VTCs with low enrollments may find it difficult to justify their continuation to policymakers who are weighing competing funding requests for limited resources.

Current study

The current study examines team members' perceptions of the future of VTCs, both for the team members' own VTC and for VTCs in general in the United States. To do this, we conducted 145 interviews with key team members from 20 VTCs around the country, including attorneys, judges, probation officers, other court team members, and clinical personnel. Below, we outline the methods of our study, before proceeding with the results.

Methods

The current study is part of a larger project focused on documenting and understanding the nature of VTCs inner workings and collaboration with various entities (e.g., community service providers, the VA).[3] An in-depth description of the methods can be found in related papers from the same project (Byrne et al., in press). This project involves a qualitative approach, wherein in-depth interviews were conducted with 145 team members from 20 VTCs across the United States.

Researchers adopted a thematic analysis approach to coding the interview data, which included deductive procedures based on the semi-structured interview protocol followed by inductive coding through iterations (Braun & Clarke, 2012). Codes from the broader project include service delivery, eligibility, perceived veteran needs, and more from the perspective of VTC team members. For the current analysis, we focus on information coded in relation to discussions about the future of VTCs, both in terms of the interviewee's specific VTC, and VTCs generally in the United States. The first and second authors engaged in an iterative, focused coding process to accommodate inductive codes that emerged through the initial coding process to discern more specific and nuanced themes (Locke et al., 2022). Specifically, whenever interviewees discussed the future of VTCs, it was assigned the code Future of VTCs. When appropriate, the comment was also assigned a subcode depending on whether the context of the comment referred to the relative short term (e.g., within the next 10 years) or long term (10 year or more) future of VTCs. We then produced analytic memos reflecting the larger themes emerging from this round of coding, which were collectively reviewed by the entire research team to produce the final iteration of the findings.

Findings

Understanding team member perspectives on what the future may hold for Veterans Treatment Courts (VTCs), both for participants' specific VTC and as a type of specialty court overall, is important to fully understanding the VTC model, and potential opportunities and challenges moving forward. Our analysis of 145 interviews across 20 VTCs revealed four overarching themes about what team members expect, or hope for, regarding VTCs in the future. These four themes reflect: the need for continued funding and increased resources; desires to expand participation in VTCs; hope and uncertainty about the future of VTCs; and depending on specific people to ensure the future of VTCs.

These themes are useful not only for understanding team member's perspectives on the current and future operations of VTCs, but also to help identify important challenges or opportunities to continuing or expanding VTC operations going forward. Throughout the findings, we present the quotes verbatim to preserve the tone and language of the participants.

Show me the money: the need for continued funding and increased resources

Many team members noted the importance of maintaining and/or increasing both the amount of funding and the overall level of resources available to VTCs. In many cases, this discussion focused on the danger of potentially losing a primary funding source for the VTC, such as a grant, and the need for stability in funding and resource streams moving forward.

The future of VTCs depends on stable funding sources

There was a common perception among participants that without a stable funding source, VTC operations would be heavily disrupted, if not discontinued entirely. Some noted that while reduced funding may still allow the VTC to operate to some extent, it would mean cutting certain VTC staff positions, having some screening tools not be available, and/or substantially reducing the number of participants in the VTC.

> There's a lot of stuff working against us, and if the funding were not to be renewed, our program would run 'cause I'm a state job. The two case managers are a state job, but the peer recovery specialist and the community liaison are grant. If the state didn't pick those up, those would go and we wouldn't have the screening tools to use for our tox screens, the remote breathalyzer, anything like that and we would not be able run the program successfully. – *Court Coordinator, Site 14*

> I don't see our standard of who we accept changing very much unless I do not get funding from the county and then we're gonna have to cut a third of our clients and not let them into veteran's court and they're gonna have to go to some other court, which would be heart-breaking to me. – *Court Coordinator, Site 18*

While stable funding would seemingly solve many of the potential problems facing VTCs, both now and in the future, one District Attorney acknowledged that this is complicated by political realities surrounding taxation and budgeting decisions.

> Long term, money's the solution. I just don't know—I mean, I know it's out there. It would just require taking money from other people and taxing large corporations, but politics is rough. – *District Attorney, Site 1*

Thus, there is not only the issue of ensuring stable funding for VTCs, but also an explicit understanding that politics can play a big role in *whether* VTCs are funded or not. This is particularly important given the short and long terms effects of the COVID pandemic on the economy *and* state budgets. In some cases, vital funding and services came from sources outside of the traditional state budgeting system, such as from the VA itself.

Reliance on the VA for funding and services

Participants noted a heavy reliance on the VA itself, primarily for providing vital services to eligible veterans participating in the VTC. Indeed, interviewees noted that VA collaboration (and the provision of services) was necessary for the VTC to continue operating successfully and serving the most clients. Without such support from the VA, the VTCs would see substantial disruption to their ability to provide veterans with a full range of treatment services, and costs for services not provided by or funded by the VA might need to be paid for by the veterans themselves.

> [The VTC will be around] as long as the VA is there. If we removed VA, the services would come out of pocket for clients. Right now, most clients are at least 80% service connected. - *VJO Specialist, Site 7*

> We got a [federal] grant that's for three years. It helps a lot. It helps tremendously because we're trying to wean ourself off of the state stuff, get it down to minimum stuff. We can do that if we can get the VA to give us more services. If we get the guys—I can't make the guy go there. - *Judge, Site 4*

> I do [think VTCs will be around long term]. I really do. I'm hoping that these outside treatment agencies, it's gonna be easier to get the VA to cover—the VA has a lot of money. It's like, come on, guys. Help these people out. I do see it in 10 years because it's progressed like it has to this point in a positive. I truly believe that. - *Court Coordinator, Site 9*

Desire for VTCs to increase program and service offerings

Some interviewees discussed not only the reliance on the VA for funding and services, but also the desire to increase the other types of programs and services provided to VTC participants. These took the form of transportation services as well as various types of substance abuse programming.

> I think one of the things that they [the VTC] also need to do is there really has to be a transportation component in these courts. - *Probation Chief, Site 20*

> I would definitely like to grow into us [DRUG AND ALCOHOL TREATMENT PROGRAM] being a bigger part [of the VTC]. We've been having meetings with the local health network. We're looking at in an MAT [MEDICATION ASSISTED TREATMENT] doctor in here as well as psych hours here, when we do this partial program, which would definitely open up the door to provide more of them services. - *Treatment Program Director, Site 8*

If federal funding was lost, someone would step up to fund VTCs

Some participants voiced their belief that if their VTC somehow lost federal funding, a replacement source of funding would be found. Given the fact that the most recent proposed FY2024 Budget[4] includes a reduction in federal spending for Veterans Treatment Courts from 35 million (in 2023) to 25 million (in 2024), we may soon find out whether team members predictions were accurate. This was typically grounded in beliefs about the public's perception that veterans are an important group to support.

> Well, I would like to think that all treatment courts would continue even if federal funding disappeared. I think if any—the court that stands the best chance at sticking around is veteran's court. Because I think across the country, certainly in [STATE], and I think a lot of other places, too. Look, we know what our soldiers have been through. We've seen it like no other era before in terms of what they've done. - *Prosecutor, Site 5*

> [In response to a question about what might happen if BJA funding goes away] "I think that states would absolutely step up to the plate [with funding] and recognize that we asked a lot of them [the veterans]." - *Prosecutor, Site 5*

> At least from the current district attorney's perspective, from my understanding, I think that even if there wasn't a larger funding pool that they would want to figure out some way to keep that going here. - *Public Defender, Site 13*

While this hopeful attitude is likely useful in getting interviewees through their day-to-day routines working in the VTC, it is not clear how realistic these hopes are. That is, in the face of dramatic state budget cuts and multiple potential programs all jockeying for limited resources, it is simply not guaranteed that VTCs would automatically be protected and funded over other high-priority programs.

Widen the VTC support net: desires to expand participation in VTCs

In discussing the future of VTCs, many interviewees noted ways that the VTC should expand participation through a variety of methods. These methods include not only broadening the criteria for veteran eligibility, but also increasing efforts for the identification and screening of potential VTC participants who are in the justice system, as well as increasing the overall awareness of the VTC program. These views match the first recommendation in the report on justice-involved veterans by the Council on Criminal Justice (2023b, p. 5), to both improve the processes of identifying veterans in the criminal justice system and to adopt a uniform definition of "military veteran."

Expanding to cover more veterans

Interviewees noted desires for the VTC to increase not only the overall number of participants, but also broadening both the types of veterans and the types of crimes that would be eligible for the program.

> I'd like to see every veteran on their first misdemeanor coming to this program, getting the services they need in this program. - *Public Defender, Site 1*

> I think that it's going to be increasing in numbers and dealing not only with the misdemeanors but probably with other type of crimes. I think it's going to increase. - *VA Treatment Provider, Site 2*

One interviewee noted that future expansion would likely occur not only in VTCs, but across the full range of specialty courts.

> I think that with the way that there's not as much help in prison, this accountability court—not only Veteran's Treatment Court, but all the accountability courts—will have to be expanded. I think if we have a lot of people that are coming in that are innovative, not just in our county, but people that are investigating innovative ways or creative ways to expand it, I think it'll be expanded in all accountability courts. - *Prosecutor, Site 4*

Expansion requires better identification and screening of eligible veterans

Yet in discussing future expansion, interviewees also noted the need to have better identification and screening procedures. These would assist not only in identifying potentially eligible veterans, but also screening for those veterans and cases that have the best chance at succeeding in the VTC program. This implies a balance between expanding participation in the VTC to more veterans, while also still screening out those individuals who are unlikely to succeed in the program, including those with other than honorable discharges (OTHs).[5],[6]

> We average about five veteran arrests a day. If we could get the majority of those into our veteran's court, I do think we could rapidly expand. It's just a matter of getting those people identified and making sure that everyone involved is educated about veteran's court. – *Prosecutor, Site 3*

> I think that now, with this new policy that they've done, with alerting and getting more people referred, the judge won't have any choices but to start accepting more people. – *VJO Specialist, Site 3*

> Whenever a person is unsuccessful in these kind of programs, I think it's because they don't self-realize, and then we try to push a little bit too hard. I feel like with those OTHs, that would probably be a barrier or a fence that we're gonna have to push through. That's why at least if we are going to expand, it's gonna have to be a narrow group of OTHs and maybe the vetting process is gonna have to be a little bit deeper to identify those people who would be successful. Then once we sort of see that and start to get some success rate with those OTHs, maybe word in the community can start to go out and we can start to expand it further. I think I would like to see it expand, but I do think it's gonna have to be a slow process and a very narrow process to begin with. – *Assistant District Attorney, Site 6*

Expansion requires increased awareness of the VTC program

As part of the increased *identification* of eligible veterans, interviewees noted the need for increased *awareness* of the VTC program among a broad swath of team members. The belief was that if more individuals (veterans or otherwise) knew about the VTC program, participation would naturally increase.

> I think it's just a matter of just educating and letting everybody know that this is probably their best available option. – *Prosecutor, Site 3*

> Also, it's just we have to touch as many people as possible. That's why I feel like we need to get the word out more. – *District Attorney, Site 1*

One interviewee noted that while they felt their own VTC would continue, they did not know how they could increase participation from veterans in their area, or even if there *was* a need for expansion. In other words, they were unclear whether there would be an increased need in the future, or if the VTC was already effectively identifying and serving veterans in the area.

> Yeah. I believe it will last. For our area, I don't know how we can reach more veterans and the thing is maybe the veterans are not getting in trouble in our area to be offered treatment court. – *Community Treatment Provider, Site 5*

Optimism and regret about future expansion

One interviewee's optimism that VTCs would continue to expand was tempered with regret that such an expansion would even be needed. This taps into an underlying conflict of the justice system itself, in that while the short-term goal is to increase participation to effectively serve all those who are eligible, the long term societal goal might be to reduce the *need* for programs like the VTC.

> On the one hand, I wanna see it treating more people. On the other hand, I want it to not have to treat more people. I want it to just not need to be bigger. I wanna see people out of this system completely as much as we can. – *Public Defender, Site 1*

I've got high hopes ... i think: hope and uncertainty about the future of VTCs

Many interviewees expressed hope that their VTC, or VTCs in general, would continue in the future. However, these hopes were typically mentioned with either justifications for such hope, or with caveats tempering the extent of such hope.

Hopeful because of a belief that VTCs are important

Some interviewees notes that they were hopeful VTCs would continue simply because they believed VTCs were important and needed for society.

> I am a strong believer, a true believer in veterans court, and I hope it continues. – *Assistant State Attorney, Site 2*

> Well, I certainly hope it won't fade away, and I think it's so important. – *Assistant State Attorney, Site 2*

> I really hope it's not a fad. I guess I'm young, and I'm trying to look on the bright side and all this. I personally think these types of courts are the way that we should be going, interagency, working together to help somebody get services. At the end of the day, that's what a lot of people in custody need, is access to services, and they don't have it. *–Public Defender's Office, Site 11*

Hopeful because VTCs serve a unique and continued need

Other interviewees mentioned that VTCs served the unique and continuing needs of veterans. This included noting the expectation that VTCs would continue as long as the population of justice-involved-veterans continued, which was largely ensured due to recent conflicts.

> I hope so. I think it will as long as we—'cause of course certain areas have more of a population. As far as [COUNTY], as long as there continues to be a population, then yes, I think it will be. – *Court Coordinator, Site 4*

> Oh, I certainly hope so because we got a lot of guys from the last two wars who have a lot of issues, and they're gonna be around. – *Mentor Coordinator, Site 14*

In one case, an interviewee noted that VTCs provided a clear difference from other types of specialty courts in terms of serving veterans' needs.

> I have other forms of diversion and mental health that don't involve veterans, and I can tell you, there is a clear difference in that connection, and so they benefit from being together, even if it's remote, and hearing the progress each one of them is making or where they're falling short. They care about each other, and because of this connection to their military service, so I would hope we wouldn't lose that because I think there's a lot to their healing and participation because they're together. – *Judge, Site 1*

Expansion is desired, but other forces make things very uncertain

Not all interviewees were entirely optimistic about the future of VTCs. Some noted that while they would like to see expansion, there were societal, economic, and political forces that may constrain any expansion plans, or even cast doubt on whether VTCs would continue.

> I think right now expansion or anything like that, I don't know where this is all gonna end up going with the way our economy is and everything that's going on. – *Court Coordinator, Site 8*

> Our justice system has been completely turned on its head in [STATE], and we are struggling to maintain some semblance of sanity. I'll just put it that way. It is a daily struggle. [. . .] Frankly, it's kind of a shitshow right now, so I don't know [if VTCs will be around in the future]. – *Prosecutor, Site 10*

> I would say that because of how political these things are, I'm not so sure. I think right now in this climate, I think veterans courts are pretty secure at least in my purview of what I work with. To project what will happen several years from now, I would say probably yes, but I think if I take a page out of what I've experienced with mental health court and even with veterans court, I think there's going to be political forces that go back and forth that will inform these courts and how they're funded and how willing people are to fund them. – *Probation Officer, Site 5*

> Hopefully it's bigger. Hopefully we're encompassing more veterans. Hopefully our statutes are a little bit broader to allow for more relief. What about the case they got and they didn't know about veterans' court but they should have? That would be nice. Hopefully better known in the community. I think, though, that the opposite might happen. [The VTC] might be smaller. They might be less well-known, and there might be less of a demand. We're seeing that in some areas just because the war has ended for now. The internal wars a lot of our folks are fighting at home are still goin' strong, and they're gonna need the help, but I think as time goes on, that's gonna dissipate. I don't know what's gonna happen next month in [LOCATION]. They might be keepin' us in business. I don't know. I hope not. I think there'll still be need to 'em. – *Prosecutor, Site 16*

One interviewee summed up their tempered optimism with this concise response:

> God, I hope it doesn't fade out. – *Deputy Public Defender, Site 18*

Hope, but tempered with pragmatism about continued funding and participants

In other cases, interviewees express hopes that were tempered with a lack of certainty about continued participants and/or funding availability.

> I guess it's gonna depend on the veteran population and where it's at in 10 years because if it's a Veterans Treatment Court, it's obviously specific. If you don't have the people to utilize it, then it may not be [around in 10 years], but right now I think it's a successful program, and I think that we have the right people doing it. As long as we have veterans that can apply and are eligible for it, and we can help them because we all know the underlying reasons are there, then we should do it. – *Assistant Director (County VA), Site 8*

> I hope so because I do think and believe wholeheartedly that it is beneficial. It's much needed. Now, as you know, when it comes to sustainability, people look at numbers. Each court, especially if it's grant-funded, I believe they are required to have a certain number of veterans to sustain the grant money. It also depends on once the grant money, whatever the contract time period is, has run out if the county or city or whatever will pick up that cost. It just depends on how important the county thinks this service is to their constituents. – *VJO, Site 4*

Shark tank revisited? Needing buy-in to ensure the future of VTCs

Many interviewees noted that the future of VTCs depended on buy-in from specific people either involved in the VTC process itself, or who provided political support and/or financial resources. The list of "key players" included judges, district attorneys, politicians, and in one case, mentors.

Investment from judges

Multiple interviewees mentioned the importance of judicial buy-in for ensuring the continuation of the VTC. In particular, these responses indicated that their VTC continues primarily because the current judge or chief justice is a strong believer in the VTC model, and it would continue to operate as long as that judge was present.

> We have all sorts of specialty things popping up and our chief justice is certainly a proponent of problem solving courts. I think as long as she's around we'll stick around here. They send us out new tallies of how many problem solving courts have started in [STATE] and how proud they are of that. It could be a flash in the pan, but I hope not because I really do think it helps people on all levels. - *Judge, Site 7*

> I will say yes, and here's why. Number one, Judge [NAME] loves this court. She loves doing this. As long as she's on the bench—even so, what I've noticed is judges like to have something named after themselves, something that they're doing. - *Prosecutor, Site 7*

> I think in particular we're seeing the judge's investment in this being a critical component to criminal justice.- *Case Manager, Site 1*

One judge broadened this list to not only include judges like themselves, but also other key court personnel, and particularly the District Attorney, as vital to the continued operation of the VTC.

> I think that if the judges are committed to it, and the court is committed to it, the DA is committed to it, it'll be around a long time, a long time. - *Judge, Site 4*

Investment from district attorneys

Like the last quote suggests, the list of key players keeping a VTC running with their buy-in was broader than just a supportive judge. Two attorneys noted specifically that District Attorneys were vital to the continued operation of VTCs. Specifically, the indication was that if DAs stopped believing in the utility of VTCs, then that factor alone would the future of these courts would be much more uncertain.

> I hope so. I think it lasting is unfortunately may be dependent on someone on the DA's office and their feelings as to its usefulness and utility. I certainly hope so for our clients and I certainly hope so. -*Public Defender, Site 13*

> I hope it continues to flourish. Again, I also think it depends who's in charge of the administration. I know that right now, those of us in collaborative courts at the DA's office are real believers in collaborative courts. We're big proponents of them and we believe that they're effective and very necessary. I don't know if that will change over the years. I hope not. - *District Attorney, Site 18*

Investment from politicians

Another interviewee pointed out that support from politicians would be vital to the future of VTCs. While they noted that being "pro-veteran" was an easy political stance to take, this is also aided by wars that have been fought over the last two decades that produced a large veteran population for local politicians to cater to.

> That, of course, translates to, like you said, politicians campaigning on being pro-veterans. That's especially relevant in the last 20 years because of the wars. It all funnels up to that point where it becomes political and about campaigning on certain things than actually delivering on managing those resources. My guess is, yeah, [COUNTY]'s got enough veterans where the politicians campaign on it. They're constantly talking about it, so makes it—makes the program easier to sustain. - *Probation Officer, Site 12*

Investment from the next generation of mentors

One interviewee lamented the lack of new, younger mentors becoming involved in the VTC. Specifically, they noted the current mentor population was continuing to increase in age, without a clear source for new mentors to replace those that leave the program.

> We can see the writing on the wall. We have a number of mentors who are retired attorneys, who are also veterans. I was just noticing one coming into court last week, and he's moving very gingerly and very carefully. Over the five years, I've watched this gentleman tremendously age. The writing is on the wall for a number of them. They needed to take a break. [...] We definitely have to recruit, but [NAME] and I are old folk. How are we gonna recruit some of these younger mentors? That's a conundrum right now. - *Mentor Recruiter, Site 18*

Discussion

The overall takeaway from these interviews is that even though most participants fully expected that VTCs would continue to operate in both the short and long-term future, there was not a clear agreement either that this future was guaranteed, how VTCs would change over time, or what would be needed to keep them going. Instead, participants noted not only the need for continued stability in funding, but also needing increased resources overall, both to better serve existing clients and for future expansion efforts. In some cases, interviewees were confident that even if federal funding were to decrease or stop, *someone* would step in to continue funding what was seen as a vital resource for justice involved veterans, particularly given the "easy political win" that VTCs represent.

In terms of beliefs about future expansion, interviewees noted different ways that VTCs could better serve the justice-involved-veteran population. One idea involved expanding eligibility options for veterans accused of a variety of crimes and with a variety of backgrounds. Yet this raises questions about balancing efforts to increase eligibility and better serve justice-involved veterans, without unduly causing "net widening" and the resulting negative consequences it could cause to individuals. For example, net widening might take what otherwise would be a relatively minor offense, punished with a small fine, and turn it into a higher-stakes, more resource-intensive VTC process. The VTC process not only could take months or years to successfully resolve, but failure could lead to more detrimental consequences than what was originally facing the justice-involved veteran. Yet this may still represent a better option than other diversionary specialty courts, as Herzog et al. (2019) found some VTC participants chose to go through the VTC process instead of drug court because they perceived VTCs as inherently more lenient and less prone to failure.

In other cases, interviewees noted that expanding the VTC required not only better identification and screening of eligible veterans by VTC personnel, but also increasing the overall *awareness* of the program itself in the community. Influencing these actions is also the timing of the VTC process, specifically whether it operates as a pre-adjudication, a post-adjudication model, or both.[7] This timing has important impacts for not only when veterans would be considered by the VTC, and how that would influence awareness campaigns, but also what potential benefits a veteran might see from their participation (e.g., sentencing reductions vs. case dismissal). Indeed, Holliday et al. (2023) suggest placing more focus on veteran-specific programs that would intervene earlier in the justice process (e.g., pre-plea), rather than as a diversion from incarceration. Further, the Council on Criminal Justice (2023a) recommends jurisdictions create laws allowing justice-involved veterans to file for expungement of their criminal records after successfully completing some form of veteran-specific programming. While we do not compare views between team members in pre- and post-adjudication VTCs in this manuscript, we plan to explore this issue in future research.

Many interviewees pinned their hopes that VTCs would continue in the future on perceptions about the importance of offering a specialty court that served the unique (and continuing) needs of the justice-involved-veteran population. While this veteran population was generally seen as currently stable, due to the impact of recent conflicts, there was also some uncertainty that this population would remain stable in the longer term, and/or that the funding for VTCs was always guaranteed to come through.

However, underlying all of these perceptions is the ultimate (albeit elusive) goal of no longer needing *any* VTCs, due to veterans' treatment and service needs being fully served by the pre-or-post separation programming offered by the DoD and/or VA *before* they become justice-involved. While perhaps unrealistic to expect VTCs to become entirely obsolete, investing more resources to programming for newly separated veterans *prior* to judicial involvement might show broader benefits to the veteran population overall compared to post-judicial-involvement investments. However, this should not be seen as a zero-sum game. Any increase in resources devoted to military-separation programming, meant to help keep veterans from becoming justice-involved, should not result in reduced funding for existing VTC programs that are designed to help veterans who *do* become justice-involved.

Finally, interviewees identified several specific positions that were perceived as needing "buy in" to ensure the future of VTCs. These included buy-in from judges, DAs, as well as politicians. Further, one interviewee noted the aging population of mentors in the VTC, and expressed a need for the "next generation" of mentors to become involved in VTC for the mentoring program to be able to continue to operate effectively. As mentoring has been found to be a key component in what makes a VTC successful (Herzog et al., 2019), the aging mentor population means there is a constant ticking time bomb that VTCs must deal with to ensure their future success. Overall, this broader theme touches on a number of issues highlighted earlier, including increasing awareness about the VTC programming, as well as monitoring changes in the veteran population both overall and in terms of their specific backgrounds and needs.

The current research study, part of a broader study on VTCs across the country, was not without limitations. Perhaps the clearest limitation is that this rich qualitative data is based on interviewees from only 20 VTCs across the country. While the selection of VTCs and interviewees ensured a broad inclusion of viewpoints and regional differences, these findings are not necessarily generalizable to *all* VTCs in the U.S. Still, these findings highlight the diverse views about the future of VTCs, and many of the issues brought up by interviewees, such as the need for stable funding sources, are likely to be relevant concerns for many VTCs.

Another limitation is that these data come from semi-structured interviews, which are by nature less standardized than if data were collected via surveys. For instance, the interviewers may not have asked the "future" question using the same wording from interview to interview, and thus any differences in how the question was asked may have influenced how it was interpreted and answered by the interviewees. Further, the somewhat random nature of what was discussed or highlighted earlier in the interview could have influenced answers to the "future" question, which typically came near the end of a given interview. These are common limitations in any research study using semi-structure interviews, and what is lost due to a lack of strict standardization in asking the question is made up for in the rich detail and nuance of the data.

Conclusion

Overall, the general sense of the interviewees in the current study is that VTCs are likely to be around for a long time. There was a belief that VTCs were valuable to both veterans and society overall, and also that this importance would be clear to politicians and the public. That said, there were numerous concerns about issues such as ensuring a stable source of funding, continued "buy in" from key team members within and external to the VTC, and resource issues linked to desires to expand the VTCs in terms of both participation and eligibility criteria. Still, interviewees in general felt quite hopeful and optimistic that VTCs *would* continue to exist and may even expand, even if they felt some unease about *how* this would occur. Given the existing research suggests that VTCs can have an important role to play in effectively supporting justice-involved veterans, and may have more benefits compared to a traditional justice-system response, it seems vital to ensure that VTCs are able to continue operating in the future.

Notes

1. For an overview, see Byrne et al. (in press).
2. It should be noted that the evaluation research examining the effectiveness of VTCs is limited to a small number of quasi-experimental studies. While no systematic review of these studies has been conducted to date, our review of this research reveals that effects of these programs would be ranked as "unknown," due to this evaluation shortfall. Recognizing the need for high quality evaluation research, NIJ has contracted with researchers from American University to conduct a multi-site RCT of the Veterans Treatment Court model. The results from this evaluation will not be available until 2027.
3. The current research project was approved by the George Mason University Institutional Review Board (09132022).
4. See https://www.justice.gov/d9/2023-03/ojp_fy_2024_presidents_budget_final_draft_clean_3.17.23.pdf.
5. In this regard, it seems clear that you would not expand the target population of veterans to those seen as most likely to fail in the program without first considering that they might fail because of one or more program requirements, such as zero tolerance substance use policies.

6. OTH: other than Honorable Discharge. For an overview of discharge status, see Hummer et al. (in press) and Veterans Legal Clinic at the Legal Services Center of Harvard Law School (2016).
7. Out of the 20 VTC sites in our study, at the time of the interviews, 2 operated mainly as a pre-adjudication model, 7 were mainly post-adjudication, and 11 operated as both.

Acknowledgments

The authors would like to thank the members of our Community Advisory Board for their invaluable feedback on an earlier draft of this article.

Disclosure statement

No potential conflict of interest was reported by the author(s).

Funding

This study was funded under the Justice Community Opioid Innovation Network (JCOIN) Coordination and Translation Center (CTC) (U2CDA050097, MPI Taxman/Rudes). The contents of this publication are solely the responsibility of the authors and do not necessarily represent the official views of the NIH, or the participating sites.

ORCID

Kelly M. Socia http://orcid.org/0000-0003-0560-3399
Sabrina S. Rapisarda http://orcid.org/0000-0001-5148-8630
Kimberly R. Kras http://orcid.org/0000-0002-0592-0418
Don Hummer http://orcid.org/0000-0003-3026-0287
James M. Byrne http://orcid.org/0000-0001-9216-9871

References

Ahlin, E. M., & Douds, A. S. (2016). Military socialization: A motivating factor for seeking treatment in a veterans' treatment court. *American Journal of Criminal Justice*, *41*(1), 83–96. https://doi.org/10.1007/s12103-015-9332-4

Baldwin, J. M., Hartley, R. D., & Brooke, E. J. (2018). Identifying those who served: Modeling potential participant identification in veterans treatment courts. *Drug Court Review*, *1*, 11–32.

Braun, V., & Clarke, V. (2012). *Thematic analysis*. American Psychological Association.

Burns, S. L. (2010). The future of problem-solving courts: Inside the courts and beyond. *University of Maryland LJ Race, Religion, Gender & Class*, *10*, 73.

Byrne, J. M., Kras, K. R., Hummer, D., Socia, K. M., & Rapisarda, S. S. (in press). Community participatory research on veterans in specialized programming: Project overview and initial findings. *Victims & Offenders*.

Casey, T. (2004). When good intentions are not enough: Problem-solving courts and the impending crisis of legitimacy. *Southern Methodist University Law Review*, *57*, 1459–1520.

Council on Criminal Justice. (2023a). *Alternatives to prosecution and incarceration for justice-involved veterans: A model policy framework*. https://counciloncj.foleon.com/veterans-commission/model-policy-framework

Council on Criminal Justice. (2023b). *Honoring service, advancing safety: Supporting veterans from arrest through sentencing*. https://counciloncj.foleon.com/veterans-commission/report-1/

DeMatteo, D., LaDuke, C., Locklair, B. R., & Heilbrun, K. (2013). Community-based alternatives for justice-involved individuals with severe mental illness: Diversion, problem-solving courts, and reentry. *Journal of Criminal Justice*, *41*(2), 64–71. https://doi.org/10.1016/j.jcrimjus.2012.09.002

Easter, M. M., Swanson, J. W., Crozier, W. E., Robertson, A. G., Garrett, B. L., Modjadidi, K., & Swartz, M. S. (2021). North Carolina specialty courts, treatment access, and the substance use crisis: A promising but underfunded model. *Psychiatric Services*, *72*(12), 1471–1474. https://doi.org/10.1176/appi.ps.202000868

Hartley, R. D., & Baldwin, J. M. (2019). Waging war on recidivism among justice-involved veterans: An impact evaluation of a large urban veterans treatment court. *Criminal Justice Policy Review*, *30* (1), 52–78. https://doi.org/10.1177/0887403416650490

Herzog, J. R., Ferdik, F., Scott, D., Denney, A., & Conklin, S. (2019). Participants' perceptions of veterans treatment courts: A qualitative assessment and systems model. *Journal of Veterans Studies*, *4*(2), 78–93. https://doi.org/10.21061/jvs.v4i2.108

Holliday, S. B., Ayer, L., & Skrabala, L. (2023). Identifying promising prevention strategies and interventions to support justice-involved veterans. *Veterans' Issues in Focus*, RAND Corporation, PE-A1363-8. https://doi.org/10.7249/PEA1363-8

Hummer, D., Byrne, J. M., Rapisarda, S. S., Socia, K. M., & Kras, K. R. (in press). No veteran left behind? Perspectives on VTC eligibility criteria for justice-involved veterans in multiple jurisdictions across the United States. *Victims & Offenders*.

Johnson, R. S., Stolar, A. G., McGuire, J. F., Clark, S., Coonan, L. A., Hausknecht, P., & Graham, D. P. (2016). US veterans' court programs: An inventory and analysis of national survey data. *Community Mental Health Journal*, *52*(2), 180–186. https://doi.org/10.1007/s10597-015-9972-3

Knudsen, K. J., & Wingenfeld, S. (2016). A specialized treatment court for veterans with trauma exposure: Implications for the field. *Community Mental Health Journal*, *52*(2), 127–135. https://doi.org/10.1007/s10597-015-9845-9

Kras, K. R., Rapisarda, S. S., Hummer, D., Socia, K. M., Byrne, J. M., & Taxman, F. (in press). At risk and underserved: Veterans treatment court team member perspectives on service delivery challenges. *Victims & Offenders*. https://doi.org/10.1080/15564886.2023.2275195

Landolfi, J., & LeClair, D. P. (1976). *A profile of Vietnam era veterans incarcerated in Massachusetts correctional institutions*. Massachusetts Department of Correction. (Publication #9036-27-250-7/76CR).

Locke, K., Feldman, M., & Golden Biddle, K. (2022). Coding practices and iterativity: Beyond templates for analyzing qualitative data. *Organizational Research Methods*, *25*(2), 262–284. https://doi.org/10.1177/1094428120948600

Pratt, T. C., & Turanovic, J. J. (2019). A criminological fly in the ointment: Specialty courts and the generality of deviance. *Victims & Offenders*, *14*(3), 375–386. https://doi.org/10.1080/15564886.2019.1595247

Rapisarda, S. S., Kras, K. R., LeMoyne, G., Hummer, D., Socia, K. M., & Byrne, J. M. (in press). Veterans treatment courts: A nationwide review of U.S. enacting and eligibility state statutes. *Victims & Offenders*.

Rowen, J. (2020). Worthy of justice: A veterans treatment court in practice. *Law & Policy*, *42*(1), 78–100. https://doi.org/10.1111/lapo.12142

Shah, S. (2014). Authorization required: Veterans treatment courts, the need for democratic legitimacy, and the separation of powers doctrine. *Southern California Interdisciplinary Law Journal*, *23*, 67.

Shannon, L. M., Birdwhistell, S., Hulbig, S. K., Jones, A. J., Newell, J., & Payne, C. (2017). Examining implementation and preliminary performance indicators of veterans treatment courts: The Kentucky experience. *Evaluation and Program Planning*, *63*, 54–66. https://doi.org/10.1016/j.evalprogplan.2017.03.003

Stacer, M. J., & Solinas-Saunders, M. (2020). Justice-involved veterans: A critical review and future research. *Critical Military Studies*, *6*(1), 41–66. https://doi.org/10.1080/23337486.2018.1435384

Tanielian, T. L. (2008). *Invisible wounds of war: Psychological and cognitive injuries, their consequences, and services to assist recovery* (Vol. 1). Rand Corporation.

Tayyeb, A. R., & Greenburg, J. (2017). Bad papers": The invisible and increasing costs of war for excluded veterans. *Health*, *104*(10), 1805–1811.

Tsai, J., Finlay, A., Flatley, B., Kasprow, W. J., & Clark, S. (2018). A national study of veterans treatment court participants: Who benefits and who recidivates. *Administration and Policy in Mental Health and Mental Health Services Research*, *45*(2), 236–244. https://doi.org/10.1007/s10488-017-0816-z

Tsai, J., Flatley, B., Kasprow, W. J., Clark, S., & Finlay, A. (2016). Diversion of veterans with criminal justice involvement to treatment courts: Participant characteristics and outcomes. *Psychiatric Services*, *68*(4), 375–383. https://doi.org/10.1176/appi.ps.201600233

U.S. Department of Veterans Affairs. (2021). *Fact sheet: Veterans treatment courts and other veteran-focused courts served by VA veterans justice outreach specialists*. https://www.va.gov/HOMELESS/docs/VJO/Veterans-Treatment-Court-Inventory-Update-Fact-Sheet-Jan-2021.pdf

Veterans Court Coordination Treatment Act of 2019. 34 U.S.C. 10651 and 10701. (2020). Public Law 116-153. https://www.govinfo.gov/app/details/PLAW-116publ153

Veterans Legal Clinic at the Legal Services Center of Harvard Law School. (2016) *Disabled American veterans (DAV) distinguished lecture series – Judge Rober Russell*. Retrieved November 17, 2016, from https://www.youtube.com/watch?v=srzZwOCPc5g&t=1338s

Yerramsetti, A. P., Simons, D. D., Coonan, L., & Stolar, A. (2017). Veteran treatment courts: A promising solution. *Behavioral Sciences & The Law*, *35*(5–6), 512–522. https://doi.org/10.1002/bsl.2308

Protecting but Not Protected: Sexual Assault in the Military

Emily K. Meinert and Ericka A. Wentz

ABSTRACT

The purpose of this study was to uncover common themes among tweets shared by victims of military sexual assault (MSA) and make suggestions for policy implications. By using Twitter as a unique data source, researchers were able to analyze self-report data that were not available elsewhere. Results of this qualitative study indicate leadership has a profound impact on MSA. Leaders failed victims in several ways: some were the offenders, some hindered the reporting process, and others ridiculed the victim. Researchers suggest reevaluation of current programs, creation of training programs for military leaders, and adequate resources be made available to MSA victims.

Introduction

Private First Class (PFC) Vanessa Guillén experienced an unthinkable reality while serving in the U.S. Army: persistent sexual harassment followed by murder at the hands of a fellow soldier. At only 20 years old, Guillén confided in her mother that one of her sergeants in the Army, her superior, was sexually harassing her (Find Vanessa Guillen, 2020). Guillén was never able to officially report the sexual harassment before she disappeared on April 22, 2020. Her remains were found two months later.

Statistics consistently illuminate the pervasiveness of sexual assault. At the civilian level, approximately 20% of U.S. women have experienced sexual assault during their lifetime while 2.6% of U.S. men reported the same (NISVS, 2015). Within military populations, the Department of Defense's Annual Report on Sexual Assault in the Military reported unwanted sexual contact prevalence rates of active duty service members for women as 8.4% and men as 1.5% during FY2021 (Department of Defense, [DOD], 2022). Even though these percentages highlight the pervasiveness of sexual assault and sexual harassment within the military and that MSA is a crime disproportionately experienced by women, research within this vein is lacking. Specifically, there is not enough literature on the topic to compare its prevalence and impact relative to sexual assault in the general population. Furthermore, it is reasonable to consider that current service members might be less likely to reveal their experiences using traditional research methods such as surveys or focus groups. Therefore, it is important to examine sexual assault and its impact within the general population to adequately frame the current study on military sexual assault.

Sexual assault victims (who may also refer to themselves as survivors) face lifelong effects after sexual assault. For example, body image issues are common among victims, as are issues with their sex lives (Bell et al., 2014). These adverse effects of sexual assaults can follow victims for the duration of their lives. Despite the relative abundance of studies to learn about sexual assault within the general population, research focusing on sexual assaults that occur among the military population is sparse.

Sexual assault in the military has made national headways due to the recent murder of U.S. Army soldier, Vanessa Guillén. Guillén disappeared on April 22, 2020, and her remains were found on June 30th (Diaz et al., 2020). While there is no official report of sexual harassment, Guillén confided in a few fellow soldiers and friends. Upon discovery of her remains, a hashtag went viral encouraging other military service members to share their stories of sexual assault or harassment that occurred within the military: #IamVanessaGuillen. The national attention from this hashtag sparked monumental change in the way the military handles reports of sexual misconduct and sexual harassment (Aguilera, 2021). The National Defense Authorization Act (NDAA), which in part aims to change the reporting policy in the military to encourage victims of sexual assault to make an official report, was passed by the Senate on December 15th, 2021 (Aguilera, 2021). In addition to requiring that formal complaints of sexual assault be investigated by an independent investigator, the passing of the NDAA ensures that, for the first time in military history, sexual harassment is classified as a crime (Aguilera, 2021). On December 27th, 2021, President Biden signed the NDAA into act, and it has since taken effect (The United States Government, 2021). Although such changes are welcome enhancements to current MSA policies and practices, it is crucial to expand on what little is known about MSA.

The current study collected and analyzed qualitative data from Twitter. By using this unique and innovative data source, we can uncover themes in military sexual assault that might have otherwise gone unnoticed, with hopes of suggesting policies that may help to reduce the occurrence of military sexual assault. To the researchers' knowledge, to date, this is the first study to use social media (specifically, tweets garnered from Twitter) to examine characteristics of military sexual assault. The goals of this paper are to determine common themes that exist among MSA victims and to suggest policy changes to improve the military's response to sexual assault.

Literature review

Due to the lack of available data on MSA experienced by males, the following review of research focuses predominantly on female experiences with MSA (Bell et al., 2014; Hankin et al., 1999; Mengeling et al., 2014; Skinner et al., 2000).

Military sexual assault (MSA) and its lasting effects on victims

The United States military consists of the following branches: Army, Navy, Marine Corps, Air Force, Coast Guard, National Guard, and Space Guard (U.S. Department of Defense, 2021). The military's culture is centered around patriarchy which values leadership, rank, solidarity, and being tough (Castro et al., 2015). Thus, masculinization is rampant within the military, which contributes to a culture in which sexual violence against women is normalized (Bell et al., 2014).

One of the major difficulties faced by MSA survivors is coming to terms with the fact that someone within their own ranks, either a peer or a leader, has victimized them. The military emphasizes the importance of unity and trust within units, as it is crucial for their effective functioning. The concept that one's life depends on the support and camaraderie of fellow service members, along with the accompanying feelings of solidarity and cohesion, is shattered in cases of MSA (Andresen et al., 2019). This institutional betrayal deeply undermines the very culture that all branches of the military strive diligently to create and uphold.

In the 2019 fiscal year, the military received almost 8,000 sexual assault reports that involved a service member, which was 3% higher than the previous fiscal year (DOD, 2020). More recently, in the 2021 fiscal year, DOD revealed an even higher number of sexual assault reports: 8,866. While not all of these occurred during a service member's military service, 6,236 reports from fiscal year 2019 did (DOD, 2020). This represents approximately 120 reports of military sexual assault (MSA) per week. It is important to note these are only *reported* cases and the actual rate of MSA is likely significantly higher. In fact, one study that examined the prevalence of MSA through self-administered surveys found that 55% of the female veteran sample were sexually harassed while in the military and 23% of the sample were sexually assaulted while in the military (Skinner et al., 2000). Similar studies yielded comparable results: 23% of a sample of female veterans reported that they were sexually assaulted while serving (Hankin et al., 1999). More recently, research found that 18% of a sample of active-duty servicewomen reported they were sexually assaulted while in the military (Mengeling et al., 2014).

Military sexual trauma (MST) is commonly referred to when discussing the various effects MSA can cause to an individual throughout their lifetime. One study found that a positive screening for MST doubled the likelihood of mental health care after the screening (Kimerling et al., 2008). Post-traumatic stress disorder (PTSD) has been linked to MSA (Campbell & Raja, 2005; Lucas et al., 2018). Campbell and Raja (2005) looked at secondary victimization and PTSD symptomatology and found a significant positive relationship between the two. However, PTSD is not the only mental illness linked to MST.

Mental health care is exceedingly important for victims of MSA. Of victims who met the criteria for depression in one study, 50% received recent mental health treatment (Hankin et al., 1999). Screening for MST at the Veterans Health Administration increases the likelihood of mental health treatment upon positive screening (Kimerling et al., 2008). This is important for a number of reasons. Proper access to mental health care can reduce suicidal ideation among MSA victims. In one study examining veterans with MST, 77% reported suicidal ideation during their lifetime (Monteith et al., 2019). Within the same sample, 75% reported their first suicide attempt after experiencing MST. In addition, a recent RAND study found trauma from sexual assault to be a significant predictor of both mental and physical health outcomes for men and women, with the most profound effects seen among women (Jaycox et al., 2023). The authors noted that women who experienced MSA self-reported higher rates of depression, anxiety, PTSD, and poor physical health than male MSA survivors, and posited that the reason for the disparity between the sexes is due to the rate of MSA being five times higher for women than men.

Depression is a common effect of sexual assault (Hankin et al., 1999). Within their study, Hankin et al. (1999) compared a sample of MSA victims to a sample of non-victims and found depression was far more common in MSA victims (60% vs. 33%, respectively). Another study found that 65% of their sample of servicewomen who were sexually assaulted in the military reported feeling depressed (Campbell & Raja, 2005). Women, who are the primary victims of sexual assault, often struggle to seek treatment when they are surrounded by men (Bell et al., 2014). According to Bell et al. (2014), 66% of women prefer a female medical staff member to perform the medical exam. However, due to the large portion of men in the military, victims of MSA are likely to encounter men during the process of reporting, which may contribute to the reluctance of victims to report the crime.

Reporting MSA

In the military, service members are presented with two different options for reporting sexual assault: restricted reports and unrestricted reports (U. S. Army SHARP, 2020). With both options, the first step in reporting requires that victims approach their assigned specialist to make a report. In the Army, where Vanessa Guillén served, this person is called the SHARP (Sexual Harassment/Assault Response & Prevention) specialist (U. S. Army SHARP, 2020). While a SHARP specialist is specific to the Army, each branch has their own similarly assigned specialists.

Restricted reports are intended for victims who wish to keep information about their case and report confidential. These reports are not intended for victims who seek prosecution and/or punishment for their perpetrator. Restricted reports represent an official accusation that an incident took place; however, they will not help a service member who wishes to transfer units. Unrestricted reports are just the opposite. The details of the case are known, the perpetrator can face punishment, and the service member is eligible for transfer if they wish (U. S. Army SHARP, 2020). Regardless of the type of report filed, many victims of MSA struggle with the notion of reporting, at all. The real prevalence of MSA is unknown due to reporting rates as low as 25% in one study (Mengeling et al., 2014) to as high as 59% in another (Campbell & Raja, 2005). More recently, research has revealed that the likelihood of officially reporting MSA increased with lower military rank (Mengeling et al., 2014).

With rates of non-reporting as high as 75%, some studies explored the various reasons why a victim may not report MSA (Mengeling et al., 2014). The same study found victims did not report due to not understanding the process of reporting, embarrassment, potential negative career effects, lack of response or action, lack of confidentiality, and self-blame. A common hurdle victims of sexual assault face is blame, whether internally or from individuals they disclose to (Ahrens et al., 2009; Ash et al., 2017; Kennedy & Prock, 2018). Another study reported fear of retaliation, from their command to fellow troops, as a reason for victims not to report MSA (Groves, 2013).

Campbell and Raja (2005) found MSA victims were met with a variety of responses upon attempting to report the incident officially. Regarding the reporting process itself, 70% were encouraged not to report, 65% had no one willing to take the report, and 70% were told that their case was not significant enough to report (Campbell & Raja, 2005). Of those who reported officially, 78% were asked if they resisted their perpetrator, 67% were asked if they were using drugs or alcohol at the time of the assault, and 83% were made to feel reluctant to find additional help (Campbell & Raja, 2005). Emotionally speaking, 65% of MSA victims felt guilt or blame, 70% felt nervous or anxious, and 70% felt distrust toward others (Campbell & Raja, 2005).

Initially, a victim of MSA may fear disbelief or dismissal when considering whether to report the incident(s) (Ahrens, 2006). This fear is very common and is one of the several leading reasons why victims choose not to report (Bell et al., 2014). A subsequent consequence of reporting sexual assault in the military is the potential for repercussions (Human Rights Watch, 2015). These repercussions can include threats of violence, social retaliation, unfair work assignments, career advancement loss, disciplinary action, or administrative or involuntary discharge (Human Rights Watch, 2015). There are also several professional retaliations including: altered performance evaluations, missed promotions, skipped training opportunities, lost awards and privileges, potential demotion, and altered job duties.

MSA is often perpetrated by one's superior or peer within the military (Campbell & Raja, 2005; Mengeling et al., 2014). One study found that 82% of sexually assaulted servicewomen were sexually assaulted by a supervisor or peer also in the military during active duty (Campbell & Raja, 2005). Further, another study found similar rates of MSA committed by fellow military personnel (80%) (Mengeling et al., 2014). As with sexual assaults in the general population, military sexual assaults often have lasting traumatic effects on victims.

Victims of MSA often quickly find available resources to be inadequate (Groves, 2013). While some military bases claim to offer resources for MSA victims, this is not always true. These programs may only exist when discussed, yet the bases may not have the resources they claim to. If the resources do exist, the programs are not always effective for MSA victims. Zero tolerance policies exist within every branch of the military with regards to sexual assault; however, these policies are not actually applied in every MSA case. Like other special populations (e.g., college students), the military has shifted their focus and resources toward the prevention of sexual assault.

Prevention

Prevention strategies and policies are of utmost importance to protect members of the military from falling victim to sexual assault (Kimerling, 2017). Programs like SHARP serve to reduce the rates of MSA and aid victims (U. S. Army SHARP, 2020). Programs to assist victims need improvement as well in order to best serve victims. Kimerling (2017) drew attention to the significance of increased access to mental health treatment for victims of MSA. Easy access to this kind of treatment has the potential to save the lives of struggling victims (Kimerling, 2017).

Military leadership

Leadership serves as a key factor within the military, as quality leadership has the ability to empower victims to report and even prevent instances of MSA (Sadler et al., 2017). Politics play a large role within this leadership, as it can enhance the masculinization of the military (Hutchison, 2013). Characteristics and qualities commonly associated with military leaders tend to be more masculine, which supports the hierarchy of the military. The military is based on rank, which is why it relies on leadership so heavily.

Some leadership training material, such as the training material for the Air Force, does not cover social influence within the military (Hutchison, 2013). Without being properly trained on social influence, leaders are not always aware of the impact their behavior may have on their subordinates. Leadership can cause a blur between social influence and control. This means that actions that are meant to influence subordinates to perform their job, are actually means to control those individuals. This can lead to some senior leaders being able to label their potentially abusive behavior as "high standards" (Hutchison, 2013). Several negative leader behaviors like this were reported in one study, which classify such behavior as "toxic leadership" according to the Center for Army Leadership (Sadler et al., 2017).

Military leaders with more of the stereotypical masculine behaviors were both more likely to commit MSA and promote an environment conducive to MSA (Sadler et al., 2017). Thus, military leaders play a crucial role in servicewomen's likelihood of MSA victimization. Beyond the impact of military leaders' behaviors on MSA, leaders have been shown to be the primary offender in some cases. Approximately 66% of MSA was committed by someone in a higher rank than the victim and 50% were committed by the victim's supervisor in a recent study (Sadler et al., 2017). Considering that MSA is often perpetuated by leaders and other military members, it is imperative that researchers use novel approaches to ascertain the extent to which MSA occurs and its characteristics, such as social media.

Hashtag movements and MSA

The social media platform, Twitter, is where the hashtag, #IAmVanessaGuillen has gained the most momentum. On Twitter, users can share their stories candidly in a tweet and add the hashtag, #IamVanessaGuillen, to the end of it in order to spread awareness. By sharing their victimizations on social media, victims have a sense of anonymity that they would not have in-person (Sills et al., 2016). Online forums allow a safe space for victims to share their stories, receive support, and heal (Bogen et al., 2019; Fawcett & Shrestha, 2016; Littleton, 2010). This allows a unique opportunity for researchers to learn more about MSA by analyzing the tweets made (voluntarily) by victims.

The hashtag, #IAmVanessaGuillen was created to honor Vanessa Guillén and to spread awareness about sexual assault in the military and its prevalence. While this is the first hashtag of its kind for military sexual assault, there have been previous social media movements regarding sexual assault. This new movement is similar to the #MeToo movement that arose during the Harvey Weinstein allegations. The #MeToo hashtag became very popular with victims sharing their stories of sexual assault. This movement also lead to the #WhyIDidntReport movement. While similar, the #WhyIDidntReport movement focused specifically on those who did not report their victimizations.

Current study

The social media forum, Twitter, allows for a unique perspective for researchers to investigate qualitative data while avoiding personal emotional harm. Users are able to post tweets using the hashtag on their own. This eliminates the need to interact with victims and risk potential emotional trauma by discussing MSA that they might have attempted to repress. Instead, the victims are free to share what details they are comfortable with sharing. To the best of the researchers' knowledge, this is the first study to utilize Twitter data to examine MSA. Thus, the purpose of this research was to seize this unique opportunity for uncharted research into military sexual assault to discover common themes among the tweets and make suggestions to improve policies and programs focusing on MSA.

This study attempted to answer the following research questions:

(1) What common themes are present among tweets involving military sexual assault?
(2) What policy implications can be inferred from tweets that would improve how MSA is approached within the military?

Methodology

The purpose of the current study was to uncover common themes in MSA victims' disclosures of the incidents on Twitter. Specifically, this study examined tweets with the hashtag, #IamVanessaGuillen to better understand MSA and to formulate policy implications surrounding the reporting and handling of MSA incidents.

Data source

The data from which the research was drawn stems from Twitter. Twitter is a social media platform that enables users to create tweets of 280 characters or less (Ash et al., 2017). Twitter is used frequently among young adults; at least 36% of adults aged 18–29 in America use Twitter (Greenwood et al., 2016; Smith & Anderson, 2018). Despite the seemingly contradictory approach of using Twitter to study a sensitive topic such as MSA, research has suggested there may be an, "online disinhibition effect" whereby people reveal things that they would not otherwise reveal through face-to-face interactions (Suler, 2005). Stated differently, Twitter allows MSA victims the ability to seek social support at the time of their own choosing through an online platform without the stigma they would likely encounter in person. Additionally, users who shared their stories on Twitter were supporting a fellow officer (i.e., Vanessa Guillén) by telling their own stories. This also creates an incentive for others to speak out on their own experiences as well as bring global awareness to MSA by amplifying the voices of marginalized groups, including survivors of MSA. Using Twitter as a data source allows researchers to examine cases of MSA that may never have been officially reported, as victims are free to disclose any information they feel comfortable sharing. Twitter users are able to create a username of their choosing as well as the name that appears with their account, so users can make their accounts to be unidentifiable, adding a sense of anonymity. Additionally, users are able to keep their account set to private if they choose, and these tweets would not be included in this analysis as they are not publicly available. This creates a unique opportunity for research as this data source helps to avoid any potential harm and revictimization associated with other methods (e.g., surveys, interviews) because victims were not asked specific questions. Instead, they share what information they want at their own discretion. Prior research highlights the use of Twitter as a data source in providing "micro-narratives" of victimizations experienced by users, as the data offers a small story of each victim, allowing them to be captured and included in research (Storer et al., 2018). This allows for a distinct opportunity to conduct research and contribute to what little is known about instances of MSA.

Data collection

Data was initially observed using Twitter's Advanced Search option. For this search, tweets that contained the hashtag #IamVanessaGuillen were collected for analysis. Any retweets that also used the hashtag were excluded from the study while the original tweets were retained for analysis. A specific time frame was also used for data collection. To ensure the tweets are related to the Vanessa Guillén case, only the tweets using the hashtag #IamVanessaGuillen that were posted within the first week after her remains were discovered (June 30, 2020-July 7, 2020) were included in the study. This time frame is important for the study because the first week after Guillén's remains were discovered was when the hashtag gained national momentum, so it can be inferred that the majority of tweets relevant to this research were captured within that time frame.

While all tweets that are posted within the time frame and using the hashtag #IamVanessaGuillen were collected, only relevant tweets were analyzed in the study. In order to be analyzed in the study, a tweet needed to specify a military sexual assault that was perpetrated against the Twitter user who posted the tweet. Therefore, duplicates and retweets were not included in the study. Indirect experiences, or an experience shared by someone that was not the original victim, were also not included in the study. While secondary victimization is important, the current study focuses on the perspective of victims, thus, indirect experiences were excluded. Tweets that were advertisements or news stories about the hashtag or Vanessa Guillén's case were excluded. Finally, tweets that did not mention the military were excluded from the study. The inclusion of tweets only pertaining to military sexual assault ensure the findings are representative of military populations.

The software program, "Twitterscraper" was employed to extract all the tweets and threads that contained the hashtag #IamVanessaGuillen from June 30, 2020 to July 7, 2020. Twitter's Advanced Search option was an initial observation, and Twitterscraper was used to collect the data that we observed in the initial search. Twitterscraper is a free program that can be configured to capture the entire tweet, including the username, time and date, tweet, hashtags used, attachments, etc. Extracted tweets were compiled into an excel document for analysis.

The initial search yielded 3,182 tweets. Two researchers performed an initial read-through of the tweets and excluded news stories, tweets that did not disclose a military victimization, tweets not in English, and tweets that were simply supporting Vanessa Guillén but not instances of the Twitter user's experiences as an MSA victim. There were several tweets ($n = 25$) that disclosed a military sexual assault victimization from an alternative perspective. Those tweets were not included in the analysis because they were indirect experiences (e.g., a friend or family member was victimized). Additionally, there were a large number of tweets ($n = 116$) that only used the hashtag, IAmVanessaGuillen, and nothing else. Those tweets were not included in the analysis, yet the researchers felt this was important to note because it is plausible that those individuals might have been victims of MSA who did not wish to disclose details of their victimization. Therefore, a total of 293 tweets were included in this study.

Analytic technique

This qualitative exploratory study used a thematic analysis to determine common themes among the tweets (Lune & Berg, 2016). The tweets were read in several phases to determine whether they met the standard for inclusion in the study, to develop common themes, and to code the tweets with corresponding themes.

Qualitative data (i.e., tweets) was examined in stages through an exploratory review. In the first stage, two researchers read through each tweet independently and omitted tweets that were not pertinent to the study (e.g., tweets that described incidents that happened to someone other than the Twitter user, news stories, retweets). The researchers then met to discuss and resolve discrepancies. A final sample of tweets ($n = 293$) was agreed on by the research team. After the initial read-through, each researcher generated a list of predominant themes that emerged from the tweets, which were then discussed within a peer debriefing (Lee et al., 2014). The initial list of themes included offender gender, rank of victim and offender, branch of military, circumstances of event (sexual assault, sexual harassment, rape, or physical assault), reporting (i.e., whether the victim disclosed they made an official report or not), and MST. Upon the generation of themes, a second read-through took place to establish more specific patterns and themes within each of the initial themes. Subsequently, each tweet was coded with any potential matching theme. Researchers discussed discrepancies to account for inter-rater reliability and ensure accuracy. Finally, a third read-through was completed where the researchers checked for any mistakes or missed themes. Researchers were then able to establish more specific patterns and themes within each of the general themes; therefore, the following themes were added: *negative leadership response*, *normative behavior*, and *offender in a higher rank than victim*.

After the coding phase was completed, the researchers investigated the themes further and determined how frequently each theme was discussed and potential policy implications for improvement.

Results

Throughout data analysis, five common themes emerged from the data: offender rank higher than the victim, leadership issues, victim ridiculed, effects of MSA, and normative behavior.

Table 1 above highlights the descriptive results for various MSA characteristics. While this table provides a basic understanding of these tweets, it is important to acknowledge that this is a qualitative study and this data may not be fully generalizable to the entire MSA population. When tweets did mention their branch of the military, this was coded and revealed that most were in the Navy ($n = 28$, or 10% of tweets) or Army ($n = 23$, or 7.8% of tweets). The sex of the victim was not assumed based on the Twitter username, but was only coded when stated. Coding found that of the 27 cases where sex was stated, 93% of victims were female and 7% were male. The sex of the offender was more frequently reported at 103 cases and were 98% male and 2% female. Finally, the circumstances of the assault were divided into four categories with sexual harassment occurring most frequently ($n = 75$, 26%), followed by sexual assault ($n = 71$, 24%). Within each category, only tweets that specifically

Table 1. MSA characteristics ($n = 293$).

Branch of Military			Number of Cases
	Army		23
	Navy		28
	Marine Corps		5
	Air Force		12
	National Guard		1
Sex			
	Sex of Victim	Male	2
		Female	25
	Sex of Offender	Male	101
		Female	2
Circumstances of the Incident			
	Sexual Harassment		75
	Sexual Assault		71
	Rape		35
	Physical Attack		1

*Data is not mutually exclusive.

mentioned each category were included. We identified five themes across the data, including the offender having a higher rank than the victim, leadership issues, the victim being ridiculed, effects of MSA, and normative behavior. These themes are discussed below.

Offender rank higher than victim

The most common theme evident throughout the tweets examined was that the offender was of a higher rank than the victim. This means that the offender was someone who the victim reported to, took orders from, and/or someone whom the victim may have seen on a daily basis. It is important to remember that the number of tweets that fall into this theme include only those tweets that specifically mentioned this situation. This occurrence may actually be more common than represented in this study.

Superior ranking military members who sexually assaulted lower-ranked service members put the victims in a very uncomfortable situation when it comes to potentially reporting the assault. An example of a tweet illustrating this is below.

> #IamVanessaGuillen I was raped in my barracks room as a private by a Sgt. I was so afraid of reporting it because I left my door unlocked which was a security violation. I was afraid of being punished. I carry guilt because Idk who else he raped because I didn't come forward.

Other victims expressed their opinions that the military is protecting higher ranking military officers who are sexually assaulting their subordinates.

> The MILITARY PROTECTS E8 and E9 males who abuse their power. I told my E8 no to all of his sexual advances and I lost my tour. Came back to my @NationalGuard unit and my leadership believed my [harasser] over me. Lost everything & that predator is still at large #IAMVANESSAGUILLEN.

In the Army, victims of MSA are supposed to report the assault to a SHARP specialist, if they choose to report. In one case, the Twitter user described an assault committed by his unit's SHARP specialist.

> I didn't want to report my abuser because he was another male and I was embarrassed. He said he was sure I was gay because I smiled at him a lot.
> He was my army unit's Sexual Harassment/Assault Response and Prevention Supervisor.
> #IAMVANESSAGUILLEN.

Other Twitter users expressed that their situations had turned dangerous when their perpetrators began threatening them. In the case of tweets like the following, the perpetrator who threatened the victim was the victim's superior.

> #IAMVANESSAGUILLEN I was sexually assaulted by my superior while I was completely unconscious, so unconscious I couldn't remove the tampon forced inside of me for [three] days. The next day he told me it would ruin MY career to report it. I had been at the command for 4 months.

Others wrote about their superior, who was also their attacker, getting away with it even after the victim reported the crime.

> 2012 at a new duty station, when a Sgt thought he could "make my day better." The judge and jury apologized to me personally. He was found not guilty for lack of physical evidence because I got away. 2 years to the day later he attacked a 14 year old girl. #IAMVANESSAGUILLEN.

> I was 19. He was a Superior. I was called a liar because "he's been in the military for a long time, and on one has ever said anything like this about him before." Then he did it again. And they moved him to another unit.
> #IAMVANESSAGUILLEN

Within this theme, victims shared their stories of being victimized by their superiors. The identity of their perpetrator may have affected the victim's choice on reporting MSA. Cases like the examples above lead victims to have a sense of distrust in their leadership.

Leadership issues

Another theme uncovered was how twitter users expressed problems they encountered with their non-offender leadership while attempting to or reporting MSA. In these cases, the victims' leader failed to help the victim, or in some cases, even made the situation worse for the victim. Again, it is important to note that this only includes the tweets that specifically mentioned encountering issues with their leadership which may not represent all the incidents.

Victims who did report MSA to their leader were often met with rejection and an unwillingness to move the report up the chain of command.

> #IAMVANESSAGUILLEN I was a soldier in HHC 197th Infantry Brigade Mechanized Separate. In the fall of 84 while on CQ I was assaulted by 2 men. I reported the assault to my CO and was told to "drop it since I didn't see [their] face" he didn't want the attention on his unit.

One tweet mentioned that their leader knew about the MSA, yet chose not to formally respond to it.

> #iamvanessaguillen #wearevanessaguillen One of my former NCOs recently apologized to me because he witnessed the first time I was sexually assaulted and he never made a statement. It hurts to stand alone then find out your leadership knew all along.

Other users took to Twitter to express their feelings that their leaders were valued more than the victim.

> And anxiety. I'm constantly looking around and I'm always alert. #FortHood taught me a lot, however the biggest thing I was taught was that integrity only matters when it's convenient to the higher ranks. #IAMVANESSAGUILLEN #IAMNICOLEEDWARDS #IAMSTRONG.

One case mentioned superiors who were harassing the victim themselves, which caused issues for the victim when trying to report. The victim's leader was directly preventing them from completing their job.

> In Dec '94, less than 11 mos after reporting to my 1st command, a US Navy ship in HI, my LPO (Leading Petty Officer) & EDO (Engineer Duty Officer) told me if I wanted my JQR (Job Qualification Requirement) signed, I had to show them my breast or be punished.

In some cases, like the examples above illustrate, military leadership played a role in MSA. While some participated in the MSA, others failed the victims in other ways. They may have failed to move the victim's report further up the chain of command, neglected to take a report from the victim, ridiculed the victim, or even discouraged the victim from making a report.

Victim ridiculed

In this study, several Twitter users told their stories of being ridiculed after reporting MSA. For the purpose of this analysis, victims being ridiculed could include: victim was blamed, made fun of, and/or humiliated due to being assaulted. This may have happened at the hands of leaders or peers but resulted in the victim feeling fault for the MSA. This theme only included tweets that specifically mentioned being ridiculed as a result of being a victim of MSA.

Some Twitter users explained that their units found out about the MSA and the victim was ridiculed by the entire unit. When the victims' units found out about the MSA, the victims faced even further victimization at the hands of their fellow service members.

> I'm [victim's name] and #IAMVANESSAGUILLEN the real secret reason why I got out of the military is because for the last year and a half I was harassed by my whole company because I "snitched" on the "great" [soldier] that sexually assaulted me.

> I decided not to submit a formal complaint because the victim's advocate was never in their office. I just wanted it to go away. Then those men started circulating my picture. Saying I was a coward for not reporting it. Constant bullying for not reporting. #IAMVANESSAGUILLEN.

Victims of MSA also expressed their displeasure with the investigative process of reporting. During the investigation, the victims felt re-victimized due to the investigation being made public to their units.

> I was assaulted at a port call. He got off with nothing, I faced an investigation and almost lost my job because he was enlisted and I was an officer. The organization I trusted for support betrayed me and my depression spiraled out of control. #IAMVANESSAGUILLEN.

> Oh did I mention the SHARP rep basically told the entire unit. Everyone knew. Nothing happened to the chaplain even though witnesses came forth. He was allowed to make MAJ and transferred after 2 years. He's still a chaplain. #IAMVANESSAGUILLEN.

MSA victims also shared their experiences with having their sexual histories shared in response to them reporting.

> #IAMVANESSAGUILLEN
> I was [a part] of a fire department program involving minors. My sexual history was explicitly shared with over 130 fellow cadets, and my leadership told me it was a personal problem and declined to do anything.

Being the victim of MSA can be incredibly traumatizing to victims. Aside from the potential physical harm to the victim, there were likely additional effects that may result after the MSA, such as military sexual trauma.

Effects of MSA

The theme effects of MSA refers to the potential lifelong effects that may impact a victim for the rest of their life. Only the cases that specifically mentioned MST, PTSD as a result of MSA, or being traumatized were coded as effects of MSA.

Several Twitter users within this study expressed a similar message: the perpetrator received a promotion, yet the victim got MST.

> He got promoted, all I got was PTSD #IAmVanessaGuillen
> I was 20 years old, serving in the US Navy. My Chief was a physical therapy technician, he offered treatment [for] an injury. He sexually assaulted me. I reported it and had my career threatened. He got promoted. I am the face of military sexual trauma. #IAMVANESSAGUILLEN

As previously mentioned, victims may deal with adverse effects of their assault for years, if not their entire lives. Some users expressed how common this is among MSA victims.

> I was [an] E3 when I was raped by another service member while being stationed overseas. I have a lifetime of trauma while he is still in the Army. This happens more than you know. #IamVanessaGuillen #JusticeForVanessaGuillen

Another Twitter user explained having PTSD as a result of MSA and how the leadership's response to a previous MSA influenced their decision to report.

> They talked down on the last person who reported, and I was new and didn't want anyone to hate me. I now have service connected PTSD. #IAMVANESSAGUILLEN

MSA affects victims in many different ways. As victims in this study expressed, the way the military (e.g., leadership, fellow service members, etc.) responded to MSA affected how the victim felt.

Normative behavior

In some cases, victims are met with normative behaviors upon reporting MSA. These behaviors attempt to normalize sexual assault. This theme only includes tweets that mentioned specific behaviors deemed to be normative.

> #IAMVANESSAGUILLEN
> I had a female sergeant tell me, "as a pretty girl in the military you're just gonna have to get used to how the guys will treat you."
> Why do we have to normalize being sexualized? Just because it's a "man's military." Things need to change.

With the military being male-dominated, women are more likely to be viewed as targets upon entry. Some were actually told that their gender will subject them to harassment, as if that behavior is normal.

> I was told I would never be a part of the good ol boys club. Ended up getting molested by one of the good ol boys and laughed at by [the] commander when I took him to court. He kept his job and they only gave him hard labor for 2 months and my reputation was over. @#IAMVANESSAGUILLEN

While some normative behaviors were aimed at women's presence in a male-dominated field, other normative behavior focuses on the men's reactions to women being present.

> I was told that it's just what men do by my superiors #IAMVANESSAGUILLEN

Additionally, due to the small portion of women in the military, some women felt blamed for how the men react to their roles within the military.

> #IamVanessaGuillen when I got to my first duty station I was the only female in replacement. The NCOs told me I was [going to] be trouble. Like it was my fault

Normative behaviors most likely occur more than what is present within this analysis.

Discussion

The purpose of this study was to examine MSA Twitter data to uncover common themes of disclosure, military branch, and social media use among MSA victims. Specifically, two research questions guided this research: 1) What common themes are present among tweets involving military sexual assault? and 2) What policy implications can be made to improve the current procedures for reporting sexual assault within the military? To accomplish these goals, this study used self-report data from Twitter to discover common themes among military sexual assault victims. By utilizing Twitter as a data source, this study fills a gap in previous research on MSA victimization whereby victims self-disclosed reported or unreported MSA. This study also contributes to literature by highlighting the impact military leadership has on MSA and how often MSA is committed by a higher-ranking service member.

Limitations

While using self-report data from social media has its advantages, this study also has limitations. One key limitation evident in this study is the inability to dictate what information Twitter users share in their tweets. There is no way to clarify what each user meant, and no follow-up questions were asked of Twitter users who used the IamVanessaGuillen hashtag. Thus, researchers were limited to the words in the tweet when classifying tweets into themes. Further, tweets are limited to 280 characters, which limits the content for analysis. This limited the analysis due to a lack of uniform information in every tweet. Another limitation of the present study is that demographic information (e.g., Twitter user's gender, race, ethnicity, age) was not collected unless they were explicitly stated in the user's tweet. For example, unless a Twitter user specified their gender in the tweet, no information could be collected on the victim's gender. Very few tweets disclosed the victim's sex ($n = 27$, or 9.2%; of those, 93% were female). Additionally, most Twitter users did not disclose which branch of the military the MSA occurred in often. Only about one quarter of the tweets shared what branch the victimization happened in ($n = 69$, or 23.5%).

Another limitation in using Twitter data to examine themes among MSA victims is the possible lack of generalization to the entire MSA victim population. In addition, Twitter users have the option to restrict their tweets so that only their followers can view them. As a result, the current research was unable to capture tweets from users whose accounts are private. The tweets examined in this study only include those who felt comfortable sharing their experience publicly. As such, these tweets may not be representative of all MSA victims.

This research uncovered themes that were largely linked with leadership and consistent with prior research (Cornelius & Monk-Turner, 2019; Hutchison, 2013; Sadler et al., 2017). Victims shared stories of their leaders sexually assaulting them, hindering the reporting process, or participating in normative behavior. The most common theme present throughout the tweets was an issue with leadership. This shows that there is something wrong in the way leaders are behaving in the military and/or the culture promoted by leaders, with regard to MSA.

Theoretical considerations

The results of this study may partially be explained by social dominance theory (Sidanius & Pratto, 2001). This theory posits that group dynamics of power and control influence individuals' actions (Sidanius & Pratto, 2001). Group inequalities create environments that breed criminal behavior and justifications for incorrect actions. Within military populations, these group dynamics are evident as considering the military's focus on leadership and rank, beliefs and morals can become blurred due to group dynamics. The military values rank and leadership above all else; so high-ranking service members are seemingly valued more than lower-ranked service members. Thus, when rank is considered within the framework of MSA, victims face a social power that is bigger than they are.

Social dominance theory is also applicable to the results as many victims of MSA in this study felt bound by their rank and powerless against their offenders (Sidanius & Pratto, 2001). The most common theme identified in this study was the offender held a rank higher than the victim's, which can lead to a power differential making the MSA more complex. Additionally, many victims faced issues with leadership as a result of the MSA. These results display the unhealthy focus the military has on rank and leadership, especially in situations such as MSA. Victims felt that they could not report to their leaders because the offender was in a higher rank than they were. Essentially, the military's ranking system can be compared to socioeconomic status in some civilian studies of sexual assault, whereby victims have more difficulty reporting crimes against offenders in higher social classes than the victims. Victims were struggling to report someone in a higher social class than they were. As evidenced by some of the tweets in this analysis, some of these offenders were the leaders that the victims were supposed to trust. In one case, the offender was even the SHARP specialist. The military has set procedures for how a service member should report MSA, though oftentimes it is not feasible. The victim cannot be expected to report MSA to their leader or superior officer if that superior officer is the one who sexually assaulted the victim.

In a similar vein, we found support for DeKeseredy's male peer support theory within the findings of the current study. This theory suggests that male friendships may promote an environment conducive to sexual harassment or assault (DeKeseredy, 1988; DeKeseredy & Schwartz, 2013). Within the military population, this may occur when male-dominated groups bond together and support each other, which may lead to the minimization of female service members. Specifically, our study found male service members often ridiculed the victim for being assaulted and did not report crimes they witnessed. An environment of male peer support, as DeKeseredy argues, would promote these types of normative behaviors (DeKeseredy, 1988; DeKeseredy & Schwartz, 2013). Without proper leadership to combat this negative peer support, the military environment will continue to be conducive to MSA.

Reasons why victims in this study chose not to report the MSA may be explained by the Intimate Partner Violence Stigmatization model (Overstreet & Quinn, 2013). Within this model, three main constructs of victims' help-seeking behaviors are presented. These constructs include cultural stigma, anticipated stigma, and stigma internalization (Overstreet & Quinn, 2013). Though these constructs were intended to explain help-seeking behaviors of IPV victims, they can also be applied to victims of MSA. Cultural stigma represents the unfavorable cultural beliefs held by society, which is easily applied within military populations. Military culture surrounds rank, honor, and leadership, so reporting one's leader for such a heinous act goes against cultural beliefs. Anticipated stigma refers to the reactions a victim anticipates receiving upon disclosure. Within military populations, disclosing MSA victimization may be construed as weak, which can lead victims to believe they will not be taken seriously. Stigma internalization encompasses the victims' personal negative beliefs. Service members may have preconceived notions of how cases of MSA are handled, which may deter them from reporting.

Additional results can be explained through implicit leadership theory (Verlage et al., 2012). This theory proposes individuals have implicit expectations of how leaders should behave, which may affect the way they respond to leaders' demands. Leaders in the military are expected to run their units with honor and integrity, though this is not always what happens. As shown in this analysis, some leaders are not meeting these expectations. Additionally, victims of MSA may have trusted their superiors due to their implicit expectations, only for the trust to be broken. Conversely, implicit leadership theory proposes that subordinates' observations of their superiors influence their perceptions of whether superiors are true leaders or not. This may explain why many victims of MSA in this study chose not to report the incident. It is plausible to consider MSA victims would only be willing to report the incident if they perceive their leader(s) to be competent to respond to the disclosure appropriately.

Policy implications

The results of this analysis highlight the potential ineffectiveness of programs such as SHARP. While these programs were put in place to ensure MSA cases were handled correctly, this is not what is always happening. Specialists put in charge within these programs are sometimes ill-equipped to lead or represent such programs. Our study highlighted cases where the SHARP supervisor was the perpetrator, making it all the more hard for the victim to seek support. While having the programs in place is important, the more crucial piece is ensuring leaders take these programs seriously. The training cannot serve its purpose if the leaders are not engaged in preventing MSA victimization. In a similar vein, bystander intervention training should be required of all military personnel. Mujal et al. 2021) found strong empirical support for bystander interventions in reducing rape myths and increasing engagement to lessen sexual assaults. Such training is especially important in all military branches to ensure their high emphasis on camaraderie is ensured within all aspects of military service.

Further, there are many programmatic and policy improvements needed within the military and among military leaders. Robust leadership training that has been validated is critical in order to reduce negative responses from superior officers that victims in this study faced. This training should focus on the potential impact that leaders' responses have on MSA victims' decision to report. A recent study found victims of sexual harassment or gender discrimination who received a positive response from their superiors when reporting experienced less emotional distress than victims whose reports were negatively received (Daneil et al., 2019). This in turn increased victims' intentions of remaining in the military. Additionally, leadership training could help weed out any service members that are not well-fit to be leaders. The improvements should also apply to cultural issues within the military; therefore, leaders should foster a climate of true equality whereby violent acts such as MSA are not tolerated. In this regard, both bystanders and victims would be empowered to report and feel confident in the process and outcomes after reporting, and potential offenders would be deterred from committing the act.

As described earlier, the military has a different reporting process for sexual assault than civilian cases. Restricted reporting offers more privacy to the victim, however it prevents the offender from facing punishment. Unrestricted reporting, on the other hand, is public so that the offender can face punishment. The current reporting process for MSA in the military is not effective. Instead of two routes for reporting, one method should be implemented. The victims' privacy should be protected, but the offender should still face punishment for the crime they committed. Having a reporting method where the offender is not held accountable does little to encourage reporting.

It is essential that victims of MSA are provided adequate resources for their mental, physical, and emotional health. As previously mentioned, access to mental health resources significantly helps victims of sexual assault (Kimerling, 2017). Thus, it is imperative that military officials work to make resources more readily available to victims of MSA. As well, the resources need to be effective for the victims, meaning the resources are actually available to the victims and staffed with trained professionals.

Conclusion

With the results of this analysis, we have a better understanding of what is not working with the military's response to MSA. The candid responses by victims of MSA in this study showed they felt failed by their leadership and fellow service members. Victims expressed that current procedures in place do not work. Programs such as SHARP, in the Army, are not always useful when SHARP specialists are also sexually assaulting service members. While this is not always the case, other Twitter users expressed their distrust in these programs after their victimizations were shared with their units.

By utilizing Twitter as the data source for this analysis, we add self-report data to research where previous literature has largely relied solely on reported cases of MSA. This allowed for research about MSA victims who did not report to be included in this study. Collecting data for this analysis from Twitter, a publicly based social media platform, ensured that victims of MSA were not subjected to potential trauma when discussing a traumatic event that other methods may have caused (e.g., interviews, surveys). Twitter users offered a perspective that has not yet been studied within military sexual assault, to the best of the researchers' knowledge. Finally, this unique data source allowed researchers to make suggestions for policies to prevent and better respond to MSA.

While the results from this study are largely similar to the results previously obtained from survey and interview research on sexual assault, using Twitter as the data source offers some unique contributions to sexual assault research. First, using social media to disclose incidents of MSA empowers victims to control the narrative surrounding the issues they feel need to be addressed within the military, something that otherwise might be lacking within results from surveys, interviews, and other methods of MSA data collection. Victims may also feel less isolated and have a greater level of support by seeing countless disclosures of MSA on Twitter. Such disclosures and the associated support of other victims may offer victims a therapeutic benefit and may encourage more victims to report their own victimizations. Additionally, social media has a global audience; therefore, sensitive topics such as sexual assault are brought to light for all to see and learn from. In this way, victims of MSA can gain allies from people who themselves were not victimized. As an example, the #MeToo hashtag was used on Twitter more than 19 million times (55,319 times per day, on average) between October of 2017 and September of 2018, illustrating the immense reach of social media (Pew Research Center, 2018). Furthermore, recent research has found that victims of workplace sexual assault were more likely to be believed and the perpetrators were more likely to be held accountable as a result of the #MeToo movement, an impact that survey research has yet to yield (Pew Research Center, 2022). For all of these reasons, sexual assault researchers may wish to consider the inclusion of social media to collect data as doing so may offer both healing benefits for the victims and global illumination of the pervasiveness of MSA and its effects on victims.

Based on the results of this study, future research should focus on the effect military leadership has on MSA victimization disclosure. In subsequent studies, researchers should consider conducting follow-up interviews or surveys with social media users to ask guided questions regarding their disclosures, interviews with former military service members about MSA, or evaluations on the effectiveness of military leadership. Additionally, this study yielded 116 tweets that exclusively used the hashtag #IamVanessaGuillen with no other content. These tweets might represent Twitter users who felt uncomfortable sharing their victimization stories, yet Guillén's case resonated with them. Using the hashtag alone may have been their way of saying they were also a victim of MSA without fully disclosing this. Future studies should explore the reasons behind this. With further research, programs, and policies, the military can improve its response to MSA victims so that soldiers do not succumb to the same fate as Vanessa Guillén.

Acknowledgments

The authors wish to thank Drs. Sarah Hupp-Williamson and Dave Ayers for their helpful guidance throughout the entirety of this project.

Disclosure statement

No potential conflict of interest was reported by the author(s).

ORCID

Emily K. Meinert http://orcid.org/0000-0002-9882-1995
Ericka A. Wentz http://orcid.org/0000-0001-9502-634X

References

Aguilera, J. (2021, December 30). Vanessa Guillen's death transforms sexual assault reporting. *Time*. https://time.com/6129740/vanessa-guillen-sexual-misconduct-military/?fbclid=IwAR3dlHuqU5B15ayOoHYPFwyEH1JSFdZL4nxZCFx3p2YFPaCw0PbfwAOZyEA

Ahrens, C. E. (2006). Being silenced: The impact of negative social reactions on the disclosure of rape. *American Journal of Community Psychology*, *38*(3–4), 31–34. https://doi.org/10.1007/s10464-006-9069-9

Ahrens, C. E., Cabral, G., & Abeling, S. (2009). Healing or hurtful: Sexual assault survivors' interpretations of social reactions from support providers. *Psychology of Women Quarterly*, *33*(1), 81–94. https://doi.org/10.1111/j.1471-6402.200801476.x

Andresen, F. J., Monteith, L. L., Kugler, J., Cruz, R. A., & Blais, R. K. (2019). Institutional betrayal following military sexual trauma is associated with more severe depression and specific posttraumatic stress disorder symptom clusters. *Journal of Clinical Psychology*, *75*(7), 1305–1319. https://doi.org/10.1002/jclp.22773

Ash, E., Sanderson, J., Kumanyika, C., & Gramlich, K. (2017). "Just goes to show how these hoes try to tear men down": Investigating twitter and cultural conversations on athletic ability, race, and sexual assault. *Journal of Sports Media*, *12*(1), 65–87. https://doi.org/10.1353/jsm.2017.0003

Bell, M. E., Turchik, J. A., & Karpenko, J. A. (2014). Impact of gender on reactions to military sexual assault and harassment. *Health & Social Work*, *39*(1), 25–33. https://doi.org/10.1093/hsw/hlu004

Bogen, K. W., Bleiweiss, K., & Orchowski, L. M. (2019). Sexual violence is #notokay: Social reactions to disclosures of sexual victimization on Twitter. *Psychology of Violence*, *9*(1), 127–137. https://doi.org/10.1037/vio0000192

Campbell, R., & Raja, S. (2005). The sexual assault and secondary victimization of female veterans: Help-seeking experiences with military and civilian social systems. *Psychology of Women Quarterly*, *29*(1), 97–106. https://doi.org/10.1111/j.1471-6402.2005.00171.x

Castro, C. A., Kintzle, S., Schuyler, A. C., Lucas, C. L., & Warner, C. H. (2015). Sexual assault in the military. *Current Psychiatry Reports*, *17*(7), 1–13. https://doi.org/10.1007/s11920-015-0596-7

Cornelius, C., & Monk-Turner, E. (2019). I'll trade you skittles for a blowjob: Assessing the role of anti-female memes in military sexual harassment and assault. *Journal of Political & Military Sociology*, *46*(1), 221–260. https://doi.org/10.5744/jpms.1008

Daneil, S., Neria, A., Moore, A., & Davis, E. (2019). The impact of leadership responses to sexual harassment and gender discrimination reports on emotional distress and retention intentions in military members. *Journal of Trauma & Dissociation*, *20*(3), 357–372. https://doi.org/10.1080/15299732.2019.1571887

DeKeseredy, W. S. (1988). *Woman abuse in dating relationships: The role of male peer support*. Canadian Scholars' Press.

DeKeseredy, W. S., & Schwartz, M. D. (Eds.). (2013). *Male peer support and violence against women: The history and verification of a theory*. Northeastern University Press.

Department of Defense. (2020). *Appendix B: Statistical data on sexual assault*. https://www.sapr.mil/sites/default/files/3_Appendix_B_Statistical_Data_on_Sexual_Assault.pdf

Department of Defense. (2022). *Annual report on sexual assault in the military: Fiscal Year 2021*. https://www.sapr.mil/sites/default/files/public/docs/reports/AR/DOD_Annual_Report_on_Sexual_Assault_in_the_Military_FY2021.pdf

Diaz, J., Cramer, M., & Morales, C. (2020). *What we know about the death of Vanessa Guillen*. https://www.nytimes.com/article/vanessa-guillen-fort-hood.html

Fawcett, H., & Shrestha, L. (2016). Blogging about sexual assault: A thematic analysis. *Journal of Forensic Practice*, *18*(1), 39–51. https://doi.org/10.1108/JFP-05-2015-0032

Greenwood, S., Perrin, A., & Duggan, M. (2016). Social media update 2016. *Pew Research Center*, *11*(2).

Groves, C. (2013). Military sexual assault: An ongoing and prevalent problem. *Journal of Human Behavior in the Social Environment*, *23*(6), 747–752. https://doi.org/10.1080/10911359.2013.795064

Hankin, C. S., Skinner, K. M., Sullivan, L. M., Miller, D. R., Frayne, S., & Tripp, T. J. (1999). Prevalence of depressive and alcohol abuse symptoms among women VA outpatients who report experiencing sexual assault while in the military. *Journal of Traumatic Stress*, *12*(4), 601–612. https://doi.org/10.1023/A:1024760900213

"Home". *Find Vanessa Guillen*. 2020, August 11. findvanessaguillen.com/

Human Rights Watch. (2015). *Embattled: Retaliation against sexual assault survivors in the US military*. https://www.hrw.org/report/2015/05/18/embattled/retaliation-against-sexual-assault-survivors-us-military

Hutchison, P. J. (2013). Leadership as an ideograph: A rhetorical analysis of military leadership training material. *Journal of Leadership Studies*, *7*(3), 24–37. https://doi.org/10.1002/jls.21293

Jaycox, L. H., Morral, A. R., Street, A., Schell, T. L., Kilpatrick, D., & Cottrell, L. (2023). Gender differences in health among U.S. service members: Unwanted gender-based experiences as an explanatory factor. *Rand Health Quarterly*, *10*(2), 8.

Kennedy, A. C., & Prock, K. A. (2018). "I still feel like I am not normal": A review of the role of stigma and stigmatization among female survivors of child sexual abuse, sexual assault, and intimate partner violence. *Trauma, Violence, & Abuse*, *19*(5), 512–527. https://doi.org/10.1177/1524838016673601

Kimerling, R. (2017). No mission too difficult: Responding to military sexual assault. *American Journal of Public Health*, *107*(5), 642–644. https://doi.org/10.2105/AJPH.2017.303731

Kimerling, R., Street, A. E., Gima, K., & Smith, M. W. (2008). Evaluation of universal screening for military-related sexual trauma. *Psychiatric Services*, *59*(6), 635–640. https://doi.org/10.1176/ps.2008.59.6.635

Lee, J. L., DeCamp, M., Dredze, M., Chisolm, M. S., & Berger, Z. D. (2014). What are health-related users tweeting? A qualitative content analysis of health-related users and their messages on twitter. *Journal of Medical Internet Research*, *16*(10), e237. https://doi.org/10.2196/jmir.3765

Littleton, H. L. (2010). The impact of social support and negative disclosure reactions on sexual assault victims: A cross-sectional and longitudinal investigation. *Journal of Trauma & Dissociation*, *11*(2), 210–227. https://doi.org/10.1080/15299730903502946

Lucas, C. L., Goldbach, J. T., Mamey, M. R., Kintzle, S., & Castro, C. A. (2018). Military sexual assault as a mediator of the association between posttraumatic stress disorder and depression among lesbian, gay, and bisexual veterans. *Journal of Traumatic Stress, 31*(4), 613–619. https://doi.org/10.1002/jts.22308

Lune, H., & Berg, B. L. (2016). *Qualitative research methods for the social sciences.* Pearson Higher Ed.

Mengeling, M. A., Booth, B. M., Torner, J. C., & Sadler, A. G. (2014). Reporting sexual assault in the military: Who reports and why most servicewomen don't. *American Journal of Preventive Medicine, 47*(1), 17–25. https://doi.org/10.1016/j.amepre.2014.03.001

Monteith, L. L., Holliday, R., Schneider, A. L., Forster, J. E., & Bahraini, N. H. (2019). Identifying factors associated with suicidal ideation and suicide attempts following military sexual trauma. *Journal of Affective Disorders, 252,* 300–309. https://doi.org/10.1016/j.jad.2019.04.038

Mujal, G. N., Taylor, M. E., Fry, J. L., Gochez-Kerr, T. H., & Weaver, N. L. (2021). A systematic review of bystander interventions for the prevention of sexual violence. *Trauma, Violence, & Abuse, 22*(2), 381–396. https://doi.org/10.1177/1524838019849587

NISVS. (2015). *NISVS 2015 data brief: Sexual violence by any perpetrator.* https://www.nsvrc.org/statistics

"Our Forces." *U.S. Department of Defense,* March 8, 2021. https://www.defense.gov/Our-Story/Our-Forces/

Overstreet, N. M., & Quinn, D. M. (2013). The intimate partner violence stigmatization model and barriers to help seeking. *Basic and Applied Social Psychology, 35*(1), 109–122. https://doi.org/10.1080/01973533.2012.746599

Pew Research Center. (2018). *How social media users have discussed sexual harassment since #MeToo went viral.* Pew Research Center. https://www.pewresearch.org/short-reads/2018/10/11/how-social-media-users-have-discussed-sexual-harassment-since-metoo-went-viral/

Pew Research Center. (2022). *More than twice as many Americans support than oppose the #MeToo movement.* Pew Research Center. https://www.pewresearch.org/social-trends/2022/09/29/more-than-twice-as-many-americans-support-than-oppose-the-metoo-movement/

Sadler, A. G., Mengeling, M. A., Booth, B. M., O'Shea, A. M. J., & Torner, J. C. (2017). The relationship between US military officer leadership behaviors and risk of sexual assault of reserve, national guard, and active component servicewomen in nondeployed locations. *American Journal of Public Health, 107*(1), 147–155. https://doi.org/10.2105/AJPH.2016.303520

Sidanius, J., & Pratto, F. (2001). *Social dominance: An intergroup theory of social hierarchy and oppression.* Cambridge University Press.

Sills, S., Pickens, C., Beach, K., Jones, L., Calder-Dawe, O., Benton-Greig, P., & Gavey, N. (2016). Rape culture and social media: Young critics and a feminist counterpublic. *Feminist Media Studies, 16*(6), 935–951. https://doi.org/10.1080/14680777.2015.1137962

Skinner, K. M., Kressin, N., Frayne, S., Tripp, T. J., Hankin, C. S., Miller, D. R., & Sullivan, L. M. (2000). The prevalence of military sexual assault among female veterans' administration outpatients. *Journal of Interpersonal Violence, 15*(3), 291–310. https://doi.org/10.1177/088626000015003005

Smith, A., & Anderson, M. (2018). Social media use in 2018. *Pew Research Center, 1.*

Storer, H. L., Rodriguez, M., & Franklin, R. (2018). "Leaving was a process, not an event": The lived experience of dating and domestic violence in 140 characters. *Journal of Interpersonal Violence, 36*(11–12), NP6553–NP6580. https://doi.org/10.1177/0886260518816325

Suler, J. (2005). The online disinhibition effect. *International Journal of Applied Psychoanalytic Studies, 2*(2), 184–188. https://doi.org/10.1002/aps.42

United States Army SHARP. (2020). *Sexual harassment/assault response & prevention: Reporting options.* https://www.sexualassault.army.mil/policy_restricted_unrestricted_reporting.aspx

The UnitedStates Government. (2021, December 27). *Statement by the president on S. 1605, the national defense authorization act for fiscal Year 2022.* The White House. https://www.whitehouse.gov/briefing-room/statements-releases/2021/12/27/statement-by-the-president-on-s-1605-the-national-defense-authorization-act-for-fiscal-year-2022/

Verlage, H., Rowold, J., & Schilling, J. (2012). Through different perspectives on leadership: Comparing the full range leadership theory to implicit leadership theories. *Journal of Organizational Learning and Leadership, 10*(2), 68–91.

OPEN ACCESS

Military Sexual Assault, Post-Service Employment, and Transition Preparation among U.S. Military Veterans: New Directions for Research

Adam J. Pritchard

ABSTRACT

Unlike studies of military sexual trauma (MST) among active-duty service members, most studies of veterans with MST have been clinical in nature, focused on estimating population prevalence rates, improving clinical responses or treatments, or have associated MST with subsequent health-related risk behaviors such as alcohol or drug abuse. The present study seeks to broaden our understanding of the corollaries of military sexual assault by considering the relationship between being a survivor of military sexual assault and post-service employment and transition experiences. Using secondary data from a survey of the members of a national organization for post-9/11 veterans, this exploratory study examines bivariate and multivariate relationships between self-reported experiences of military sexual assault and specific post-transition outcomes commonly used as indicators of a successful career transition from military to civilian life including employment status, time from transition to employment, and veterans' perceptions of being prepared for their transition out of the military. Analysis from this study suggests that military sexual assault is impactful in the domains of employment and transition readiness. This paper's findings point to a need to consider a range of inter-related social determinants of health and well-being when providing post-service career support for veterans.

Introduction

The problem of sexual assault and harassment within the military ranks is not a new one, having been studied in various forms since the 1960s. Institutional attention to addressing the problem of military sexual trauma (MST) increased significantly in the 1990s in part due to new policies, research, and efforts by Veterans Affairs (VA) to improve clinical screening and treatment (Allard et al., 2011; Purtle, 2016; Suris & Lind, 2008). Still, in the decades that followed, only disparate studies could be identified to establish a baseline prevalence for MST, with many studies lacking deliberate sampling or methodological consistency (Turchik & Wilson, 2010; Wilson, 2018). These limitations in defining the problem kept much of the focus of veteran-oriented research on estimating prevalence rates through clinical data and practice. From the beginning, much of this research has centered around psychological trauma, particularly among female soldiers and veterans (Himmelfarb et al., 2006; Martin et al., 2000) but also among men (Peterson et al., 2011), and has continued into recent years to largely focus on post-traumatic stress disorder (PTSD) or other health-related outcomes (Jaycox et al., 2022). Given the largely clinical focus of research into MST to-date, comparatively little research exists that examines the impacts of MST or military sexual assault on veterans outside of health-care contexts. The present study explores whether experiences of military sexual assault impact other areas of a veteran's life, in this case, by examining employment and transition experiences based on a non-clinical, national sample of US veterans.

Research studies that specifically focus on veteran survivors of military sexual assault that go beyond direct trauma treatment are rare but are still largely medical in nature. Most recently, experiences of military sexual trauma have been linked to a wide variety of other adverse health and wellness outcomes such as addiction (Beckman et al., 2022), impact on sexual functioning in relationships (Blais & Livingston, 2021), or other risk behaviors (Forkus et al., 2021). One recent study did consider the impact of military sexual assault on the outcome of a vocational employment program, however this too was in the context of a broader medical rehabilitation program and thus not generalizable (Gross et al., 2022). Blais and Livingston (2021) utilize a non-clinical sample of service members or veteran women recruited via social media and identify psychological correlates linking MST to reduced sexual function, but this sample is limited in that it only examines partnered women. Due to the clinical (mostly VA-related) nature of most other data sources used to study MST, there are significant limitations on our ability to accurately measure and estimate the prevalence of MST among veterans in the general population (Wilson, 2018) and also to accurately understand the broader impacts of MST beyond for those in direct treatment. Wilson (2018) aptly points out that "more research is urgently needed using diverse methodologies . . . [because] our ability to provide adequate MST services to our military personnel and veterans hinges on accurate detection of the phenomenon" (593). While her focus is on improvements in treatment and primary prevention, many social services that support veterans across a range of needs should also consider how military sexual assault can be an important, yet not often considered, obstacle to successful outcomes.

The present study seeks to explore this gap in the research on how military sexual assault impacts outcomes for veterans beyond the better-studied contexts of physical and mental health. Extending the work of addressing sexual trauma beyond the clinical context is also a way to address the needs or experiences of the many "invisible" victims of sexual assault who do not come forward with their experiences, which data suggests may even be more common in the military (U.S. Commission on Civil Rights, 2013) than in other contexts where underreporting is also a serious concern. The prevalence of MST may also be underestimated in VA-related populations, given estimates that the majority of veterans are not enrolled in VA health care (Holder & Day, 2017), especially considering that individuals who experience sexual trauma may face disqualifying discharge or harbor mistrust toward military-related institutions. This paper's analysis is exploratory in nature, conducting secondary analysis on a dataset from a national survey of mostly post-9/11 veterans about a variety of personal, political, and social issues. The intention of this paper is to explore the relationships between military sexual assault, post-service employment, and preparation for transition, providing direction for future research that integrates these domains into efforts to better understand and mitigate the impacts of military sexual trauma on veterans.

Background

Efforts to support veterans who had previously experienced military sexual assault as a service member include several important milestones, notably a 1992 mandate to the Department of Veterans' Affairs (VA) naming military sexual trauma as an area of concern (Allard et al., 2011). More recently, a 2012 report commissioned by the Obama administration (U.S. Commission on Civil Rights, 2013) set the stage for a new round of reforms spanning the past decade. This internal effort was strengthened in response to high-profile incidents at military bases and VA health centers around the country and increasing public pressures to address sexual assault and harassment issues in the entertainment industry, professional workplaces, and college campuses during this same period. Most recently, the 2022 National Defense Authorization Act (NDAA) and a number of executive orders signed by President Biden have sought to specifically strengthen reforms within the Military Code of Justice and enact new procedural responses to sexual assault and harassment reports within the military (Mason, 2022). While these recent reforms are an important step forward for current service members, there are an estimated 18 million veterans including 3.7 million post-9/11 veterans (Vespa, 2020) who previously served during periods where much less support was offered to active duty survivors of military sexual trauma.

Early research examining sexual assault experiences among soldiers helped to set the agenda for understanding MST; namely, the focus was placed on the psychological effects of sexual trauma and the particularly negative impacts it had on female service members (Martin et al., 1998, 2000). Importantly, the experiences of sexual harassment in this early research were also linked to unit cohesion and combat effectiveness (Rosen & Martin, 1998), suggesting that sexual assault could have a direct impact on military effectiveness, leading to an increasing emphasis on sexual assault as a form of psychological trauma by U. S. legislators (Purtle, 2016). The implication of this work made MST an important consideration for other areas of concern, such as military readiness, retention and recruitment, both physical and psychological danger to service members (Szitanyi, 2020), and general well-being for active duty soldiers (Holland et al., 2016). This research and policy agenda linked military sexual assault to psychological trauma, moral injury, and physical combat risks, which has clear and urgent implications for many service-disabled veterans or those with mental health needs, however this narrow focus on military-specific forms of trauma (and the related research funding priorities supporting this work) led researchers to generally neglect inquiries into how other veterans might experience corollary impacts from sexual assault and harassment experienced during service.

A substantial part of the extant research on veterans focuses on the transition from military service to being a veteran. Theory on military transition has recognized the importance of addressing past trauma in order to develop a new self-narrative, building upon the idea that a meaningful work and career can be a mechanism for successful veteran transition (Haynie & Shepherd, 2011). Other theory considers the ecological context in which a veteran transitions as important for clinical interventions (Elnitsky et al., 2017). Within efforts to understand and support veterans' transition, however, research studies that consider the role of military sexual assault are relatively sparse. These tends also focus only on women veterans, with very few studies considering socioeconomic factors such as employment (Maya & Kimberley, 2018). Research has, however, begun to consider a wider range of social determinants of health, adding important context to a veteran's transition needs and challenges. Notable in these efforts are research projects by The Veterans Metrics Initiative (TVMI) at Pennsylvania State University or the D'Aniello Institute for Veterans and Military Families (IVMF) at Syracuse University, whose studies highlight transition challenges such as navigating VA benefits or dealing with service-connected disabilities or examine benefits of a wide range of employment and career-preparation opportunities provided to veterans (Bradbard & Maury, 2021; Perkins et al., 2020). To date, however, almost no research exists which unites the clinically focused work on military sexual trauma with efforts to understand socio-demographic correlates of military separation and transition. The fact that the study of military sexual assault and its implications for veterans has so far been siloed into healthcare research represents a significant gap in the literature.

The few extant studies looking at military sexual assault in the context of employment or well-being outcomes, discussed below, clearly suggest that MST impacts outcomes. Research combining VA medical and employment program records has found that MST is linked to a lack of competitive employment at program completion (Gross et al., 2022). Moreover, this relationship may create a vicious cycle; research on adult trauma and PTSD consistently shows a relationship between low income or unemployment and dropping out of treatment programs (Matthieu & Ivanoff, 2006).

One key transition challenge for survivors of MST may be related to a heightened sense of institutional mistrust caused by the military's response (or lack of response) to their assault experiences (Bourke, 2022). Once these service members become veterans, this mistrust may be extended to other governmental services such as the VA. Previous research has found that veterans who experienced MST, and particularly those who experienced retaliation for reporting, are less likely to access not only treatment but other needed support as well (Holland et al., 2016). Extant literature also suggests that sexual trauma can have other complex interactions with certain unique properties of military service. For instance, research among female service members has shown that many had experienced more instances of sexual trauma than other women, even prior to joining the military, itself an independent risk factor for subsequent adult sexual victimization (Martin et al., 1998; Turchik & Wilson, 2010). Outside of research specifically focused on veterans or service members, people with disabilities and particularly disabled women have been found to be more vulnerable to sexual victimization in national population-based studies (Basile et al., 2016; Mailhot Amborski et al., 2021). Therefore, it is not unexpected that there could also be connections between service-connected disabilities and subsequent risk of victimization among women veterans.

Despite the relative sparseness of research specifically linking military sexual assault or MST to veteran outcomes beyond clinical and health-care contexts, enough evidence exists in what research has been previously published to suggest that this area represents a substantial gap in our knowledge of how best to support veterans who are also survivors. The analyses in this paper focus on answering the question of whether there are differences between military sexual assault survivors and other veterans across variables measuring employment (both current and at the time of transition) and ratings of preparedness for their transition from the service that may provide direction for future research investigating how military sexual assault influences non-medical needs such as employment and transition support.

Methods

Sample and data collection

This study analyzed data collected by a recent national survey of predominately post-9/11 veterans, exploring several topics related to veterans' service, post-transition experiences, and opinions on topics important to U.S. military veterans. A module on sexual assault and harassment was one of the topics surveyed. In the fall of 2021, Iraq and Afghanistan Veterans of America (IAVA) and the D'Aniello Institute for Veterans and Military Families at Syracuse University (IVMF) fielded the *2022 IAVA Membership Survey* (Pritchard et al., 2022). The survey was open from September 2021 through October 2021, with a reminder e-mail each week (8 total) sent from representatives of IAVA. No incentives were provided to participants, and the survey was protected from unauthorized or bot participation by sending to a controlled distribution list rather than using an anonymous link. The study and the necessary confidentiality protocols were reviewed and approved as exempt by the Syracuse University IRB (IRB #21–245), and consent was obtained via the landing page of the online survey within Qualtrics. The online survey was sent to 111,634 valid e-mail addresses for members provided by IAVA, resulting in 7,417 started surveys (6.6%) and 5,524 completed surveys (74.5% completion rate). The final valid survey sample includes 5,157 participants, including 691 female veterans (14%), approximately proportional to the female population of recent US veterans (Vespa, 2020). For the purposes of this paper, the data presented will be based on the subsample of participants with a valid response (e.g., not left blank) on the military sexual assault screening item, who as a group do not significantly differ from the overall sample on basic demographics. The overall survey and analytic sample demographics are presented in Table 1.

Measures

This paper uses items from throughout the survey to conceptualize the topics investigated in this analysis. Specifically, this survey makes use of the survey's measures of military sexual assault and reporting experiences, measures of veteran employment outcomes, and items examining veterans' perceptions of their level of preparedness for transitioning from military to civilian life.

Military sexual assault

The main screening item for military sexual assault was measured using the following binary (yes/no) question: "Are you a survivor of military sexual assault? (This includes things like unwanted touching, someone exposing themselves or unwanted sexual contact)." This measure is used throughout the analysis of specific topics to distinguish those veterans reporting prior military sexual assault experiences from those who did not; in other words, participants selected yes on this item if they self-identify as a survivor of military sexual assault due to their experiences. Table 2 provides results from this measure and follow-up questions, including veterans' experiences with reporting sexual assault incidents and their perceptions of the military's response.

For those indicating an experience of military sexual assault, a follow-up item asked, "Did you report the incident?," which triggered additional branching logic. Those who did

Table 1. Survey and sample demographic comparison.

	Entire survey (N = 5,157)	Analysis sample (n = 4,407)	
	n (%)	n (%)	p
Sex			
Male	4203 (84.4)	3726 (84.5)	.682
Female	691 (13.9)	610 (13.8)	.991
Other	85 (1.7)	62 (1.4)	.247
Total valid	n = 4979	n = 4398	
Age			
18–30	54 (1.1)	43 (1.0)	.662
31–40	1497 (29.6)	1297 (29.4)	.887
41–50	1571 (31.1)	1357 (31.2)	.806
51–65	1497 (28.7)	1296 (29.4)	.868
Over 65	458 (8.9)	391 (8.9)	.769
Total valid	n = 5059	n = 4403	
Race and ethnicity[a]			
White	3844 (77.6)	3445 (78.6)	.249
Black or African American	387 (7.8)	333 (7.6)	.696
Hispanic, Latino, or Spanish	569 (10.4)	486 (11.1)	.543
American Indian or Alaskan Native	199 (3.6)	167 (3.4)	.606
Asian	184 (3.4)	164 (3.7)	.946
Native Hawaiian or Pacific Islander	42 (0.8)	37 (0.8)	.984
Other	261 (4.8)	221 (5.0)	.620
Total valid	n = 4953	n = 4383	
Veteran status			
Veteran (yes)	4888 (94.8)	4168 (94.6)	.653
Post-9/11 veteran (yes)	4655 (90.3)	4002 (90.8)	.365
Total valid	n = 5157	n = 4407	
Enlistment status			
Enlisted	3734 (72.4)	3276 (76.2)	.192
Officer/warrant officer	1094 (21.2)	1024 (23.8)	.192
Total valid	n = 4828	n = 4300	

[a]This item is coded as select all that apply, so counts indicate yes on a given category and the percentage reflects the percent of cases. Individuals endorsed a mean of 1.1 categories.

Table 2. Military sexual assault survey items.

	Total	Male	Female	Sex diff.
	N (% total)	N (% males)	N (% females)	p
Experienced military sexual assault	526 (11.9)	151 (4.1)	358 (58.7)	.000*
If experienced (n = 526) did you report?	178 (33.8)	36 (23.8)	134 (37.4)	.002*
If not reported (n = 348) why not?				
Did not think anything would be done	242 (69.9)	68 (60.2)	167 (74.6)	.007*
Fear of retaliation by my peers or chain of command	195 (56.4)	48 (42.5)	142 (63.4)	.000*
Concerned about impact on my career	189 (54.6)	52 (46.0)	132 (58.9)	.025*
Doubted that my chain of command would believe me	176 (50.9)	47 (41.6)	125 (55.8)	.014*
Concerned that my peers would treat me differently	171 (49.4)	65 (57.5)	102 (45.5)	.038*
Did not want to be involved in an investigation	161 (46.5)	47 (41.6)	111 (49.6)	.167
Worried I was less valued than perpetrator	117 (33.8)	27 (23.9)	86 (38.4)	.008*
Worried that people would think I was weak	114 (32.9)	47 (41.6)	66 (29.5)	.026*
Worried family/friends would treat me differently	57 (16.5)	29 (25.7)	26 (11.6)	.000*
Other	60 (17.3)	30 (26.5)	29 (12.9)	.002*
If reported (n = 178) did you experience retaliation?	112 (62.9)	17 (47.2)	90 (67.2)	.024*
View of trained military prosecutor rather than commander to handle complaint				
More likely to report	267 (51.0)	60 (40.0)	196 (54.9)	.002*
Would not change my decision	242 (46.2)	82 (54.7)	156 (43.7)	.024*
Less likely to report	15 (2.9)	8 (5.3)	5 (1.4)	.011*

*$p < .05$.

not report their assault experiences were given a multiple response list of prompts for "Why did you not report this?" (see Table 2). If they indicated that their assault was reported, survey participants were asked the yes/no follow-up question "Did you experience any kind of retaliation after reporting?" and also "If instead of your commander, a trained military prosecutor had the authority to make the decision to move forward with your case, which of the following impacts would it have had on your decision to report?" with response options of "I would have been more likely to report," "I would have been less likely to report," or "It would not have made a difference in my decision."

Employment

Measures used for classifying veteran employment included three questions from the survey. Employment status was measured by asking "Which best describes your current employment situation?" with six response options ranging from "Employed Full Time (35 + hours per week)" to "Disabled or otherwise unable to work" (see Table 3). Employment at transition was measured with the question "How long were you without a job after transitioning out of the military?," which included seven response options ranging from "Less than 3 months" to "Opted to attend school" (see Table 3).

Transition

Transition from military service to civilian life was measured using a scale. Five items asked about perceptions of preparation for specific aspects of transition ("Using the following

Table 3. Key measures by military sexual assault survivor status.

	Military sexual assault		
	Yes	No	
	N (%)	*N* (%)	*Sig. (p)*
Current employment			
Full-time	216 (44.2)	2091 (60.1)	.000*
Part-time	39 (8.0)	185 (5.3)	.009*
Unemployed, looking for work	33 (6.7)	170 (4.9)	.040*
Unemployed, not looking for work	25 (5.1)	81 (2.3)	.000*
Retired, not employed	48 (9.8)	509 (14.6)	.002*
Disabled or otherwise unable to work	128 (26.2)	443 (12.7)	.000*
Time until employment after transition			
Less than 3 months	57 (15.2)	666 (28.8)	.000*
3–6 months	69 (18.4)	489 (21.1)	.119
Between 6 and 9 months	33 (8.8)	226 (9.8)	.285
Between 9 and 12 months	27 (7.2)	168 (7.3)	.490
Over 12 months	129 (34.5)	421 (18.2)	.000*
Never unemployed	8 (2.1)	79 (3.4)	.098
Opted to attend school	51 (13.6)	267 (11.5)	.121
How prepared were you to navigate (1 = very unprepared, 5 = very prepared)			
Transition from military to civilian life	2.52 (1.350)	3.00 (1.357)	.000*
Transition to post-service employment	2.41 (1.400)	3.00 (1.394)	.000*
Access to post-service education	2.92 (1.397)	3.24 (1.317)	.000*
Resources available in your local community	2.03 (1.253)	2.59 (1.298)	.000*
Healthcare and benefits system	2.47 (1.382)	2.90 (1.351)	.000*
Overall scale (Cronbach's alpha = 0.878)	2.42 (1.023)	2.86 (1.098)	.000*
Mean length of service in years	6.87 (3.506)	7.18 (3.378)	.235

* $p < .05$.

Levene's test indicates unequal variance in individual scale items, so *p*-values presented for those items are calculated using the more conservative, non-parametric Mann–Whitney U test.

scale, how prepared were you to successfully navigate the following …?") on a 5-point Likert-type scale ranging from 1 = "very unprepared" to 5 = "very prepared" with 3 as neutral (Cronbach's Alpha = 0.878). The transition topics measured are listed in Table 3.

In addition to these subjective measures of transition, the mean length of military service in years was calculated based on two other questions in the demographic section of the survey: "What year did you join the military?" and "What year did you separate from the military?"

Data analysis

The data analysis was conducted using IBM SPSS Statistics 27 and involved two types of analysis. First, t-tests comparing veterans who reported military sexual assault to veterans who did not were used to explore the bivariate relationships between study variables and military sexual assault. In certain circumstances (i.e., with ordinal items in the transition scale), additional tests such as Levene's test for unequal variance and Mann–Whitney U are used and are indicated in the tables where applicable. In Table 2, t-tests are also used to compare military sexual assault experiences by sex. Second, regression analysis (multinomial logistic regression or ordinary least-squares regression as appropriate) is used to control for demographic variables while examining the relationships between military sexual assault experiences and employment or transition measures.

Results

Military sexual assault

Details of veterans' experiences with military sexual assault are summarized in Table 2. Overall, 526 respondents or 12% of the sample self-identified as a survivor of military sexual assault, defined in the question as "having experienced sexual assault or things like unwanted touching, someone exposing themselves, or unwanted sexual contact."

Most participants self-identifying as a survivor of military sexual assault are female (70%) and survivors comprise 4% of male survey participants and 59% of female participants. Among male survivors, 24% reported the incident, and about half of those who reported (47%) said they experienced some form of retaliation after reporting. Among female survivors, 37% reported the incident and 67% said they experienced retaliation for having reported. This high rate of retaliation among those who did report their assault is commensurate with the perceptions of the 66% of survivors overall who did not report the incident, 56% of whom did not do so out of "fear of retaliation by my peers or chain of command." Table 2 also shows veterans' opinions about having an independent investigator outside of their chain of command handle complaints. After this survey was conducted, a version of this proposed change was implemented in the 2022 National Defense Authorization Act (NDAA) and will go into effect December 27, 2023, as Public Law 117–81.

Employment

Data examining the relationship between experiences of military sexual assault and current employment, as well as the time until securing employment upon transitioning out of the military, are presented in Table 3. Current employment status significantly differed between military sexual assault survivors and other veterans. Military sexual assault survivors are less often employed full time (44.2% vs 60.1%, $p = .000$), less often retired (9.8% vs 14.6%, $p = .002$), and are disabled and not working almost twice as often as other veterans (26.2% vs 12.7%, $p = .000$).

To determine if these relationships are significant when controlling for demographic differences, current employment status was further analyzed using multinomial logistic regression. Using full-time employment (>36 hours) as the reference category, military sexual assault was considered in a model using dummy variables to control for sex (1 = male), age (1 = over 40 years old), and officer/enlisted status (1 = officer). Race was measured using a multiple-response item, included in models by coding as 1 if the racial/ethnic category was endorsed and 0 if that category was not endorsed. For example, individuals who endorsed both white and Hispanic are coded as both white = 1 and Hispanic = 1 although most individuals endorsed only one category (mean is 1.1 endorsed categories), and only individuals endorsing at least one category are included in the analysis. For brevity, only the results from this model for categories where military sexual assault is significant are presented in Table 4. When these controls are considered, military sexual assault remains a significant predictor for both unemployed categories and for disability, but is no longer significant for veterans who are not working due to retirement. Relative to veterans who are full-time employed, unemployed veterans (looking for work) are 2.2x more likely to be military sexual assault survivors (exp(B) = 2.190), unemployed veterans (not looking for work) are 2.2x more likely to be military sexual assault survivors (exp(B) = 2.186), and veterans who are disabled or otherwise unable to work are 3.7x more likely to be survivors of military sexual assault (exp(B) = 3.668).

Table 3 also reports on the time elapsed between separation from the military and securing employment reported by veterans. Overall, 24.1% of those veterans experiencing military sexual assault had a job secured before leaving the military, compared to 33.5% of those who had not experienced military sexual assault ($p = .000$). Veterans without military sexual assault experiences had secured employment in less than 3 months after transition at nearly twice the proportion of those who experienced assault (28.8% vs 15.2%, $p = .000$), whereas the opposite is true of those taking over 12 months after transition to find employment. More than one-third (34.5%) of survivors of military sexual assault reported going more than 12 months before securing employment after transition compared to only 18.4% of other veterans ($p = .000$).

Once again, follow-up analysis using multinomial logistic regression was used to control for demographic variables to better validate these apparent differences. This analysis compared individuals who reported some delay to employment (categories "Less than 3 months" through "Over 12 months") and excluded those with no employment gap or those who attended school. Ordinal regression was ruled out for this analysis due to uneven distribution of cumulative probabilities for the categories or violations of parallel line tests when appropriate link functions were considered. In such cases, multinomial regression is advised as an alternative (Hosmer et al., 2013). Once again for brevity, Table 5 presents only results from this model for the category "Over 12 months" where military sexual assault was a significant category predictor. Consistent with the bivariate results even when controlling for available demographics, veterans who took over 12 months to secure employment were 2.6x more likely to be military sexual assault survivors than those securing employment in less than 3 months (exp(B) = 2.566).

Table 4. Multinomial logistic regression model comparing current employment status and military sexual assault (reference category = full-time employment).

	B	S.E.	Sig.	EXP(B)	CI – low	CI – High
Unemployed, looking for work						
Intercept	−2.321	0.372	**0.000**			
Sex (male = 1)	0.334	0.275	0.225	1.396	0.814	2.394
Age (over 40 years old = 1)	−0.002	0.163	0.990	0.998	0.725	1.373
Enlistment (officer/warrant = 1)	−0.170	0.204	0.405	0.844	0.566	1.258
White	−0.701	0.244	**0.004**	0.496	0.307	0.800
Black	0.427	0.295	0.148	1.532	0.859	2.732
Hispanic	−0.011	0.270	0.966	0.989	0.583	1.677
Asian, Hawaiian, or Pac Islander	−0.296	0.388	0.447	0.744	0.348	1.593
Amer Indian or Alaskan	0.074	0.409	0.856	1.077	0.483	2.402
Military sexual assault survivor	0.784	0.270	**0.004**	2.190	1.290	3.717
Unemployed, not looking for work						
Intercept	−2.867	0.474	**0.000**			
Sex (male = 1)	−0.486	0.321	0.130	0.615	0.328	1.154
Age (over 40 years old = 1)	0.086	0.218	0.693	1.090	0.711	1.669
Enlistment (officer/warrant = 1)	−0.419	0.286	0.144	0.658	0.375	1.153
White	0.016	0.344	0.963	1.016	0.518	1.995
Black	0.225	0.447	0.616	1.252	0.521	3.009
Hispanic	0.278	0.360	0.440	1.320	0.652	2.675
Asian, Hawaiian, or Pac Islander	0.263	0.474	0.579	1.301	0.514	3.292
Amer Indian or Alaskan	−0.074	0.604	0.902	0.928	0.284	3.033
Military sexual assault survivor	0.782	0.334	**0.019**	2.186	1.136	4.204
Disabled or otherwise unable to work						
Intercept	−2.147	0.250	**0.000**			
Sex (male = 1)	0.380	0.179	**0.034**	1.463	1.030	2.078
Age (over 40 years old = 1)	0.744	0.114	**0.000**	2.105	1.683	2.631
Enlistment (officer/warrant = 1)	−0.870	0.147	**0.000**	0.419	0.314	0.559
White	−0.265	0.163	0.104	0.767	0.557	1.056
Black	0.296	0.207	0.153	1.345	0.896	2.018
Hispanic	−0.069	0.181	0.704	0.934	0.655	1.331
Asian, Hawaiian or Pac Islander	−0.347	0.279	0.214	0.707	0.409	1.221
Amer Indian or Alaskan	0.891	0.210	**0.000**	2.439	1.617	3.677
Military sexual assault survivor	1.300	0.171	**0.000**	3.668	2.624	5.128

Nagelkerke's R-squared = 0.152. Significance of $p < .05$ indicated in bold. Full model also considers part-time employment and retired or no longer working. For brevity, these results are not presented as military sexual assault survivor is non-significant for these categories.

Table 5. Multinomial logistic regression model comparing the time from military transition to securing employment and military sexual assault (reference category = less than 3 months).

Over 12 months	*B*	S.E.	*Sig.*	*EXP(B)*	CI – low	CI – High
Intercept	0.195	0.299	0.514			
Sex (male = 1)	−0.399	0.210	0.057	0.671	0.445	1.012
Age (over 40 years old = 1)	−0.413	0.130	**0.002**	0.662	0.513	0.854
Enlistment (officer/warrant = 1)	0.476	0.160	**0.003**	1.610	1.176	2.203
White	−0.270	0.203	0.183	0.763	0.513	1.136
Black	0.607	0.281	**0.031**	1.836	1.057	3.187
Hispanic	0.209	0.223	0.348	1.233	0.796	1.908
Asian, Hawaiian, or Pac Islander	0.412	0.346	0.234	1.511	0.766	2.978
Amer Indian or Alaskan	0.556	0.284	0.051	1.744	0.999	3.044
Military sexual assault survivor	0.942	0.219	**0.000**	2.566	1.670	3.943

Nagelkerke's R-squared = 0.066. Significance of $p < .05$ indicated in bold. Full model also considers 3–6 months, between 6 and 9 months, and between 9 and 12 months. For brevity, these results are not presented as military sexual assault survivor is non-significant for these categories.

Transition

Veterans' ratings of preparedness for transition on a scale examining elements such as employment, education, community resources, and the healthcare system are also presented in detail in Table 3. Similar to bivariate comparisons on employment measures that showed significantly worse employment outcomes for military sexual assault survivors, all transition preparation items were rated significantly higher by veterans who indicated no military sexual assault experiences. Service members experiencing military sexual assault had, on average, slightly shorter service length than other veterans (6.87 vs. 7.18 years), but this difference was not statistically significant ($p = .235$). Time in service also had relatively large standard deviations (3.506 and 3.378, respectively), reflecting a wide range of service experiences in general that may defy a simplistic explanation.

Based on the extant literature, this study considers the possibility that both military sexual assault and time-in-service might impact transition preparation (e.g., hypothesizing that longer service is more likely to be planned, and thus better prepared where shorter service may result from unplanned or early departure). As such, both years in service and military sexual assault were considered possible predictors of transition preparedness. Once again, a regression model was employed as a follow-up analysis to further validate these apparent differences using appropriate demographic controls for sex, race, age (over/under 40 years old), and officer/enlisted status. This time, ordinary least squared regression was used due to the nature of the dependent variable (i.e., a Likert-type scale). Models are presented first for control variables only, next adding years of service, then third adding military sexual assault (Table 6). Both independent variables are statistically significant when added, and years of service are statistically significant in both models. Years of service are positively associated with better preparation (0.04 increase in the scale mean per - service year), while military sexual assault is negatively associated with better preparation for transition (0.44 decrease in the scale mean if a survivor). Also notable is that being an officer (rather than enlisted) was a strong positive predictor of transition preparation (0.39 increase in the scale mean if an officer), while American Indian/Alaskan Native ethnicity was a strong negative predictor of transition preparedness (0.44 decrease in the scale mean if American Indian/Alaskan Native).

Table 6. OLS regression model transition preparedness scale versus years of service and military sexual assault experiences.

	MODEL 0 – Controls			Model 1 – years of service			Model 2 – military sexual assault		
	B	t	Sig.	B	t	Sig.	B	t	Sig.
Constant	2.311	17.150	***0.000***	2.076	13.950	***0.000***	2.350	14.374	***0.000***
Male	0.102	1.161	0.246	0.084	0.958	0.338	−0.170	−1.570	0.117
Over 40 years old	0.033	0.428	0.669	0.004	0.057	0.955	−0.003	−0.037	0.970
Officer/warrant officer	0.441	3.544	***0.000***	0.396	3.188	***0.001***	0.393	3.186	***0.001***
White	0.159	1.427	0.154	0.164	1.481	0.139	0.163	1.488	0.137
Black	0.234	1.508	0.132	0.238	1.543	0.123	0.239	1.560	0.119
Hispanic	0.011	0.098	0.922	0.017	0.150	0.881	0.008	0.066	0.947
Asian, Hawaiian or Pac Islander	0.037	0.249	0.803	0.029	0.195	0.846	−0.018	−0.121	0.904
Amer Indian or Alaskan	−0.427	−2.304	**0.021**	−0.441	−2.391	**0.017**	−0.443	−2.419	**0.016**
Years in service				0.037	3.631	***0.000***	0.038	3.799	***0.000***
Military sexual assault survivor							−0.442	−3.920	***0.000***
F	3.112			4.263			5.426		
R-squared	0.023			0.035			0.049		
Adj. *R*-squared	0.016			0.027			0.040		
R-squared change	0.023			0.012			0.014		

$N = 1{,}064$. Significance of $p < .05$ indicated by bold, and $p < .01$ indicated by bold and italics.

Discussion

The data presented in this paper explore post-service correlates of military sexual assault based on an exploratory analysis of data from a national sample of U.S. military veterans who participated in a wide-ranging survey through one of the nation's largest membership organizations for post-9/11 veterans. Unlike most other research on veterans and military sexual assault, which focuses on clinical encounters with military sexual trauma (MST), this study seeks to highlight important associations beyond those typically examined through clinical or a service-seeking population. It is, therefore, the goal of this paper to highlight areas in which military sexual assault seems to have a differential impact on a veteran's post-service experiences, and direct future research toward deeper investigations into the mechanisms behind, and ultimately opportunities to respond to, these apparent relationships.

Overall, this study's findings are aligned with previous research indicating that military sexual assault is common, particularly among women; around 4.1% of male and 58.7% of female veterans indicated having such an experience. Prevalence rates are high in this sample, around twice that of studies with assault-only measures that exclude harassment (1.9% of men and 23.6% of women) and closer to measures that do include sexual harassment as well as assault (8.9% of men and 52.5% of women) as calculated via meta-analysis (Wilson, 2018). One possibility is that participants in the present study responded based on any adverse sexual experiences in the military and includes many types of harassment due to the nonspecificity of the measure ("Are you a survivor") used in the survey. Another possibility is that this sample differs from most other MST research (typically VA-served clinical populations) because it samples from (1) a non-clinical population that is (2) mostly post-9/11 veterans. Notably, official estimates of the proportion of veterans served by VA health care are as low as around one-third (Holder & Day, 2017), meaning that most veterans are not captured in VA clinical studies. While this study is not designed to estimate prevalence, nevertheless the high prevalence rate found here supports Wilson's (2018) urgent call to develop better population-based studies to estimate the scope of military sexual assault within veteran and active duty populations. Extant research also raises the possibility that early or bad discharge status can be related to assault experiences and can disqualify veterans from benefits like VA care and that institutional mistrust fostered by poor institutional response may contribute to a veteran's unwillingness to engage VA health care, and therefore, survivors may not be well represented in clinical VA samples (Bourke, 2022; Brignone, 2017; Holland et al., 2016). Considering other well-documented barriers to support for those experiencing sexual assault within the military, the data presented in Table 2 reflect the reality that most of those experiencing sexual assault in the military have not, by and large, felt well supported at the time of the incident. Experiences of sexual victimization, subsequent complex trauma, and associated lack of institutional support contribute to ongoing disadvantages for many veterans to whom these things happened during their military service (Bourke, 2022). Given the high rates of reported retaliation and the historical lack of institutional responsiveness, being a "squeaky wheel" within the military may carry additional unmeasured consequences including bad discharge status, lack of professional references and separation support, or other stressful stigma that may increase transition difficulties (Brignone, 2017; Holland et al., 2016). Especially for women, research has found that unwanted sexual experiences are an explanatory factor in negative impacts on service members' health (Jaycox et al., 2022; Schram et al., 2022). These impacts likely extend far beyond physical or mental health and may have different implications by gender; however, to date, little research has been conducted that demonstrates possible impacts outside of clinical populations. This study's exploratory analysis suggests that a military sexual assault can have deleterious impacts for veterans in non-clinical domains, in this case, employment and transition preparedness, as they separate from the service and possibly beyond.

Data from this study show that veterans who experienced military sexual assault during their time in the service had considerably higher barriers to obtaining employment than did other veterans. This interpretation is further supported by their subjective ratings of the transition experience, most notably perhaps in terms of feeling less prepared for life after separation. Military sexual assault experiences and shorter time-in-service are possible mechanisms that may explain this lack of preparation, although the low explanatory power of these models (and the extant literature) suggest that there are almost certainly additional factors not considered here which may also have an impact on transition readiness. While the present analysis investigates employment impacts at transition, future research should consider how enduring these employment effects may be over time. The fact that military sexual assault was also associated with lower rates of retirement and higher rates of unemployment due to disability offers support to previous research identifying connections between military sexual assault and combat-related injury (Szitanyi, 2020), and suggests that these connections are deserving of further research inquiry.

It is possible that in addition to clinically identified cases where military sexual assault contributes to MST, unreported experiences of military sexual assault or harassment may nevertheless impact a veteran's ease-of-transition and employment success via the mechanisms of an abridged military career or disrupted career transition processes. This implication is difficult to parse out since separation can be voluntary, involuntary, or through disability that itself may or may not be more likely because of, or even directly related to, military sexual assault experiences (Brignone, 2017). Data from this survey are enough, however, to recommend this hypothesis be further explored given that exploratory multivariate analyses with demographic controls showed a significant influence on transition preparedness for both time-in-service and military sexual assault. Any such inquiry would likely require a carefully designed qualitative research study since there is unlikely to be accessible, honest, quantitative data with enough detail to explore the nuanced connection between stigmatizing experiences and the personal reasons service members choose to separate.

Another theoretical possibility that may explain the ongoing impact of military sexual assault on the lives of some veterans, including employment and transition difficulties, may also lie in the linkage between sexual assault and subsequent service-connected disability (Suris & Lind, 2008; Szitanyi, 2020). Sequelae of trauma such as PTSD or anxiety occurring after sexual assault experiences may contribute to a veteran's disability status, either directly (e.g., as a mental health diagnosis), indirectly through physical injuries or mistakes made while distracted by complex trauma occurring within a high-risk work environment (e.g., deployment and training), or both (Allard et al., 2011). Given the high-stress environments in which military service members regularly operate and findings that a large proportion of military sexual assault survivors do not seek help due to actual retaliation or a perception that they will experience retaliation, there is a strong possibility that military sexual assault also increases the risk of seemingly unrelated incidents or injuries. It is possible that military sexual assault is both a cause and risk factor for some significant types of service-related injuries, trauma, or disabilities.

Limitations

The data used in this study are based on a national survey of members of an organization advocating for the needs of post-9/11 veterans. Typical limitations of self-selection in this type of survey research are present in this data (e.g., voluntary participation, overrepresentation of post-9/11 veterans, possible bias toward issues advocated by the organization), including the fact that many of the measures are less detailed than they would be in a purposive academic study owing to the reason for this survey and wide range of topics covered. This survey was conducted during the fall of 2021. Therefore, the impact of the COVID-19 pandemic cannot be specifically estimated on certain variables (e.g., current employment) or for any very recently separated veterans whose subjective experience of transition may be shaped by having occurred during the pandemic (3.1% of veterans surveyed separated in 2020 or 2021). All things considered these disruptions are likely to be minimal since one would not expect the pandemic to impact military sexual assault survivors in a different way than all other veterans.

This study relies on a single, broad question to measure a service member's experience of military sexual assault. This type of nonspecific question does not classify the types or severity of experiences that other behaviorally specific victimization measures would provide, but as-is this item prioritizes a survey participant's self-identification as a survivor regardless of their specific experiences. Since this study seeks to explore enduring impacts of military sexual assault experiences on post-service employment and transition, a measure that captures a participant's self-identification with having had sexual assault experiences still arguably measures experiences impactful enough for participants to self-identify as a survivor, and therefore it is reasonable to use this measure for the purposes indicated.

Conclusion

The exploratory analysis presented in this paper has been undertaken to inform and direct future research toward investigating the impacts of military sexual assault on veterans' post-service lives beyond just clinical concerns. In contrast and as a supplement to the body of work linking veterans' history of MST to physical and mental health outcomes, this paper highlights the need to address the post-service consequences of military sexual assault across other domains such as veteran employment and transition readiness. Military sexual assault experiences can have deleterious impacts on areas outside of health and can do so even if these experiences are not reported or disclosed to health care providers. This paper utilized data from a national survey of post-9/11 veterans, placing military sexual assault alongside other key issues facing veterans and was thereby able to identify and empirically demonstrate associations between this and other important parts of veterans' transition and post-service lives. Although this paper explored topics of post-service employment and transition, there are undoubtedly other areas or aspects veterans' experiences (e.g., higher education or disability) where additional research could produce unique insights, including but not limited to replication among other groups of veterans (i.e., pre-9/11, non-US veterans). A comprehensive approach to understanding how specific military experiences and veteran well-being are related should be standard practice in all research intended to support veterans' success. Most services for veterans already recognize the impacts of highly visible military experiences (e.g., service-connected injuries, PTSD, and family separation) on veterans' needs, but experiences such as military sexual trauma or intimate partner violence that are more often "hidden" (for personal, cultural, or structural reasons) are just as important barriers to future well-being and are deserving of similar consideration when designing interventions. The data presented in this paper represent a first step in that direction, demonstrating to researchers and practitioners the possibilities of a more integrated research agenda in support of all veterans.

Acknowledgments

The author would like to thank Walter DeKeseredy and Deborah Bradbard for their feedback on earlier versions of this manuscript.

Disclosure statement

No potential conflict of interest was reported by the author(s).

ORCID

Adam J. Pritchard http://orcid.org/0009-0005-0937-1195

References

Allard, C. B., Nunnink, S., Gregory, A. M., Klest, B., & Platt, M. (2011). Military sexual trauma research: A proposed agenda. *Journal of Trauma & Dissociation*, *12*(3), 324–345. https://doi.org/10.1080/15299732.2011.542609

Basile, K. C., Breiding, M. J., & Smith, S. G. (2016). Disability and risk of recent sexual violence in the United States. *American Journal of Public Health*, *106*(5), 928–933. https://doi.org/10.2105/ajph.2015.303004

Beckman, K. L., Williams, E. C., Hebert, P. L., Frost, M. C., Rubinsky, A. D., Hawkins, E. J., Littman, A. J., & Lehavot, K. (2022). Associations among military sexual trauma, opioid use disorder, and gender. *American Journal of Preventive Medicine*, *62*(3), 377–386. https://doi.org/10.1016/j.amepre.2021.08.020

Blais, R. K., & Livingston, W. S. (2021). The association of assault military sexual trauma and sexual function among partnered female service members and veterans: The mediating roles of depression and sexual self-schemas. *European Journal of Psychotraumatology*, *12*(1), 1872964. https://doi.org/10.1080/20008198.2021.1872964

Bourke, J. (2022). Military sexual trauma: Gender, military cultures, and the medicalization of abuse in contemporary America. *Journal of War & Culture Studies*, *15*(1), 86–105. https://doi.org/10.1080/17526272.2021.1884785

Bradbard, D. A., & Maury, R. V. (2021). *The evolution of the veteran employment landscape: Five key highlights*. Institute for Veterans and Military Families at Syracuse University.https://surface.syr.edu/cgi/viewcontent.cgi?article=1393&context=ivmf

Brignone, E. (2017). Misconduct-related discharge from active duty military service: An examination of precipitating factors and post-deployment health outcomes.

Elnitsky, C. A., Blevins, C. L., Fisher, M. P., & Magruder, K. (2017). Military service member and veteran reintegration: A critical review and adapted ecological model. *American Journal of Orthopsychiatry*, *87*(2), 114. https://doi.org/10.1037/ort0000244

Forkus, S. R., Weiss, N. H., Goncharenko, S., Mammay, J., Church, M., & Contractor, A. A. (2021). Military sexual trauma and risky behaviors: A systematic review. *Trauma, Violence & Abuse*, *22*(4), 976–993. https://doi.org/10.1177/1524838019897338

Gross, G. M., Kaczynski, R., & Resnick, S. (2022). The effect of military sexual trauma on competitive employment status following veterans health administration supported employment services. *Psychological Services*. https://doi.org/10.1037/ser0000635

Haynie, J. M., & Shepherd, D. (2011). Toward a theory of discontinuous career transition: Investigating career transitions necessitated by traumatic life events. *Journal of Applied Psychology*, *96*(3), 501. https://doi.org/10.1037/a0021450

Himmelfarb, N., Yaeger, D., & Mintz, J. (2006). Posttraumatic stress disorder in female veterans with military and civilian sexual trauma. *Journal of Traumatic Stress*, *19*(6), 837–846. https://doi.org/10.1002/jts.20163

Holder, K. A., & Day, J. C. (2017, September 14). Health insurance coverage of veterans. *Census Blogs*. United States Census Bureau. https://www.census.gov/newsroom/blogs/random-samplings/2017/09/health_insurancecov0.html

Holland, K. J., Rabelo, V. C., & Cortina, L. M. (2016). Collateral damage: Military sexual trauma and help-seeking barriers. *Psychology of Violence*, *6*(2), 253–261. https://doi.org/10.1037/a0039467

Hosmer, D. W., Lemeshow, S., & Sturdivant, R. X. (2013). Logistic regression models for multinomial and ordinal outcomes. In *Applied logistic regression* (pp. 269–311). Wiley. doi:10.1002/9781118548387.ch8.

Jaycox, L. H., Morral, A. R., Street, A., Schell, T. L., Kilpatrick, D., & Cottrell, L. (2022). *Gender differences in health among U.S. service members: Unwanted gender-based experiences as an explanatory factor*. RAND Corporation. https://doi.org/10.7249/RRA1848-1

Mailhot Amborski, A., Bussières, E.-L., Vaillancourt-Morel, M.-P., & Joyal, C. C. (2021). Sexual violence against persons with disabilities: A meta-analysis. *Trauma, Violence & Abuse*, 1524838021995975. https://doi.org/10.1177/1524838021995975

Martin, L., Rosen, L. N., Durand, D. B., Knudson, K. H., & Stretch, R. H. (2000). Psychological and physical health effects of sexual assaults and nonsexual traumas among male and female United States army soldiers. *Behavioral Medicine*, *26*(1), 23–33. https://doi.org/10.1080/08964280009595750

Martin, L., Rosen, L. N., Durand, D. B., Stretch, R. H., & Knudson, K. H. (1998). Prevalence and timing of sexual assaults in a sample of male and female U.S. army soldiers. *Military Medicine*, *163*(4), 213–216. https://doi.org/10.1093/milmed/163.4.213

Mason, J. (2022, June 16). What soldiers need to know about the army's new approach to sex crimes. *Task & Purpose*. https://taskandpurpose.com/analysis/army-sharp-program-change/

Matthieu, M., & Ivanoff, A. (2006). Treatment of human-caused trauma: Attrition in the adult outcomes research. *Journal of Interpersonal Violence*, *21*(12), 1654–1664. https://doi.org/10.1177/0886260506294243

Maya, E., & Kimberley, S.-E. (2018). Gender in veteran reintegration and transition: A scoping review. *Journal of Military, Veteran and Family Health*, *4*(1), 5–19. https://doi.org/10.3138/jmvfh.2017-0004

Perkins, D. F., Aronson, K. R., Morgan, N. R., Bleser, J. A., Vogt, D., Copeland, L. A., Finley, E. P., & Gilman, C. (2020). Veterans' use of programs and services as they transition to civilian life: Baseline assessment for the veteran metrics initiative. *Journal of Social Service Research*, *46*(2), 241–255. https://doi.org/10.1080/01488376.2018.1546259

Peterson, Z. D., Voller, E. K., Polusny, M. A., & Murdoch, M. (2011). Prevalence and consequences of adult sexual assault of men: Review of empirical findings and state of the literature. *Clinical Psychology Review*, *31*(1), 1–24. https://doi.org/10.1016/j.cpr.2010.08.006

Pritchard, A. J., Powell, S., & Horr, T. (2022). *2022 IAVA member survey*. https://iava.org/wp-content/uploads/2022/03/2022_IAVA_Member_Survey.pdf

Purtle, J. (2016). "Heroes' invisible wounds of war:" Constructions of posttraumatic stress disorder in the text of US federal legislation. *Social Science & Medicine, 149*, 9–16. https://doi.org/10.1016/j.socscimed.2015.11.039

Rosen, L. N., & Martin, L. (1998). Sexual harassment, cohesion, and combat readiness in U.S. army support units. *Armed Forces and Society, 24*(2), 221–244. https://doi.org/10.1177/0095327x9702400202

Schram, B., Canetti, E., Orr, R., & Pope, R. (2022). Injury rates in female and male military personnel: A systematic review and meta-analysis. *BMC Women's Health, 22*(1), 310. https://doi.org/10.1186/s12905-022-01899-4

Suris, A., & Lind, L. (2008). Military sexual trauma: A review of prevalence and associated health consequences in veterans. *Trauma, Violence & Abuse, 9*(4), 250–269. https://doi.org/10.1177/1524838008324419

Szitanyi, S. (2020). Violated bodies: Combat injuries and sexual assault in the U.S. military. In S. Szitanyi (Ed.), *Gender trouble in the U.S. military: Challenges to regimes of male privilege* (pp. 89–118). Springer International Publishing. https://doi.org/10.1007/978-3-030-21225-4_4

Turchik, J. A., & Wilson, S. M. (2010). Sexual assault in the U.S. military: A review of the literature and recommendations for the future. *Aggression and Violent Behavior, 15*(4), 267–277. https://doi.org/10.1016/j.avb.2010.01.005

U.S. Commission on Civil Rights. (2013). *Sexual assault in the military*. https://www.usccr.gov/files/pubs/docs/09242013_Statutory_Enforcement_Report_Sexual_Assault_in_the_Military.pdf

Vespa, J. E. (2020). *Those who served: America's veterans from World War II to the war on terror* (ACS-43). https://www.census.gov/content/dam/Census/library/publications/2020/demo/acs-43.pdf

Wilson, L. C. (2018). The prevalence of military sexual trauma: A meta-analysis. *Trauma, Violence & Abuse, 19*(5), 584–597. https://doi.org/10.1177/1524838016683459

Index

Page numbers in **bold** refer to tables and those in *italic* refer to figures.